Perspectives on Juvenile Justice

Legal, Social, and Policy Issues

snova
New York

Law, Crime and Law Enforcement

Deviance in Business: Seriousness of Harmful Occupational and Corporate Convenience
Petter Gottschalk
ISBN: 979-8-89530-459-4
eBook ISBN: 979-8-89530-524-9

Hypocrisy in International Criminal Justice
Farhad Malekian
ISBN: 979-8-89530-205-7
eBook ISBN: 979-8-89530-311-5

Critical Women's Issues
Gary I. Lilienthal, PhD (Editor)
ISBN: 979-8-89530-002-2
eBook ISBN: 979-8-89530-126-5

Corporate Manslaughter by Unsafe Food: An Australasian Perspective
S. M. Solaiman
ISBN: 979-8-89113-776-9
eBook ISBN: 979-8-89113-851-3

Understanding the Fentanyl Crisis
Michael K. Reyes (Editor)
ISBN: 979-8-89113-830-8
eBook ISBN: 979-8-89113-869-8

Conundrums of Paternalism in International Criminal Justice
Farhad Malekian
ISBN: 979-8-89113-284-9
eBook ISBN: 979-8-89113-743-1

More information about this series can be found at
https://novapublishers.com/product-category/series/law-crime-and-law-enforcement/

David Y. Reyes
Editor

Perspectives on Juvenile Justice

Legal, Social, and Policy Issues

snova
New York

Library of Congress Cataloging-in-Publication Data

ISBN: 979-8-89530-669-7 (Hardcover)
ISBN: 979-8-89530-726-7 (eBook)

Published by Nova Science Publishers, Inc. † New York

Contents

Preface

Research and data on youth and delinquency are critical for identifying opportunities and developing strategies to support positive development through prevention and intervention. Responses to youth misbehavior by youth-serving systems—including education, child welfare, behavioral health, and justice systems—can play an important role in promoting or disrupting youths' healthy social and emotional development.

Understanding the complexities of juvenile delinquency requires a multifaceted approach that integrates legal, social, and psychological perspectives. This book aims to provide a comprehensive analysis of various aspects of juvenile justice, from federal criminal law to the impact of incarceration on young offenders.

Chapter 1

Juvenile Delinquents and Federal Criminal Law: The Federal Juvenile Delinquency Act and Related Matters*

Charles Doyle

Summary

The Federal Juvenile Delinquency Act (JDA) gives federal authorities three options when a juvenile violates federal criminal law. First, they can refer the juvenile to state authorities.

Second, they can initiate federal delinquency proceedings. Third, if a case is retained in the federal system and involves a serious offense, they can petition the federal court to transfer the juvenile for trial as an adult. The JDA applies to those charged before the age of 21 with a breach of federal criminal law occurring before they reached the age of 18.

The JDA generally favors referring juveniles to state authorities, but it permits federal delinquency proceedings where state courts cannot or will not accept jurisdiction. Given the preference for state juvenile proceedings and the fact that a violation of federal law will ordinarily support the assertion of state juvenile court jurisdiction, most juveniles who violate federal criminal law never come in contact with federal authorities. Many of those who do are returned to state officials to be processed through the state court system.

Most juvenile delinquency cases that do remain in the federal system have historically arisen in areas beyond state jurisdiction, primarily in Indian country. Thus, the majority of federal delinquency proceedings have involved Native Americans. Federal prosecutors may also elect to

* This is an edited, reformatted and augmented version of Congressional Research Service Publication No. RL30822, updated May 9, 2023.

In: Perspectives on Juvenile Justice: Legal, Social, and Policy Issues
Editor: David Y. Reyes
ISBN: 979-8-89530-669-7

initiate federal proceedings if the state courts are unwilling or unable to assume jurisdiction, or the state has no adequate treatment plans, or the juvenile is charged with a crime of violence or with drug trafficking.

Federal juvenile delinquency proceedings require neither grand jury indictment, public trial, nor trial by jury. The constitutional rights available to juveniles at delinquency proceedings are otherwise much like those found in adult criminal trials. Juveniles found delinquent may be released under suspended sentence, placed on probation, ordered to pay restitution and/or sentenced to detention. The period of detention, if any, may not exceed the term which might be imposed upon an adult offender for the same misconduct. The period of detention may be followed by a period of juvenile delinquent supervision, revocation of which in serious cases may result in detention until the individual is 26 years of age.

A U.S. district court may, and in some cases must, transfer a juvenile for criminal trial as an adult. A juvenile may also request a transfer to trial as an adult. Discretionary transfers come in two varieties. A court may transfer a juvenile who, when 13 years of age or older, is alleged to have committed aggravated assault, murder, attempted murder, armed robbery, or armed rape. A court may also transfer a juvenile who, when 15 years of age or older, is alleged to have committed drug trafficking or a violent felony. The court orders or denies the transfer petition after considering the seriousness of the offense, the age and maturity of the juvenile, the juvenile's prior delinquency record, the results of past rehabilitative efforts, and the availability of existing rehabilitative programs. A court must order a transfer when a juvenile has a prior comparable conviction or juvenile adjudication and is charged with committing a violent offense or a drug trafficking offense at the age of 16 or older.

This report begins with a brief discussion of the evolution of the treatment of juvenile criminal offenders in the United States. It then analyzes in detail the various provisions of the JDA.

Introduction

Juvenile offenders who violate federal criminal law are generally the responsibility of state juvenile court authorities.[1] The Federal Juvenile Delinquency Act (JDA) permits federal delinquency proceedings when state courts cannot or will not accept jurisdiction or, in the case of a limited number

[1] This report is available in an abridged version as CRS Report R47548, Juvenile Delinquents and Federal Criminal Law: The Federal Juvenile Delinquency Act and Related Matters in Short, by Charles Doyle.

of crimes, when there is a substantial federal interest. In the more serious of these cases, the juvenile offender may be transferred for trial as an adult. The rise in serious juvenile crime, the contraction of state juvenile court jurisdiction, and the expansion of federal criminal law have all contributed to the increased prevalence of federal delinquency proceedings, as described here.

History of Federal Delinquency Law

In early America, the law held that a child, until the age of 7, lacked the maturity necessary to be held criminally responsible. Thereafter, the law rebuttably presumed incapacity until the child reached the age of 14, by which time acquisition of the intellectual capability to entertain criminal intent was assumed. As an early nineteenth century commentator explained,

> Under the age of seven years, indeed, it seems that no circumstances of mischievous discretion can be admitted to overthrow the strong presumption of innocence which is raised by an age so tender. During the interval between seven and fourteen, the infant is prima facie supposed to be destitute of criminal design; but this presumption diminishes as the age increases, and even during this interval of youth, may be repelled by positive evidence of vicious intention. For a tenderness of years will not excuse a maturity in crime;
>
> . . . since the power of contracting guilt is measured rather by the strength of the delinquent's understanding, than by days and years. Thus, children of thirteen, eight, and ten years of age, have been executed for capital offenses, because they respectively manifested a consciousness of guilt, and a mischievous discretion or cunning. After the age of fourteen, an infant is on the same footing with those of the mature years.[2]

A child found capable of the requisite intent was subject to trial and punishment as an adult; other children were set free.

In the early twentieth century, the states established juvenile court systems so that children accused of conduct that would be criminal in an adult might

[2] 3 JOSEPH CHITTY, A PRACTICAL TREATISE ON CRIMINAL LAW 724 (3d Am. ed. 1836); *accord* 1 JOEL PRENTISS BISHOP, COMMENTARIES ON THE CRIMINAL LAW § 368 (7th ed. 1886); ROLLIN M. PERKINS & RONALD N. BOYCE, CRIMINAL LAW 936-39 (3d ed. 1982).

be processed apart from the criminal justice system in an environment more closely attuned to their rehabilitative needs. By 1930, the Wickersham Commission reported that only the federal government continued to uniformly treat children, charged with a crime, as adults.[3] The states had instead adopted various juvenile court systems in which the "child offender [was] generally dealt with on a noncriminal basis and . . . protected from prosecution and conviction for crime . . . [They undertook] to safeguard, train, and educate rather than to punish him. [They] substituted social for penal methods; the concept of juvenile delinquency for that of crime."[4]

Attorney General Wickersham also pointed out that (1) most of the federal cases involved interstate joyriding, an offense for which juvenile court treatment was thought particularly appropriate; (2) "[t]here [were] not enough juveniles brought into the Federal courts to justify the establishment of juvenile courts by act of Congress"; and (3) "federal penal institutions are not adequately equipped to deal with this class of juvenile delinquency."[5] He recommended, and Congress agreed, that the disparity should be adjusted by authorizing the Department of Justice to return juveniles charged with violating federal law to the juvenile authorities of their home state.[6]

This solution suffered two unfortunate limitations. First, it did not account for juveniles charged with capital crimes. State law ordinarily excluded capital offenses from the jurisdiction of its juvenile courts. Second, state juvenile courts had no jurisdiction over juveniles who lived, and whose misconduct occurred upon, Indian reservations or military installations over which the state had no legislative jurisdiction.

Congress addressed these shortcomings with the Federal Juvenile Delinquency Act of 1938.[7] State juvenile proceedings remained the preferred alternative, but the Attorney General might instead elect to proceed against a juvenile as an adult, and federal juvenile proceedings became possible should both parties agree.[8] Although supplemented in 1950 by the Federal Youth Corrections Act, which afforded federal juvenile offenders tried as adults the

---

[3] National Commission on Law Observance and Enforcement [(Wickersham Commission)], REPORT ON THE CHILD OFFENDER IN THE FEDERAL SYSTEM OF JUSTICE 2 (1931).

[4] *Id.*

[5] H.R. REP. NO. 72-958, at 2 (1932).

[6] *Id.*

[7] ch. 486, 52 STAT. 764 (1938); 18 U.S.C. §§ 921–927 (1940).

[8] ch. 486, 52 STAT. at 765; 18 U.S.C. § 922 (1940).

prospect of special rehabilitative opportunities,[9] the Act remained essentially unchanged for over thirty-five years.

In 1974, Congress substantially revised the Act[10] "to provide basic procedural rights to juveniles who come under federal jurisdiction and to bring federal procedures up to the standards set by various model acts, many state codes and court decisions."[11] For the first time, crimes punishable by death or life imprisonment (primarily murder, kidnapping, and rape) were made subject to the federal juvenile system.[12] At the time, the Supreme Court's decision in *Furman v. Georgia*[13] had recently declared unconstitutional the procedure under which the vast majority of state and federal capital punishment statutes operated. It was not until two years thereafter that *Woodson v. North Carolina*[14] and *Gregg v. Georgia*[15] gave some clue as to what procedures would pass constitutional muster. When Congress established the requisite procedures to restore capital punishment as a federal sentencing option, it exempted juveniles.[16]

In the 1974 revision of federal juvenile law, Congress curtailed what to that point had been the Attorney General's unilateral discretion to determine whether children accused of federal crimes should be tried as adults in federal criminal proceedings. Congress instead authorized the Attorney General to petition the federal court to transfer, for trial as an adult, any 16- or 17-year-old accused of a crime which carried a maximum penalty of death, life imprisonment, or imprisonment for ten years or more.[17]

Congress made the final major adjustments ten years later with changes that emphasized that at least some of the juveniles who commit serious crimes merited punishment as adults. The Sentencing Reform Act of 1984 repealed the Federal Youth Corrections Act and eliminated juvenile parole provisions.[18]

---

[9] ch. 1115, 64 STAT. 1085, 1086 (1950); 18 U.S.C. §§ 5005–5026 (1952).
[10] 88 STAT. 1133 (1974); 18 U.S.C. §§ 5031–5042 (1976).
[11] S. REP. NO. 93-1011, at 19 (1974).
[12] 88 STAT. 1133–1134 (1974); 18 U.S.C. §§ 5031, 5032 (1976).
[13] 408 U.S. 238 (1972).
[14] 428 U.S. 280 (1976).
[15] 428 U.S. 153 (1976).
[16] 18 U.S.C. § 3591.
[17] 88 STAT. 1134 (1974); 18 U.S.C. § 5032 (1976).
[18] 98 STAT.1837, 2027 (1984). Congress made modest, largely technical, adjustments thereafter on a number of occasions: P.L. 99-646, § 21(a), 100 STAT. 3596 (1986) (18 U.S.C. § 5037 (1980 & Supp. V)); P.L. 100-690, §§6467(a), 7045, 102 STAT. 4375, 4400 (1988) (18 U.S.C. §§ 5032, 5034 (1988)); P.L. 101-647, §§ 1205(n), 3599G, 104 STAT. 4831, 4832 (1990) (18 U.S.C. § 5032 (1988 & Supp. II)); P.L. 103-322, §§ 140001, 140002, 140003, 140005, 150002, 108 STAT. 2012, 2031, 2032, 2035 (1994) (18 U.S.C. §§ 5032, 5038, 5039 (1994)); P.L. 104-294, §§601(c)(1), (f)(16), (g)(1), 604(b)(40), 110 STAT. 3499,

The Sentencing Reform Act also lowered the age at which a juvenile may be transferred for trial as an adult and expanded the list of crimes that justify such a transfer.[19] Thus far at least, the courts have declined to read into this history a congressional intent to repudiate rehabilitation as a sentencing consideration in federal juvenile proceedings.[20]

Overview of Existing Federal Law

The continuing basic premise of federal juvenile law is that juvenile matters, even those arising under federal law, should be handled by state authorities whenever possible.[21] The remote second preference of federal law is treatment of the juvenile under the federal delinquency provisions.[22] Because many federal cases arise in areas beyond the reach of state authorities, i.e., primarily Indian country, the majority of federal delinquency proceedings have historically involved Native Americans.[23] In a limited, but growing, number of instances involving drugs or violence, federal law permits the trial of juveniles as adults in federal court.[24]

3500, 3502, 3509 (1996) (18 U.S.C. §§ 5032, 5037, 5038 (1994& Supp. III)); P.L. 107-273, § 12301, 116 STAT. 1986 (2002) (18 U.S.C. § 5037 (2000 & Supp. III)).

[19] 18 U.S.C. §§ 5037, 5032.

[20] United States v. Lopez, 860 F.3d 201, 210 (4th Cir. 2017) ("Rather, the JDA [Juvenile Delinquency Act] is intended to ensure that at the time they are brought into the criminal justice process, juveniles will have the benefit of a system that is tailored to their special needs and vulnerabilities and, in particular, to their special receptivity to rehabilitation."); United States v. Juvenile, 347 F.3d 778, 786–87 (9th Cir. 2003) ("Moreover, if the primary goal of the federal juvenile justice system is no longer rehabilitation, as the government asserts, then the lessened due process protections afforded under the system would become extremely problematic."); *see also* United States v. M.R.M., 513 F.3d 866, 869 (8th Cir. 2008); United States v. Patrick V., 359 F.3d 3, 10–11 (1st Cir. 2004) (each citing United States v. R.L.C., 503 U.S. 291, 298 (1992) (opinion of Souter, J.)).

[21] 18 U.S.C. § 5032. Section 5032 does recognize an exception for minor offenses committed within federal enclaves: "A juvenile alleged to have committed an act of juvenile delinquency, *other than a violation of law committed within the special maritime and territorial jurisdiction of the United States for which the maximum authorized term of imprisonment does not exceed six months*, shall not be proceeded against in any court of the United States unless …." *Id.* (emphasis added.).

[22] *Id.*

[23] United States v. Juvenile Male, 492 F.3d 1046, 1049 n.3 (9th Cir. 2007) (per curiam) ("Because of the structure of the FJDA, Native American youth are disproportionately subject to federal court jurisdiction for their delinquency offenses."); *see generally* Amy J. Standefer, Note, *The Federal Juvenile Delinquency Act: A Disparate Impact on Native American Juveniles*, 84 MINN. L. REV. 473 (1999).

[24] 18 U.S.C. § 5032.

Under the JDA,[25] a juvenile is an individual under 18 years of age, or an individual between 18 and 21 years of age alleged to have committed a federal offense when under 18 years of age.[26]

The Act does not apply to individuals over 21 years of age or to conduct committed after a person turns 18.[27] Federal authorities, however, may prosecute as an adult any individual whose active participation in a conspiracy or racketeering enterprise bridges his or her eighteenth birthday.[28] Once the federal courts have found a juvenile delinquent, however, a court that revokes a juvenile's delinquent supervised release may order the juvenile held until age 26.[29]

---

[25] 18 U.S.C. §§ 5031 (definitions), 5032 (delinquency proceedings in district courts; transfer for criminal prosecution), 5033 (custody prior to appearance before magistrate judge), 5034 (duties of magistrate judge), 5035 (detention prior to disposition), 5036 (speedy trial), 5037 (dispositional hearing), 5038 (use of juvenile records), 5039 (commitment), 5040 (support), 5042 (revocation of probation), 5043 (juvenile solitary confinement); *see also* Davis Jaffe & Darcie McElwee, *Federally Prosecuting Juvenile Gang Members*, 68 DOJ J. FED. L. & PRAC.15 (2020); JM §§ 9-8.000 to 9-8.220 (Jan. 2020), https://www.justice.gov/jm/jm-9-8000-juveniles.

[26] "For purposes of this chapter, a 'juvenile' is a person who has not attained his eighteenth birthday, or for the purpose of proceedings and disposition under this chapter for an alleged act of juvenile delinquency, a person who has not attained his twenty-first birthday, and 'juvenile delinquency' is the violation of a law of the United States committed by a person prior to his eighteenth birthday which would have been a crime if committed by an adult or a violation by such a person of section 922(x) [relating to unlawful possession of a handgun or handgun ammunition by a juvenile]." *Id.* § 5031. Nevertheless, as discussed below under the section captioned "Disposition," detention, detention after revocation of juvenile probation, and detention after revocation of juvenile delinquent supervision may in some cases extend until the individual is 26 years of age. *Id.* § 5037(b)-(c), (d)(6). Moreover, a court may continue to exercise jurisdiction over an individual who was under 21 years of age when proceedings began, but who turned 21 during the course of the proceeding. United States v. Woods, 827 F.3d 712, 717 (7th Cir. 2016) (citing in accord, United States v. Ramirez, 297 F.3d 185, 191–92 (2d Cir. 2002); United States v. Smith, 851 F.2d 706, 710 (4th Cir. 1988); United States v. Martin, 788 F.2d 696, 697–98 (11th Cir. 1986); United States v. Doe, 631 F.2d 110, 112-13 (9th Cir. 1980)).

[27] 18 U.S.C. § 5031; United States v. Lopez, 860 F.3d 201, 209 (4th Cir. 2017); United States v. Wright, 540 F.3d 833, 839 (8th Cir. 2008); *Ramirez*, 297 F.3d at 191–92; United States v. Male Juvenile (Pierre Y.), 280 F.3d 1008, 1017 (9th Cir. 2002).

[28] United States v. Mendez, 28 F.4th 1320, 1324 (9th Cir. 2022); United States v. Guerrero, 768 F.3d 351, 361–62 (5th Cir. 2014); United States v. Soto-Beniquez, 356 F.3d 1, 23–24 (1st Cir. 2003); United States v. Burns, 298 F.3d 523, 537 (6th Cir. 2002); United States v. Delatorre, 157 F.3d 1205, 1209–11 (10th Cir. 1998); United States v. Thomas, 114 F.3d 228, 238–39 (D.C. Cir. 1997); United States v. Wong, 40 F.3d 1347, 1365-66 (2d Cir. 1994); United States v. Cruz, 805 F.2d 1464, 1476 (11th Cir. 1976). For a more extensive discussion of questions presented by crimes that straddle the jurisdictional age lines see, D. Ross Martin, Note, *Conspiratorial Children? The Intersection of the Federal Juvenile Delinquency Act and Federal Conspiracy Law*, 74 B.U. L. REV. 859 (1994).

[29] 18 U.S.C. § 5037(d)(6).

Federal Juvenile Offenders in State Proceedings

Criminal investigation and prosecution is first and foremost the domain of state and local governments, and conduct which violates federal criminal law is usually contrary to state law as well. For example, the federal Controlled Substances Act[30] has a state equivalent in every jurisdiction,[31] and robbery of a federal insured bank,[32] or murder of a federal employee or law enforcement officer,[33] will almost always be contrary to the state robbery and murder statutes in the state in which the offenses occur.[34] Moreover, while state crimes are the most common basis for state juvenile court jurisdiction, many state juvenile courts enjoy delinquency jurisdiction based upon a violation of federal law.[35] Thus, an individual under 18 who violates federal criminal law can move through the state juvenile delinquency system without ever coming into contact with federal authorities.

Contractions in state juvenile court jurisdiction, however, make this less likely than was once the case. Many states now define juvenile court jurisdiction more narrowly than federal law, in terms of age or crime or both.[36]

---

[30] 21 U.S.C. §§ 801–889.

[31] *E.g.*, ALA. CODE §§ 20-2-1 to 20-2-93; ALASKA STAT. §§ 11.71.010 to 11.71.900; ARIZ. REV. STAT. ANN. §§ 13-3401 to 13-3423; ARK. CODE ANN. §§ 5-64-101 to 5-64-1005.

[32] 18 U.S.C. § 2113.

[33] *Id.* § 1114.

[34] *E.g.*, CAL. PEN. CODE §§ 187–189 (murder); COLO. REV. STAT. §§ 18-3-101 to 18-3-107 (homicide); CONN. GEN. STAT. ANN. §§ 53a-54a to 53a-58a (homicide); DEL. CODE ANN. tit.11 §§ 631–641 (homicide); FLA. STAT. ANN. § 812.13 (robbery); GA. CODE ANN. §§ 16-8-40, 16-8-41 (robbery); HAWAII REV. STAT. ANN. §§ 708-840 to 708-842(robbery); IDAHO CODE ANN. §§ 18-6501 to 18-6503 (robbery).

[35] ALA. CODE § 12-15-102 ("When used in this chapter, the following words and phrases shall have the following meanings . . . (6) Delinquent Act. An act committed by a child that is designated a violation, misdemeanor, or felony offense pursuant to the law of the . . . state in which the act was committed or pursuant to federal law"); *see also* ARIZ. REV. STAT. ANN. § 8-201; CAL. WEL. & INST. CODE § 602; COLO. REV. STAT. ANN. § 19-2.5-103; CONN. GEN. STAT. ANN. § 46b-120; FLA. STAT. ANN. § 985.03; GA. CODE ANN. § 15-11-2; HAWAII REV. STAT. § 571-11; IDAHO CODE § 20-505; ILL. COMP. STAT. ANN. ch.705 § 405/5-105; IOWA CODE § 232.2; LA. CHILD. CODE art. 804; MICH. COMP. LAWS ANN. § 712A.2; MINN. STAT. ANN. § 260B.007; MISS. CODE § 43-21-105; N.D. CENT. CODE § 27-20.2-01; OHIO REV. CODE § 2152.02; 10A OKLA. STAT. ANN. § 2-1-103; ORE. REV. STAT. § 419C.005; PA. STAT. AND CONS. STAT. ANN. tit.42 § 6302; R.I. GEN. LAWS § 14-1-3; S.D. COD. LAWS § 26-8C-2; TENN. CODE ANN. § 37-1-102; TEX. FAM. CODE ANN. § 51.03; UTAH CODE ANN. § 78A-6-103; VT. STAT. ANN. tit. 33 § 5102; VA. CODE § 16.1-228; WASH. REV. CODE ANN. § 13.40.020; WIS. STAT. ANN. § 938.02.

[36] Although most juvenile courts have delinquency jurisdiction over juveniles under 18 years of age, there are a few exceptions, *e.g.*, MD. CODE, ANN., CTS. & JUD. PROC. § 3-8A-03 (at least 13); N.C. GEN. STAT. § 7B-1501 (under 16). Far more common are crime-specific limitations on juvenile court delinquency jurisdiction, *e.g.*, ALASKA STAT.§ 47.12.030

Some also permit the adult criminal trial of a juvenile either through the exercise of concurrent jurisdiction or a waiver or transfer of jurisdiction under circumstances the federal courts could not.[37]

In most instances, federal law favors dealing with juvenile offenders under state law. Federal juvenile proceedings are only possible if: relevant state courts are unable or unwilling to proceed; their juvenile programs are unavailable or inadequate; or the offense is a designated serious federal offense.[38]

Arrest and Arraignment

The JDA, 18 U.S.C. § 5033, requires that a juvenile taken into federal custody for violating federal law must be advised of his or her legal rights immediately, and the juvenile's parents or guardian must be notified immediately.[39] The courts have held that because federal custody activates the JDA requirements, these obligations only begin after a juvenile who was initially detained by state, local, or tribal officials is turned over to federal authorities.[40] The

---

(The juvenile court has no jurisdiction over juveniles who, when 16 years of age or older, are alleged to have committed an unclassified felony (*e.g.*, murder, manslaughter, rape), a class A felony (*e.g.*, first degree kidnaping, first degree robbery, first degree assault), first degree arson, or a class B felony involving the use of deadly weapon by a juvenile previously convicted (or adjudged delinquent) of a crime against an individual involving the use of a deadly weapon) or misuse of a firearm; IND. STAT. ANN. § 31-30-1-4 (the juvenile court has no jurisdiction over an individual 16 or older charged with various violent crimes, *e.g.*, murder, kidnapping, rape, robbery, and carjacking); MINN. STAT. ANN. §§ 260B.101, 260B.007 (the juvenile court has no jurisdiction over a juvenile charged with murder); N.J. STAT. ANN. § 2A:4A-26.1 (the juvenile court must waive jurisdiction over a juvenile, 15 or older, with a finding of probable cause relating to various violent crimes, *e.g.*, homicide, robbery, carjacking, rape, kidnapping or arson); PA. STAT. AND CONS. STAT. ANN. tit.42 § 6302 (delinquent acts over which the juvenile court has jurisdiction do not include murder, certain violent crimes (*e.g.*, rape, robbery, and kidnapping) committed by a juvenile, 15 or older, committed while armed with dangerous weapon or after having previously been found delinquent for committing certain violent crimes); UTAH CODE ANN. §§ 78A-6-103, 78A-5-102.5 (the juvenile court has no jurisdiction of juveniles, 16 or older, charged with murder).

[37] *E.g.*, ALA. CODE § 12-15-203 (transfer of any juvenile, 14 or older, for any crime); MO. ANN. STAT. § 211.071 (transfer of any juvenile, 12 or older, for any felony); MONT. CODE ANN. §§ 41-5-203, 41-5-206 (concurrent jurisdiction); N.H. REV. STAT. ANN. § 169-B:24 (transfer of any juvenile for any felony).

[38] 18 U.S.C. § 5032.

[39] *Id.* § 5033.

[40] United States v. Kerr, 120 F.3d 239, 241–42 (11th Cir. 1997); *cf.* United States v. Doe, 226 F.3d 672, 679 (6th Cir.2000).

notification requirement may be excused, however, when the juvenile frustrates reasonable notification efforts.[41] Much of the case law relating to the federal advice and notification provisions comes from the U.S. Court of Appeals for the Ninth Circuit, which has held that

- the word "immediate" means the same for both advice and notifications purposes;[42]
- advice given 4 hours after arrest and notification given 3½ hours after arrest has not been given "immediately";[43]
- notice given within close to an hour after arrests had been given immediately;[44]
- parental notification must include advice as to the juvenile's rights;[45]
- parental notification may be accomplished through the good offices of the surrogate or appropriate foreign consulate when the juvenile's parents reside outside of the United States;[46]
- convictions or delinquency determinations must be overturned if they are tainted by violations of section 5033 so egregious as to violate due process;[47] and
- less egregious but prejudicial violations of section 5033 may require that any resulting incriminating statements be suppressed.[48]

The juvenile must also be brought before a magistrate for arraignment "forthwith."[49] At night, on weekends, or at other times when a magistrate is not immediately available, arraignment may be within a time reasonable under the circumstances,[50] and a waiver of Miranda rights may be construed as a

---

[41] United States v. Burrous, 147 F.3d 111, 115–16 (2d Cir. 1998).

[42] United States v. Doe, 219 F.3d 1009, 1014–15 (9th Cir. 2000).

[43] United States v. Juvenile (RRA-A), 229 F.3d 737, 744 (9th Cir. 2000); *Doe*, 219 F.3d at 1014–15.

[44] United States v. Female Juvenile (Wendy G.), 255 F.3d 761, 765 (9th Cir. 2001).

[45] *Juvenile (RRA-A)*, 229 F.3d at 744; *Doe*, 219 F.3d at 1015; *Female Juvenile (Wendy G.)*, 255 F.3d at 767–77.

[46] United States v. C.M., 485 F.3d 492, 500 (9th Cir. 2007); *Juvenile (RRA-A)*, 229 F.3d at 744.

[47] United States v. Juvenile Male, 595 F.3d 885, 902 (9th Cir. 2010); *C.M.*, 485 F.3d at 505; *Juvenile (RRA-A)*, 229 F.3d at 744; *Doe*, 219 F.3d at 1016.

[48] United States v. D.L., 453 F.3d 1115, 1125–27 (9th Cir. 2006); *Juvenile (RRA-A)*, 229 F.3d at 744; *Doe*, 219 F.3d at 1017; United States v. Doe, 226 F.3d 672, 678–80 (6th Cir. 2000). Harmless violations may go unsanctioned. United States v. A.S.R., 81 F. Supp. 3d 709, 721 (E.D. Wis. 2015) (failure to advise the juvenile's parents of the juvenile's rights).

[49] 18 U.S.C. § 5033; *C.M.*, 485 F.3d at 502.

[50] *Doe*, 219 F.3d at 1015–16 (a 31-hour delay in the absence of extenuating circumstances was not reasonable); United States v. Doe, 862 F.2d 776, 780 (9th Cir. 1988) (36-hour delay

waiver of the right to timely presentation.[51] When a magistrate is available, arraignment may not be delayed simply because the government is proceeding with an abundance of caution or because the associated paperwork is tedious.[52] Once before the magistrate, the juvenile is entitled to the assistance of counsel and to have counsel appointed in the case of indigence.[53] The magistrate may also appoint a guardian ad litem, and, after a hearing before counsel, order the juvenile detained to guarantee subsequent court appearances or for the safety of the juvenile or anyone else.[54]

A juvenile under federal detention is entitled to a delinquency hearing within 30 days or to have the information charging his or her delinquency dismissed with prejudice unless he or she has contributed or consented to the delay or unless dismissal with prejudice would be contrary to the interests of justice.[55] This speedy trial requirement runs from the time the juvenile was taken into federal custody pending judicial proceedings,[56] but does not attach to any period of state detention;[57] to any period during which the juvenile was being held for purposes other than the pendency of delinquency proceedings;[58] to any time when the juvenile is not being detained;[59] to delays attributable to the juvenile's deception;[60] to the period between an admission or guilty plea

---

was unreasonable); United States v. Doe, 701 F.2d 819, 823–24 (9th Cir. 1983) (delay between 11 at night and arraignment in the morning two days later was reasonable in light of unavailability of a magistrate and the officer's press of official business); United States v. DeMarce, 513 F.2d 755, 757–58 (10th Cir. 1975) (80-hour delay unreasonable even if some of delay fell on a weekend); United States v. Nash, 620 F. Supp. 1439, 1444 (S.D.N.Y. 1985) (7-9 hour delay on a weekday unreasonable even without proof of bad faith).

[51] United States v. Jones, 566 F. Supp. 3d 956, 962–63 (D.S.D. 2021).

[52] United States v. D.L., 453 F.3d 1115, 1123–24 (9th Cir. 2006).

[53] 18 U.S.C. § 5034.

[54] *Id.* The Supreme Court has upheld state juvenile pretrial detention, Schall v. Martin, 467 U.S. 253, 256–57 (1984), and adult federal pretrial detention, United States v. Salerno, 481 U.S. 739, 741 (1987). Section 5035 states that a juvenile may only be detained in a juvenile facility or other suitable place.

[55] 18 U.S.C. § 5036.

[56] United States v. D.B., 61 F.4th 608, 612 (8th Cir. 2023); United States v. Female Juvenile, A.F.S., 377 F.3d 27, 34 (1st Cir. 2004); United States v. Wong, 40 F.3d 1347, 1371 (2d Cir. 1994); United States v. Romulus, 949 F.2d 713, 716 (4th Cir. 1991); United States v. Doe, 882 F.2d 926, 927–28 (5th Cir. 1989).

[57] United States v. Eric B., 86 F.3d 869, 873 (9th Cir. 1996); United States v. Three Male Juveniles, 49 F.3d 1058, 1063 (5th Cir. 1995); United States v. Doe, 642 F.2d 1206, 1207–08 (10th Cir. 1981).

[58] United States v. Juvenile Male, 74 F.3d 526, 528–29 (4th Cir. 1996).

[59] United States v. Doe, 149 F.3d 945, 949–50 (9th Cir. 1998) (released to half-way house pending trial); United States v. Cuomo, 525 F.2d 1285, 1290–91 (5th Cir. 1976) (released to parents under restrictive bail conditions).

[60] United States v. Doe, 49 F.3d 859, 865–66 (2d Cir. 1995).

and sentencing;[61] or to the period for which a continuance has been granted at the juvenile's behest.[62] Time spent on the government's appeal is excludable in the interest of justice,[63] as is time spent litigating the government's transfer motions,[64] but not when the juvenile was being unlawfully detained at the time of the government's motion.[65]

Initial Stages of Federal Adjudication

Federal law permits federal proceedings against a federal juvenile offender when there is no realistic state alternative or when the juvenile is accused of a serious federal crime. The government must certify that it has elected a federal forum. The certificate must assert that either

1) the state courts are unwilling or unable to proceed against the juvenile for the misconduct in question; or
2) the juvenile programs of the state are unavailable or inadequate; or
3) the offense is a drug dealing or drug smuggling violation, possession of an undetectable firearm, or a felony and crime of violence and that a substantial federal interest exists warranting the exercise of federal jurisdiction.[66]

---

[61] United States v. Juvenile Male, 939 F.2d 321, 324 (6th Cir. 1991).

[62] United States v. Doe, 226 F.3d 672, 681 (6th Cir. 2000).

[63] United States v. Doe, 94 F.2d 532, 535–36 (9th Cir. 1996).

[64] United States v. David A., 436 F.3d 1201, 1207 (10th Cir. 2006); United States v. A.R., 203 F.3d 955, 963–64 (6th Cir. 2000); United States v. Sealed Juvenile 1, 192 F.3d 488, 491–92 (5th Cir. 1999); United States v. Wong, 40 F.3d1347, 1371 (2d Cir. 1994); United States v. Romulus, 949 F.2d 713, 716 (4th Cir. 1991).

[65] United States v. Female Juvenile, A.F.S., 377 F.3d 27, 37–38 (1st Cir. 2004).

[66] 18 U.S.C. § 5032[¶1] ("A juvenile alleged to have committed an act of juvenile delinquency . . . shall not be proceeded against in any court of the United States unless the Attorney General, after investigation, certifies to the appropriate district court of the United States that (1) the juvenile court or other appropriate court of a State does not have jurisdiction or refuses to assume jurisdiction over said juvenile with respect to such alleged act of juvenile delinquency, (2) the State does not have available programs and services adequate for the needs of juveniles, or (3) the offense charged is a crime of violence that is a felony or an offense described in section 401 of the Controlled Substances Act (21 U.S.C. 841), or section 1002(a), 1003, 1005, 1009, or 1010(b)(1), (2), or (3) of the Controlled Substances Import and Export Act (21 U.S.C. 952(a), 953, 955, 959, 960(b)(1), (2), (3)), section 922(x) or section 924(b), (g), or (h) of this title, and that there is a substantial Federal interest in the case or the offense to warrant the exercise of Federal jurisdiction.") (full text appears as an addendum to this report).

"Because certification requirements are disjunctive, a single basis for certification establishes jurisdiction."[67] Although the statute calls for certification by the Attorney General, the authority has been redelegated to the various United States Attorneys.[68] A facially adequate certification is generally thought to be beyond judicial review in the absence of evidence of bad faith.[69]

Certification is jurisdictional, however, so that certification by an Assistant United States Attorney without evidence of the United States Attorney's approval is insufficient.[70] The government need not certify the want of, or unwillingness to exercise, tribal as well as state jurisdiction.[71] "The Attorney General's certification of a 'substantial federal interest' is an act of prosecutorial discretion that is shielded from judicial review."[72]

The term "crime of violence" appears, undefined, several times in section 5032. Elsewhere, the term is defined using an "elements" clause ("The term 'crime of violence' means–(a) an offense that has as an element, the use, attempted use, or threatened use of physical force against the person or property of another")[73] or a "risk" clause ("[an] offense . . . that, by its nature, involves a substantial risk that physical force against the person or property of another may be used in the course of committing the offense").[74] In one instance, section 5032, itself, uses an "element" clause and a "risk" clause rather than the term "crime of violence."

In other contexts, The Supreme Court has declared the identical language in the "risk" clause or "residual" clause unconstitutionally vague and

---

[67] United States v. JDT, 762 F.3d 984, 993 (9th Cir. 2014).

[68] 28 C.F.R. § 0.57; *JDT*, 762 F.3d at 993; United States v. Sealed Juvenile 1, 225 F.3d 507, 509 (5th Cir. 2000); United States v. White, 139 F.3d 998, 1000 (4th Cir. 1998).

[69] *JDT*, 762 F.3d at 992; United States v. Doe, 226 F.3d 672, 676–78 (6th Cir. 2000); United States v. Smith, 178 F.3d 22, 25 (1st Cir. 1999); United States v. Juvenile No. 1, 118 F.3d 298, 304–05 (5th Cir. 1997); United States v. Juvenile Male J.A.J., 134 F.3d 905, 906–09 (8th Cir. 1998); United States v. Jarrett, 133 F.3d 519, 538 (7th Cir. 1998); *In re* Sealed Case, 131 F.3d 208, 211–14 (D.C. Cir. 1997); United States v. I.D.P., 102 F.3d 507, 511 (11th Cir. 1996); United States v. Vacier, 515 F.2d 1378, 1380–81 (2d Cir. 1975); *contra* United States v. T.M., 413 F.3d 420, 423–24 (4th Cir. 2005); *see also* Matthew Dexler, Note, *Judicial Review & the Policy of Federal Abstention: A Juvenile's Right to Ensure the Existence of a "Substantial Federal Interest,"* 98 MICH. L. REV. 1007 (2000).

[70] *Sealed Juvenile 1*, 225 F.3d at 509; United States v. Angelo D., 88 F.3d 856, 859–60 (10th Cir. 1996) (certification by principal assistant authorized by the United States Attorney to act for him in his absence); United States v. F.S.J., 265 F.3d 764, 768 (9th Cir. 2001) (same).

[71] United States v. Male Juvenile (Pierre Y.), 280 F.3d 1008, 1014–16 (9th Cir. 2002).

[72] United States v. Female Juvenile, A.F.S., 377 F.3d 27, 32 (1st Cir. 2004); *cf.* United States v. Diggins, 36 F.4th 302, 318 (1st Cir. 2022) (collecting circuit cases in accord).

[73] 18 U.S.C. §§ 16(a), 924(c)(3)(A).

[74] *Id.* §§ 16(b), 924(c)(3)(B).

inoperable.[75] In the context of section 5032, prosecutors have relied on the elements clause and avoided the risk clause.[76]

If the government decides against federal proceedings, the juvenile must either be released or, under the appropriate conditions, turned over to state authorities.[77] Otherwise, the government begins the proceedings by filing an information and a statement of the juvenile's past record with the district court.[78] Most courts appear to believe that they have no jurisdiction to proceed against a juvenile until they receive evidence of the juvenile's prior record.[79] The government may proceed against a juvenile as an adult only if the child insists, or pursuant to a juvenile court transfer.[80]

Transfers

There are two types of transfers to proceed against a juvenile as an adult under 18 U.S.C. § 5032, mandatory and discretionary. A transfer is mandatory in the case of a violent felony, drug trafficking, drug smuggling, or arson, allegedly committed by a juvenile 16 years of age or older who has previously been found to have committed comparable misconduct.[81] As the language suggests,

---

[75] Johnson v. United States, 576 U.S. 591, 606 (2015); Sessions v. Dimaya, 138 S. Ct. 1204, 1223 (2018).

[76] United States v. D.D.B., 903 F.3d 684, 686 n.1 (3d Cir. 2020) ("Section 5032 also contains what has been called in other contexts, a 'residual clause' . . . The government does not rely on this clause "); United States v. Rogers, 179F. Supp. 3d 881, 886 (E.D. Wis. 2016) ("[I]n light of the legal developments in *Johnson* the government does not rely . . . on the residual clause embodied in Section 5032"); David Jaffe & Darcie McElwee, *Federally Prosecuting Juvenile Gang Members*, 68 DOJ. FED. L. & PRAC. 15, 23–24 (2020).

[77] 18 U.S.C. § 5001.

[78] *Id.* § 5032[¶10].

[79] United States v. Woods, 827 F.3d 712, 715 (7th Cir. 2016); Impounded (Juvenile I.H., Jr.), 120 F.3d 457, 460 (3d Cir. 1997); United States v. Wong, 40 F.3d 1347, 1369–70 (2d Cir. 1994); United States v. Parker, 956 F.2d 169, 170 (8th Cir. 1992); *contra* United States v. Doe, 366 F.3d 1069, 1075–77 (9th Cir. 2004).

[80] 18 U.S.C. § 5032[¶4].

[81] *Id.* ("However, a juvenile who is alleged to have committed an act after his sixteenth birthday which if committed by an adult would be a felony offense that has as an element thereof the use, attempted use, or threatened use of physical force against the person of another, or that, by its very nature, involves a substantial risk that physical force against the person of another may be used in committing the offense, or would be an offense described in section 32, 81, 844(d), (e), (f), (h), (i) or 2275 of this title, subsection (b)(1)(A), (B), or (C), (d), or (e) of section 401 of the Controlled Substances Act, or section 1002(a), 1003, 1009, or 1010(b)(1), (2), or (3) of the Controlled Substances Import and Export Act (21 U.S.C. 952(a), 953, 959, 960(b)(1), (2), (3)), and who has previously been found guilty of an act which if committed by an adult would have been one of the offenses set forth in this

the prior felony "conviction" may be either a conviction as an adult or a finding of delinquency based on conduct that would be felonious if committed by an adult.[82]

Charges that would support a mandatory transfer if brought against a 16-year-old recidivist may be used to trigger a discretionary transfer if the juvenile is 15 or older regardless of his or her prior record;[83] discretionary transfers are also possible for juveniles 13 or older in some cases of assault, homicide, or robbery.[84]

At least one federal appellate court has rejected contentions that mandatory transfers constitute an unconstitutional denial of either due process or equal protection.[85] Aside from a denial of a claim of ineffective assistance of counsel, questions of the constitutionality of the underlying prior conviction or determination may not be raised at the transfer hearing.[86]

When the transfer is discretionary, juvenile adjudication is presumed appropriate,[87] unless the government can establish its case for a transfer by a

---

paragraph or an offense in violation of a State felony statute that would have been such an offense if a circumstance giving rise to Federal jurisdiction had existed, shall be transferred to the appropriate district court of the United States for criminal prosecution").

[82] United States v. N.J.B., 104 F.3d 630, 636–37 (4th Cir. 1997); United States v. Juvenile Male #1, 47 F.3d 68, 69 (2d Cir. 1995).

[83] 18 U.S.C. § 5032[¶4] ("A juvenile who is alleged to have committed an act of juvenile delinquency and who is not surrendered to State authorities shall be proceeded against under this chapter unless he has requested in writing upon advice of counsel to be proceeded against as an adult, except that, with respect to a juvenile fifteen years and older alleged to have committed an act after his fifteenth birthday which if committed by an adult would be a felony that is a crime of violence or an offense described in section 401 of the Controlled Substances Act (21 U.S.C. 841), or section 1002(a), 1005, or 1009 of the Controlled Substances Import and Export Act (21 U.S.C. 952(a), 955, 959), or section 922(x) of this title, or in section 924(b), (g), or (h) of this title, criminal prosecution on the basis of the alleged act may be begun by motion to transfer of the Attorney General in the appropriate district court of the United States, if such court finds, after hearing, such transfer would be in the interest of justice").

[84] *Id.* ("In the application of the preceding sentence [relating to the transfers of juveniles 15 or older], if the crime of violence is an offense under section 113(a), 113(b), 113(c), 1111, 1113, or, if the juvenile possessed a firearm during the offense, section 2111, 2113, 2241(a), or 2241(c), 'thirteen' shall be substituted for 'fifteen' and 'thirteenth' shall be substituted for 'fifteenth'.").

[85] United States v. Juvenile, 228 F.3d 987, 990 (9th Cir. 2000).

[86] United States v. M.C.E., 232 F.3d 1252, 1257 (9th Cir. 2000).

[87] United States v. Doe, 58 F.4th 1148, 1156 (10th Cir. 2023); United States v. J.C.D., 861 F.3d 1, 4 (1st Cir. 2017); *Female Juvenile, A.F.S.*, 377 F.3d at 32; United States v. Ramirez, 297 F.3d 185, 192 (2d Cir. 2002); United States v. Anthony Y., 172 F.3d 1249, 1252 (10th Cir. 1999); United States v. A.R., 203 F.3d 955, 961 (6th Cir. 2000); United States v. A.R., 38 F.3d 699, 706 (3d Cir. 1994).

preponderance of the evidence.[88] Section 5032 lays out the factors for the court's consideration when it is asked to exercise its discretion to transfer a juvenile in the interest of justice for trial as an adult. "In making its determination, the court must consider six factors: (1) the age and social background of the juvenile; (2) the nature of the alleged offense; (3) the extent and nature of the juvenile's prior delinquency record; (4) the juvenile's present intellectual development and psychological maturity; (5) the nature of past treatment efforts and the juvenile's response to them; and (6) the availability of programs designed to treat the juvenile's behavioral problems."[89] The purpose of the exercise is to determine whether the prospects for the juvenile's rehabilitation are outweighed by the risk of harm that he poses if not tried as an adult.[90]

A court need not give the factors equal weight as long as the court documents its consideration of each.[91] The age factor compels the court to consider a juvenile's age both at the time of the misconduct and at the time of the transfer hearing.[92] "The older a juvenile delinquent is both at the time of the alleged offense and at the time of transfer hearing, the more the juvenile defendant's age weighs in favor of transfer."[93] In considering the child's social

---

[88] *Doe*, 58 F.4th at 1156; United States v. Juvenile Male, 889 F.3d 450, 453 (8th Cir. 2018); United States v. Under Seal, 819 F.3d 715, 718 (4th Cir. 2016); United States v. Sealed Appellant 1, 591 F.3d 812, 820 (5th Cir. 2009); United States v. David A, 436 F.3d 1201, 1214 (10th Cir. 2006); United States v. Brandon P., 387 F.3d 969, 977 (9th Cir. 2004); *Female Juvenile, A.F.S.*, 377 F.3d at 32; *Ramirez*, 297 F.3d at 192; United States v. I.D.P., 102 F.3d 507, 513 (11th Cir. 1996); United States v. T.F.F., 55 F.3d 1118, 1122 (6th Cir. 1995); *A.R.*, 38 F.3d at 703.

[89] *Doe*, 58 F.4th at 1156-57; *Juvenile Male*, 889 F.3d at 453 (citing 18 U.S.C. § 5032[¶5]); United States v. Woods, 827F.3d 712, 715 (7th Cir. 2016).

[90] *Doe*, 58 F.4th at 1157; United States v. James, 556 F.3d 1062, 1066 (9th Cir. 2009); United States v. SLW, 406 F.3d 991, 993 (8th Cir. 2005); United States v. Male Juvenile E.L.C., 396 F.3d 458, 461 (1st Cir. 2005).

[91] *Doe*, 58 F.4th at 1157; *Juvenile Male*, 889 F.3d at 453; *Sealed Appellant 1*, 591 F.3d at 820; *Anthony Y.*, 172 F.3d at 1253; United States v. Wilson, 149 F.3d 610, 614 (7th Cir. 1998); United States v. Wellington, 102 F.3d 499, 506 (11th Cir. 1996); United States v. Nelson, 90 F.3d 636, 640 (2d Cir. 1996); United States v. Juvenile Male, 40 F.3d 841, 845–46 (6th Cir. 1994); *A.R.*, 38 F.3d at 705.

[92] United States v. Male, 610 F. Supp. 3d 474, 484 (E.D.N.Y. 2022) (citing United States v. Nelson, 68 F.3d 583, 589 (2d Cir. 1995)); United States v. J.J.P., 434 F. Supp. 3d 372, 377 (D. Md. 2020).

[93] United States v. Juvenile Male, 316 F. Supp. 3d 553, 561 (E.D.N.Y. 2018); *see also J.C.D.*, 861 F.3d at 3 ("J.C.D.'s advanced age (seventeen when he allegedly committed the carjacking) favored transfer."); *J.J.P.*, 434 F. Supp. 3d at 377.

background, the courts cite the child's family life, both positive and negative, and other social interactions.[94]

The second factor calls for an assessment of both the seriousness of the misconduct alleged and the juvenile's role in the transgression.[95] The allegations are taken as true for purposes of the assessment,[96] and allegations of serious offenses argue strongly for transfer.[97]

The third factor requires the court to take into account "the extent and nature of the juvenile's prior delinquency record."[98] This may include the juvenile's arrest record in some instances.[99] A clean record, however, is no bar to a transfer,[100] but may weigh against a transfer.[101]

---

[94] *E.g.*, *Juvenile Male*, 889 F.3d at 453 ("It considered A.M.'s assertions of his upstanding social background, but found that there was no evidence to support those assertions and that photos of A.M. flashing gang symbols and handling firearms undercut them."); *J.C.D.*, 861 F.3d at 3 ("J.C.D.'s social background, and particularly the abuse he suffered as a child, disfavored transfer."); *Woods*, 827 F.3d at 718 (citing difficulties at home and in school, history of drug possession, and long association with a gang).

[95] "In considering the nature of the offense, as required by this paragraph, the court shall consider the extent to which the juvenile played a leadership role in an organization, or otherwise influenced other persons to take part in criminal activities, involving the use or distribution of controlled substances or firearms. Such a factor, if found to exist, shall weigh in favor of a transfer to adult status, but the absence of this factor shall not preclude such a transfer." 18 U.S.C. § 5032[¶5]; *Juvenile Male*, 889 F.3d at 453; *J.C.D.*, 861 F.3d at 3 ("The Magistrate Judge noted the seriousness of the alleged offense, recounting J.C.D.'s underlying conduct and concluding that 'the evidence does suggest that J.C.D. was the primary aggressor; he carried a gun, he drove, he robbed, and, perhaps worst of all, he threatened.'"); United States v. Male, 610 F. Supp. 3d 474, 489 (E.D.N.Y. 2022) ("The defendant is charged with two premeditated brutal murders committed on behalf of the MS-13 gang."): *Woods*, 827 F.3d at 718 ("[D]uring the second robbery, Woods shot the store clerk multiple times.").

[96] *Id.*; United States v. Y.C.T., Male Juvenile, 805 F.3d 356, 358 (1st Cir. 2015).

[97] *J.C.D.*, 861 F.3d at 4 (upholding the district court's transfer order following a magistrate's finding that "only the nature of the offense weighs strongly in favor of transfer,' while '[t]he remaining statutory factors weigh against it or are neutral"); United States v. Sealed Appellant 1, 591 F.3d 812, 820 (1st Cir. 2009) ("This circuit has made clear that the seriousness of the offense in particular may be given more weight than other factors."); *Male,* 610 F. Supp. 3d at 489 ("[T]he Court may weigh this factor more heavily than any other when the alleged offense is particularly serious."); *J.J.P.*, 434 F. Supp. 3d at 378.

[98] 18 U.S.C. § 5032[¶5]; *e.g.*, *Woods*, 827 F.3d at 718 (noting extensive and escalating involvement with the juvenile system).

[99] *Male*, 610 F. Supp. 3d at 490 n.12 (citing United States v. Juvenile LWO, 160 F.3d 1179, 1183–84 (8th Cir. 1998), and United States v. Wilson, 149 F.3d 610, 613 (7th Cir. 1998), as evidence of a split in the circuits).

[100] United States v. Juvenile Male, 269 F. Supp. 3d 29, 41–42 (E.D.N.Y. 2017) (citing United States v. Juvenile Male, 554 F.3d 456, 468–70 (4th Cir. 2009), in which case the Fourth Circuit affirmed the district court's transfer order relating to a juvenile with no prior record); *see also* United States v. Female, 581 F. Supp. 3d 482, 486 (E.D.N.Y. 2022).

[101] *J.J.P.*, 454 F. Supp. 3d at 379.

The fourth factor, the juvenile's "intellectual development and psychological maturity," is essentially a matter of whether the juvenile has the mind of a child at the time of the transfer petition, indicating a receptivity to rehabilitation.[102] The factor may argue strongly for the transfer of a juvenile wise beyond his years.[103] Moreover, with age, the weight the courts give to average intellectual development and maturity begins to slip away.[104] In the case of older juveniles, the courts may find evidence of reduced, or even greatly reduced, development and maturity insufficient to overcome the counterweight of a serious offense.[105]

The fourth factor attempts to predict whether the juvenile will be receptive to rehabilitative efforts. The fifth factor evaluates whether the juvenile has been receptive to past rehabilitative efforts.[106] Sometimes, the factor carries

---

[102] 18 U.S.C. § 5032[¶5].

[103] *E.g.*, *Juvenile Male*, 269 F. Supp. 3d at 42–43 ("[T]he Court finds that the defendant's intellectual development and psychological maturity … weigh strongly in favor of transfer. Dr. Bardey reported that the defendant (1) exhibited thought processes that 'were logical and goal-directed,' displayed no evidence of a thought disorder, psychotic symptoms, or symptoms of anxiety or depression; (2) appeared to be 'of average intelligence and was grossly intact cognitively;' (3) 'displayed a level of psychological and emotional maturity beyond that of the average teenager of the same age;' and (4) 'deviate[s] from the neuropsychological makeup of an immature and impulsive juvenile' in regards to his actions, the complexity of his decision making, his ability to synthesize information from different sources, and his planning ability.").

[104] United States v. Woods, 827 F.3d 712, 718 (7th Cir. 2016) (in the case of a juvenile nearly 21 years of age at the time of the transfer petition, the district "court noted that Woods had completed his GED and that there was no indication of intellectual or psychological deficits," and the appellate court found "no abuse of discretion in the court evaluating this factor as neutral"); United States v. J.J., 704 F.3d 1219, 1222–24 (9th Cir. 2013) (affirming the transfer order of a juvenile, 17 years of age at the time of the offense, after "the witnesses testified that Defendant appeared to be of average intelligence and had the maturity typical of someone in his late teens").

[105] United States v. J.C.D., 861 F.3d 1, 3–6 (1st Cir. 2017) (in the case of a juvenile "nearly eighteen" at the time of the carjacking, the appellate court affirming a transfer order issued on the basis of the seriousness of the offense in spite of a finding that the juvenile lacked "a sense of right and wrong and logic mediated by judgment"); United States v. Sealed Appellant 1, 591 F.3d 812, 822 (5th Cir. 2009) (finding the district court did not err in ordering the transfer of a juvenile charged with armed carjacking even though the district court found that the juvenile "was suffering from Conduct Disorder, PTSD, a learning disability, and had an IQ of 77, which was borderline mentally retarded or in the 'lowest range of normal").

[106] 18 U.S.C. § 5032[¶5]; *e.g.*, *Woods*, 827 F.3d at 718 ("The district court noted that 'the juvenile system has made numerous efforts to assist the Defendant, with little or no success.' The district court noted that Woods responded poorly to the various programs. The court also stressed that Woods's escalating behavior demonstrated that the numerous prior attempts to rehabilitate him did not have any positive influence and accordingly found this factor weighed in favor of transfer.").

no weight when there have been no past efforts;[107] on other occasions, the want of past treatment may favor transfer.[108]

The final factor is the availability of treatment programs for the individual either as a juvenile or an adult.[109] The juvenile's age or offense may make him ineligible for programs in some instances.[110]

Transfer hearings are considered akin to preliminary hearings. Consequently, other than the rules of privilege, the Federal Rules of Evidence, including those governing the use of hearsay, do not apply.[111] A juvenile's statements "prior to or during a transfer hearing" may not be admitted in subsequent criminal proceedings.[112] Thus, a juvenile may be required to submit to a psychiatric examination in connection with the hearing, and the court may base its transfer determinations on the results without intruding upon the juvenile's Fifth Amendment privilege against self- incrimination.[113] The court's determination of whether transfer is appropriate is immediately appealable under an abuse of discretion standard.[114]

The Supreme Court's decision in Miller v. Alabama,[115] barring imposition of a sentence of life imprisonment without parole for an offense committed while a juvenile, precludes a transfer relating to an offense punishable only by

---

[107] United States v. Juvenile Male, 554 F.3d 456, 469 (4th Cir. 2009); United States v. Juvenile Male, 269 F. Supp. 3d 29, 43 (E.D.N.Y. 2017).

[108] United States v. Male, 610 F. Supp. 3d 474, 493 (E.D.N.Y. 2022) ("In sum, because the defendant has not made a demonstrable commitment to treatment efforts, and because there are indicators that there are impediments to rehabilitation (such as [a] disciplinary infraction relating to his alleged ongoing association with the MS-13), the Court finds that this factor weighs slightly in favor of transfer.").

[109] 18 U.S.C. § 5032[¶5].

[110] United States v. Doe, 58 F.4th 1148, 1158 (10th Cir. 2023) ("The three juvenile facilities have voluntary treatment options, but juveniles must leave the facility on their twenty-first birthday."); United States v. Juvenile Male, 889 F.3d 450, 453 (8th Cir. 2018) (The court "also considered the fact that because A.M. was now eighteen there were no longer juvenile programs designed to treat his behavioral needs."); *Woods*, 827 F.3d at 718 (no juvenile programs because of offense and age).

[111] FED. R. EVID. 1101(d)(3); *Juvenile Male*, 554 F.3d at 459–60; United States v. SLW, 406 F.3d 991, 995 (8th Cir. 2005); *In re* A.M., 34 F.3d 153, 161–62 (3d Cir. 1994); United States v. Doe, 871 F.2d 1248, 1255 (5th Cir. 1989); United States v. C.P.A., 572 F. Supp. 2d 1122, 1124–125 (D.N.D. 2008).

[112] 18 U.S.C. 5032[¶8].

[113] United States v. Mitchell H., 182 F.3d 1034, 1035–36 (9th Cir. 1999); United States v. A.R., 38 F.3d 699, 703 (3d Cir. 1994).

[114] United States v. Woods, 827 F.3d. 712, 717 & n.2 (7th Cir. 2016); United States v. Y.C.T., Male Juvenile, 805 F.3d 356, 357, 358 (1st Cir. 2015); United States v. Juvenile Male, 554 F.3d 456, 463–65 (4th Cir. 2009).

[115] 567 U.S. 460 (2012).

death or life imprisonment.[116] It does not preclude a transfer with respect to an offense punishable alternatively by imprisonment for a term of years.[117] A court may order a juvenile transferred whose alleged misconduct carries both permissible and impermissible adult sentences.[118]

Delinquency Hearings

In the absence or failure of a government transfer motion and unless the juvenile insists on an adult trial, the district court, at its discretion, conducts a delinquency hearing "at any time and place within the district, in chambers or otherwise."[119] Neither the right to grand jury indictment[120] nor to a jury trial is constitutionally required.[121] The Constitution demands many of the other features of an adult criminal trial, however, including notice of charges, right to counsel, privilege against self-incrimination, right to confrontation and cross examination, proof beyond a reasonable doubt, protection against double jeopardy,[122] and application of the Fourth Amendment exclusionary rule.[123]

---

[116] United States v. Under Seal, 819 F.3d 715, 728 (4th Cir. 2016).

[117] *Cf.* United States v. Jefferson, 816 F.3d 1016, 1017–18 (8th Cir. 2016) (affirming a district court decision to reduce a pre-*Miller* sentence of mandatory life imprisonment to imprisonment for 50 years).

[118] United States v. Doe, 58 F.4th 1148, 1155 (10th Cir. 2023) ("Doe's argument is unripe [for adjudication] because her potential punishments rely upon 'contingent future events that may not occur as anticipated or indeed may not occur at all.' Doe could be acquitted, be convicted of second second-degree murder [which carries a permissible sentence], plea to a lesser-included offense, or even be convicted of first-degree murder but receive a lower sentence.") (quoting Texas v. United States, 523 U.S. 296, 300 (1998)).

[119] 18 U.S.C. § 5032[¶3]. District courts have discretion to regulate access to juvenile proceedings on a case by case basis. United States v. Three Juveniles, 61 F.3d 86, 92 (1st Cir. 1995); United States v. A.D., 28 F.3d 1353, 1359–62 (3d Cir. 1994).

[120] 18 U.S.C. § 5032[¶3] (". . . The Attorney General shall proceed by information"); *see also* United States v. C.S., 968 F.3d 237, 242 n.2 (3d Cir. 2020); United States v. Juvenile, 228 F.3d 987, 990 (9th Cir. 2000); United States v. Welch, 15 F.3d 1202, 1208–09 n.9 (1st Cir. 1993); United States v. Hill, 538 F.2d 1072, 1076 (4th Cir. 1976).

[121] McKeiver v. Pennsylvania, 403 U.S. 528, 545 (1975) (plurality op.) ("[W]e conclude that trial by jury in the juvenile court's adjudicative stage is not a constitutional requirement."); *C.S.*, 968 F.3d at 242 n.2; United States v. Male Juvenile (Pierre Y.), 280 F.3d 1008, 1021 (9th Cir. 2002); *Welch*, 15 F.3d at 1208–09 n.9; United States v. Juvenile Male C.L.O., 77 F.3d 1075, 1077 (8th Cir. 1996); *cf.* Bucio v. Sutherland, 674 F. Supp. 2d 882, 949 (S.D. Ohio 2009); United States v. Miguel, 338 F.3d 995, 1004 (9th Cir. 2003).

[122] Schall v. Martin, 467 U.S. 253, 263 (1984) (citing *In re* Gault, 387 U.S. 1, 31–57 (1967); *In re* Winship, 397 U.S. 358, 365–67 (1970); Breed v. Jones, 421 U.S. 519 (1971)); *see also* United States v. Doe, 226 F.3d 672, 680 (6th Cir. 2000) (proof beyond a reasonable doubt).

[123] United States v. Doe, 801 F. Supp. 1562, 1568 (E.D. Tex. 1992).

Disposition

Upon a finding of delinquency, the court schedules either a sentencing hearing or a hearing in anticipation of a commitment for examination prior to sentencing.[124] At sentencing, the court may dispose of a juvenile delinquency case by suspending sentence, by ordering restitution or probation, or by committing the juvenile to the custody of the Attorney General for detention.[125] The Sentencing Guidelines do not apply to detention ordered pursuant to federal juvenile delinquency proceedings.[126] Some recent cases reflect the view that a sentencing court need not opt for the least-restrictive disposition needed to secure the juvenile's rehabilitation.[127]

Unless the court suspends sentence, section 5037 establishes a series of time limits that restrict the court's authority when it orders detention,[128] when it imposes or revokes probation,[129] and when it imposes or revokes a period of juvenile delinquent supervision.[130]

Section 5037(c) provides different detention limitations depending upon whether the dispositional hearing occurs when the individual is under 18 years of age or is between 18 and 21 years of age.[131] In the case of a juvenile under 18, the court may order a term of detention no longer than the shorter of (A) the date the juvenile will turn 21; (B) the term at the top of the sentencing range under the Sentencing Guidelines that would apply had the juvenile been an adult; or (C) the maximum term of imprisonment that would apply had the juvenile been an adult.[132]

The detention limits for juveniles between the ages of 18 and 21 depend on the seriousness of the misconduct that led to the delinquency determination.

---

[124] 18 U.S.C. § 5037.

[125] *Id.*

[126] U.S. Sent'g Guidelines Manual § 1B1.12 (U.S. Sent'g Comm'n 2021); United States v. D.B., 61 F.4th 608, 614 (8th Cir. 2023).

[127] United States v. A.S., 939 F.3d 1063, 1084–85 (10th Cir. 2019) ("A.S.'s least-restrictive disposition rubric primarily stems from the decisions of the Ninth Circuit. . . . However, we are unpersuaded. We are unaware of any other circuit that has embraced the Ninth Circuit's approach. And two other circuits–the First and the Eighth–have affirmatively rejected it.") (citing United States v. Juvenile, 347 F.3d 778 (9th Cir. 2003); United States v. Patrick V., 359 F.3d 3, 10–12 (1st Cir. 2004); United States v. M.R.M., 513 F.3d 866, 869 (8th Cir. 2008)).

[128] 18 U.S.C. § 5037(c).

[129] *Id.* § 5037(b).

[130] *Id.* § 5037(d).

[131] *Id.* §§ 5037(c)(1), (2).

[132] *Id.* §§ 5037(c)(1)(A), (B), (C); *e.g.*, United States v. Sealed Juvenile, 781 F.3d 747, 750 (5th Cir. 2015).

If the misconduct would have been punishable by imprisonment for a maximum of 12 years or more, the term of detention may be no longer than the sooner of (i) five years, or (ii) the top of the Sentencing Guideline range applicable to adults under comparable circumstances.[133] If less serious misconduct led to the delinquency determination, the court may order detention for no longer than the sooner of (i) three years; (ii) the top of the Sentencing Guideline range; or (iii) the maximum term of imprisonment that an adult would have faced under the circumstances.[134]

The time limits for probation are comparable. The court may set the term of probation for a juvenile under 18 years of age at no longer than the sooner of (A) the date on which the juvenile will turn 21 years of age; or (B) five years (or one year if the misconduct in an adult would be punishable by imprisonment for not more than five days).[135] For juveniles between the ages of 18 and 21, the limit is the shorter of (A) three years; or (B) one year (if the misconduct in an adult would be punishable by imprisonment for not more than five days).[136] The adult mandatory and discretion condition statutes apply, including the requirement that any discretion conditions involve only such deprivations of liberty or property as are reasonably necessary to comply with statutory sentencing principles.[137]

The court may later revise or revoke a juvenile's probation and order the juvenile's detention for violation of his probation conditions.[138] Detention authority following revocation mirrors the court's initial detention authority with two exceptions. First, regardless of the juvenile's age at the time of revocation, the court is initially governed by the time limits that apply to the detention of juveniles between the ages of 18 and 21.[139] Second, an individual who is 21 years of age or older may not be detained beyond the age of 23, or beyond the age of 25 if the misconduct ispunishable by imprisonment for 12 years or more.[140] Subject to those restrictions, when the misconduct that

---

[133] 18 U.S.C. §§ 5037(c)(2)(A)(i), (ii), 3581(b); *e.g.*, United States v. J.A.S., Jr., 862 F.3d 543, 544 (6th Cir. 2017).

[134] 18 U.S.C. §§ 5037(c)(2)(B)(i), (ii), (iii).

[135] *Id.* §§ 5037(b)(1)(A), (B), 3561(c).

[136] *Id.* §§ 5037(b)(2)(A), (B), 3561(c).

[137] *Id.* §§ 5037(b), 3563.

[138] *Id.* §§ 5037(b), 3563(c).

[139] ". . . The term of official detention authorized upon revocation of probation shall not exceed the terms authorized in section 5037(c)(2)(A) and (B) . . ." *Id.* § 5037(b).

[140] ". . . A disposition of a juvenile who is over the age of 21 years shall be in accordance with the provisions of section 5037(c)(2), except that in the case of a juvenile who if convicted as an adult would be convicted of a Class A, B, or C felony, no term of official detention may continue beyond the juvenile's 26th birthday, and in any other case, no term of official

resulted in the delinquency determination would be punishable by a maximum term of imprisonment of 12 years or more, the court may order a term of detention no longer than the shorter of (i) five years; or (ii) the term at the top of the sentencing range under the Sentencing Guidelines that would apply had the juvenile been an adult.[141] For less serious forms of misconduct, the limit is the shorter of (i) three years; (ii) the term at the top of the sentencing range under the Sentencing Guidelines that would apply had the juvenile been an adult; or (iii) the maximum term of imprisonment that would apply had the juvenile been an adult.[142]

When a court orders juvenile detention, it may also impose a term of juvenile delinquent supervision to be served after the individual's release from detention.[143] Juvenile delinquent supervision has its own time limits and its own set of conditions. The conditions are the same as those available when the court sentences a juvenile to probation.[144] The initial term of juvenile delinquent supervision may not exceed the juvenile's 21st birthday if the individual is under the age of 18 when the detention order is issued.[145] If the individual is between 18 and 21 when the detention order is issued, the initial time limits for supervision are those that apply to detention, less the time served in detention.[146] Thus, when the misconduct that resulted in the delinquency determination would be punishable by a maximum term of imprisonment of 12 years or more, the court may order a term of supervision no longer than the shorter of (i) five years; or (ii) the term at the top of the sentencing range under the Sentencing Guidelines that would apply had the juvenile been an adult.[147] For less serious forms of misconduct, the limit is the shorter of (i) three years; (ii) the term at the top of the sentencing range under the Sentencing Guidelines that would apply had the juvenile been an adult; or

---

detention may continue beyond the juvenile's 24th birthday. . ." *Id.* § 5037(b); *see id.*, § 3581(b) (defining class A, B, and C felonies).

141 *Id.* §§ 5037(c)(2)(A)(i), (ii), 3581(b).

142 *Id.* § 5037(c)(2)(B)(i), (ii), (iii).

143 *Id.* § 5037(b), (d)(1).

144 *Id.* § 5037(d)(3); *e.g.*, United States v. Sealed Juvenile, 781 F.3d 747, 750–51 (5th Cir. 2015) ("This Court has recognized that district courts have broad discretion in imposing conditions of supervised release, subject to statutory requirements. Under 18 U.S.C. § 3563, a court may provide discretional conditions 'to the extent that such conditions are reasonably related to the factors set forth in section 3553(a) and (a)(2) and to the extent that such conditions involve only such deprivations of liberty or property as are reasonably necessary for the purposes indicated in section 3553(a)(2).'").

145 18 U.S.C. § 5037(d)(2)(A).

146 *Id.* § 5037(c)(A), (B), (d)(2)(B).

147 *Id.* §§ 5037(c)(2)(A)(i), (ii), 3581(b).

(iii) the maximum term of imprisonment that would apply had the juvenile been an adult.[148]

Violation of the conditions of supervision may lead to further terms of detention and juvenile delinquent supervision.[149] The maximum term of detention following revocation of a term of supervision is the same as the maximum term of detention following revocation of probation, lesstime served in detention.[150] That is, when the misconduct that resulted in the delinquency determination would be punishable by a maximum term of imprisonment of 12 years or more, the court may order a term of supervision no longer than the shorter of (i) five years; (ii) the term at the top of the sentencing range under the Sentencing Guidelines that would apply had the juvenile been an adult; or (iii) the time before which the individual turns 26 years of age.[151] For less serious forms of misconduct, the limit is the shorter of (i) three years; (ii) the term at the top of the sentencing range under the Sentencing Guidelines that would apply had the juvenile been an adult; (iii) the maximum term of imprisonment that would apply had the juvenile been an adult; or (iv) the time before which the individual turns 24.[152]

Section 5037(d)(6) is somewhat cryptic about the term limits on the juvenile delinquent supervision imposed after revocation. It makes no mention of the limits in place when the individual is less than 18 years of age or between 18 and 21 years of age. As for individuals over 21 years of age, it declares that the term of juvenile delinquent supervision "shall be in accordance with the provisions of section 5037(d)(1)," with the exception of the usual bars on supervision over individuals once they reach either 24 or 26 years of age depending on the seriousness of their original misconduct.

The difficulty stems in part from the fact that section 5037(d)(1) says nothing about time limits. It merely states that "[t]he court, in ordering a term of official detention, may include the requirement that the juvenile be placed on a term of juvenile delinquent supervision after official detention." One appellate court has held that "the maximum term of supervision that a court

---

[148] *Id.* § 5037(c)(2)(B)(i), (ii), (iii).

[149] *Id.* § 5037(d)(4), (5). Revocation of the term of supervision is mandatory if the individual is 21 years of age or older and violated a condition of supervision relating to possession of a controlled substance or a firearm or failure to take and pass a drug test. *Id.* §§ 5037(d)(5), 3565(b).

[150] *Id.* § 5037(c)(2), (d)(5).

[151] *Id.* § 5037(c)(2)(A)(i), (ii); *see e.g.*, United States v. Juvenile Male, 900 F.3d 1036, 1044 & n.4 (9th Cir. 2018).

[152] 18 U.S.C. § 5037(c)(2)(B)(i), (ii), (iii).

may impose under § 5037(d)(6) is determined by the requirements in § 5037(d)(2), using the juvenile's age at the time of the revocation hearing."[153]

Juvenile Records and Conditions of Custody

One of the hallmarks of the Federal Juvenile Delinquency Act is its effort to shield juveniles from some of the harsh consequences of exposure to the criminal justice system. Before and after being taken into custody, and before and after being found delinquent, it refuses to allow juveniles to be interspersed with adults who are awaiting trial for, or have been convicted of, criminal offenses.[154] In the same spirit, ordinarily federal juvenile records are sealed for all purposes other than judicial inquiries, law enforcement needs, juvenile treatment requirements, employment in a position raising national security concerns, or disposition questions from victims.[155] This does not render otherwise admissible evidence of juvenile proceedings inadmissible in criminal proceedings.[156] Moreover, in response to media requests the court will balance the competing interests, which weigh heavily in favor of confidentiality;[157] and, in light of the Crime Victims' Rights Act,[158] the court

---

[153] United States v. E.T.H., 833 F.3d 931, 939-40 (8th Cir. 2016) (Thus, "the maximum *total* period of detention and supervision that may be imposed upon revocation of a previously imposed term of supervision for a juvenile who is under age 21 at the time of revocation is (i) 3 years, (ii) the top of the Guidelines range that would have applied to a similarly situated adult defendant *unless the court finds an aggravating factor to warrant an upward departure*, or (iii) the maximum term of imprisonment that would be authorized if the juvenile had been tried and convicted as an adult, whichever is least, *see* 18 U.S.C. § 5037(c)(2)(B), 'less the term of official detention ordered.' *Id.* § 5037(d)(2)(B).") (emphasis of the court).

[154] 18 U.S.C. § 5035.

[155] *Id.* § 5038(a).

[156] United States v. Jefferson, 215 F.3d 820, 824–25 (8th Cir. 2000) (upholding admission in proceedings against adult defendants when the juvenile raised no objections and the adult defendant had no standing to object); United States v. Under Seal, 853 F.3d 706, 728 (4th Cir. 2017) (upholding disclosure of partial transcript of juvenile proceedings in the order to satisfy the government's *Brady* obligations to disclose exculpatory evidence to defendant's counsel in related adult criminal proceedings).

[157] United States v. Three Juveniles, 61 F.3d 86, 92–94 (1st Cir. 1995) (upholding lower court authority to close juvenile proceedings); United States v. A.D., 28 F.3d 1353, 1361–62 (3d Cir. 1994) (holding balance favored opening juvenile proceedings); *In re* Wash. Post Motion, 247 F. Supp. 2d 761, 762–64 (D. Md. 2003) (unsealing some records but refusing to open others where the juvenile had been charged as an adult in another jurisdiction).

[158] 18 U.S.C. § 3771.

may permit the government to notify the victim of a juvenile threat of the status of proceedings against the juvenile, without identifying him.[159]

The Sex Offender Registration and Notification Act[160] dictates when a federal juvenile delinquent must register as a sex offender,[161] notwithstanding apparent conflicts with the confidentiality provisions that govern juvenile records.[162]

Juveniles Tried as Adults

Juveniles transferred for trial as adults in federal court are essentially treated as adults, with few distinctions afforded or required because of their age. At one time, even the Sentencing Guidelines instructed sentencing judges that an offender's youth was not ordinarily a permissible ground for reduction of the otherwise applicable Sentencing Guideline range.[163] The Sentencing Commission has since amended the guideline to permit consideration of the defendant's age in atypical cases.[164]

The Constitution's Cruel and Unusual Punishments Clause limits the sentence that a court may impose upon a juvenile tried as an adult. The "death penalty cannot be imposed upon juvenile offenders."[165] Nor can life imprisonment without the possibility of parole be imposed upon a juvenile offender for a non-homicide offense.[166] Nor may a sentence of mandatory life without the possibility of parole be imposed for a homicide committed by a

---

[159] United States v. C.S., 968 F.3d 237, 246–47 (3d Cir. 2020).

[160] 34 U.S.C. §§ 20901–20932.

[161] *Id.* § 20911(8) (when the juvenile "is 14 years of age or older at the time of the offense and the offense adjudicated was comparable to or more severe than aggravated sexual abuse (as described in section 2241 of title 18), or was an attempt or conspiracy to commit such an offense").

[162] United States v. Juvenile Male, 670 F.3d 999, 1002 (9th Cir. 2012); United States v. Under Seal, 709 F.3d 257, 259 (4th Cir. 2013).

[163] U.S. Sent'g Guidelines Manual § 5H1.1 (U.S. Sent'g Comm'n eff. until Nov. 1, 2010) ("Age (including youth) is not ordinarily relevant in determining whether a sentence should be outside the applicable guideline range. . ."); United States v. Wong, 40 F.3d 1347, 1381 (2d Cir. 1994); United States v. Talk, 13 F.3d 369, 371 (10th Cir. 1993).

[164] U.S. Sent'g Guidelines Manual § 5H1.1 ("Age (including youth) may be relevant in determining whether a departure is warranted, if considerations based on age, individually or in combination with other offender characteristics, are present to an unusual degree and distinguish the case from the typical cases covered by the guidelines.").

[165] Roper v. Simmons, 543 U.S. 551, 575 (2005).

[166] Graham v. Florida, 560 U.S. 48, 82 (2010).

juvenile under the age of 18.[167] Nevertheless, a sentencing court need not find that a juvenile is permanently incorrigible before imposing a discretionary sentence of life without parole.[168]

A federal court may sentence a juvenile to a term of imprisonment which, given his life expectancy and abolition of federal parole, "amount[s] to a de facto LWOP sentence."[169]

Addendum

18 U.S.C. § 5032 (Text)

> A juvenile alleged to have committed an act of juvenile delinquency, other than a violation of law committed within the special maritime and territorial jurisdiction of the United States for which the maximum authorized term of imprisonment does not exceed six months, shall not be proceeded against in any court of the United States unless the Attorney General, after investigation, certifies to the appropriate district court of the United States that (1) the juvenile court or other appropriate court of a State does not have jurisdiction or refuses to assume jurisdiction over said juvenile with respect to such alleged act of juvenile delinquency, (2) the State does not have available programs and services adequate for the needs of juveniles, or (3) the offense charged is a crime of violence that is a felony or an offense described in section 401 of the Controlled Substances Act (21 U.S.C. 841), or section 1002(a), 1003, 1005, 1009, or 1010(b)(1), (2), or (3) of the Controlled Substances Import and Export Act (21 U.S.C. 952(a), 953, 955, 959, 960(b)(1), (2), (3)), section 922(x) or section 924(b), (g), or (h) of this title, and that there is a substantial Federal interest in the case or the offense to warrant the exercise of Federal jurisdiction.
>
> If the Attorney General does not so certify, such juvenile shall be surrendered to the appropriate legal authorities of such State. For purposes of this section, the term "State" includes a State of the United States, the District of Columbia, and any commonwealth, territory, or possession of the United States.

---

[167] Miller v. Alabama, 567 U.S. 460, 465 (2012).

[168] Jones v. Mississippi, 141 S. Ct. 1307, 1311 (2021).

[169] United States v. Grant, 9 F.4th 186, 190 (3d Cir. 2021); *see also* United States v. Portillo, 981 F.3d 181, 182 (2d Cir. 2020). Both Grant and Portillo were convicted on racketeering charges (18 U.S.C. § 1962) that involved multiple murders.

If an alleged juvenile delinquent is not surrendered to the authorities of a State pursuant to this section, any proceedings against him shall be in an appropriate district court of the United States. For such purposes, the court may be convened at any time and place within the district, in chambers or otherwise. The Attorney General shall proceed by information or as authorized under section 3401(g) of this title, and no criminal prosecution shall be instituted for the alleged act of juvenile delinquency except as provided below.

A juvenile who is alleged to have committed an act of juvenile delinquency and who is not surrendered to State authorities shall be proceeded against under this chapter unless he has requested in writing upon advice of counsel to be proceeded against as an adult, except that, with respect to a juvenile fifteen years and older alleged to have committed an act after his fifteenth birthday which if committed by an adult would be a felony that is a crime of violence or an offense described in section 401 of the Controlled Substances Act (21 U.S.C. 841), or section 1002(a), 1005, or 1009 of the Controlled Substances Import and Export Act (21 U.S.C. 952(a), 955, 959), or section 922(x) of this title, or in section 924(b), (g), or (h) of this title, criminal prosecution on the basis of the alleged act may be begun by motion to transfer of the Attorney General in the appropriate district court of the United States, if such court finds, after hearing, such transfer would be in the interest of justice. In the application of the preceding sentence, if the crime of violence is an offense under section 113(a), 113(b), 113(c), 1111, 1113, or, if the juvenile possessed a firearm during the offense, section 2111, 2113, 2241(a), or 2241(c), "thirteen" shall be substituted for "fifteen" and "thirteenth" shall be substituted for "fifteenth". Notwithstanding sections 1152 and 1153, no person subject to the criminal jurisdiction of an Indian tribal government shall be subject to the preceding sentence for any offense the Federal jurisdiction for which is predicated solely on Indian country (as defined in section 1151), and which has occurred within the boundaries of such Indian country, unless the governing body of the tribe has elected that the preceding sentence have effect over land and persons subject to its criminal jurisdiction. However, a juvenile who is alleged to have committed an act after his sixteenth birthday which if committed by an adult would be a felony offense that has as an element thereof the use, attempted use, or threatened use of physical force against the person of another, or that, by its very nature, involves a substantial risk that physical force against the person of another may be used in committing the offense, or would be an offense described in section 32, 81, 844(d), (e), (f), (h), (i) or 2275 of this title, subsection (b)(1)(A), (B), or (C), (d), or (e) of section 401 of the Controlled Substances Act, or section 1002(a), 1003, 1009, or 1010(b)(1), (2), or (3) of the Controlled Substances Import and Export Act (21 U.S.C. 952(a), 953, 959, 960(b)(1), (2), (3)), and who has previously been found guilty of an act which if committed by an adult would have been one of the offenses set forth in this paragraph or an offense in violation of a State felony statute that would have been such an offense if a circumstance giving rise to Federal jurisdiction had existed, shall be transferred to the appropriate district court of the United States for criminal prosecution.

Evidence of the following factors shall be considered, and findings with regard to each factor shall be made in the record, in assessing whether a transfer would be in the interest of justice: the age and social background of the juvenile; the nature of the alleged offense; the extent and nature of the juvenile's prior delinquency record; the juvenile's present intellectual development and psychological maturity; the nature of past treatment efforts and the juvenile's response to such efforts; the availability of programs designed to treat the juvenile's behavioral problems. In considering the nature of the offense, as required by this paragraph, the court shall consider the extent to which the juvenile played a leadership role in an organization, or otherwise influenced other persons to take part in criminal activities, involving the use or distribution of controlled substances or firearms. Such a factor, if found to exist, shall weigh in favor of a transfer to adult status, but the absence of this factor shall not preclude such a transfer.

Reasonable notice of the transfer hearing shall be given to the juvenile, his parents, guardian, or custodian and to his counsel. The juvenile shall be assisted by counsel during the transfer hearing, and at every other critical stage of the proceedings.

Once a juvenile has entered a plea of guilty or the proceeding has reached the stage that evidence has begun to be taken with respect to a crime or an alleged act of juvenile delinquency subsequent criminal prosecution or juvenile proceedings based upon such alleged act of delinquency shall be barred.

Statements made by a juvenile prior to or during a transfer hearing under this section shall not be admissible at subsequent criminal prosecutions.

Whenever a juvenile transferred to district court under this section is not convicted of the crime upon which the transfer was based or another crime which would have warranted transfer had the juvenile been initially charged with that crime, further proceedings concerning the juvenile shall be conducted pursuant to the provisions of this chapter.

A juvenile shall not be transferred to adult prosecution nor shall a hearing be held under section 5037 (disposition after a finding of juvenile delinquency) until any prior juvenile court records of such juvenile have been received by the court, or the clerk of the juvenile court has certified in writing that the juvenile has no prior record, or that the juvenile's record is unavailable and why it is unavailable.

Whenever a juvenile is adjudged delinquent pursuant to the provisions of this chapter, the specific acts which the juvenile has been found to have committed shall be described as part of the official record of the proceedings and part of the juvenile's official record.

Chapter 2

Five Things About Youth and Delinquency*

National Institute of Justice

Research and data on youth and delinquency is critical for identifying opportunities and developing strategies to support positive development through prevention and intervention. Responses to youth misbehavior by youth-serving systems — including education, child welfare, behavioral health, and justice systems — can play an important role in promoting or disrupting youths' healthy social and emotional development. The five findings below provide insights into the nature, scope, and context of youth and delinquency.

1) Youth risk-taking is part of the normative developmental process — with brain maturation continuing into early adulthood.

The cognitive control capacities needed to inhibit risk taking behaviors develop throughout adolescence — from the onset of puberty through the mid-20s. Exploration and risk taking are part of the natural developmental process during this period.[1] Research suggests environmental factors can affect youths' development and impact risk trajectories. Exposure to positive factors, such as supportive relationships and positive role models, is associated with positive developmental trajectories. Exposure to negative factors, such as

---

* This is an edited, reformatted and augmented version of U.S. Department of Justice, Office of Justice Programs, Publication No. NCJ 309129, dated July 2024.

[1] National Academy of Sciences, Engineering, and Medicine (NAS), The Promise of Adolescence: Realizing Opportunity for All Youth (Washington, DC: The National Academies Press, 2019), https://doi.org/10.17226/25388.

In: Perspectives on Juvenile Justice: Legal, Social, and Policy Issues
Editor: David Y. Reyes
ISBN: 979-8-89530-669-7

toxic stress caused by abuse and neglect, can reduce youths' control of their moods and impulses and put or keep them on at-risk trajectories.[2]

2) Engagement in offending tends to increase through adolescence and then decline.

Research has consistently found the prevalence of offending increases during adolescence and subsequently declines, with most people eventually desisting from criminal behavior altogether.[3] For example, as illustrated in Exhibit 1, data from 2020 on age-specific rates shows arrests for violent offenses increased from ages 10 to 22, stabilized from ages 23 to 29, and then declined.[4] Reduced offending behaviors happen for most youths regardless of formal intervention. Research also suggests formal punishments, including incarceration, may disrupt youths' psychosocial development and increase the risk of reoffending, dropping out of school, and involvement in the criminal justice system.[5]

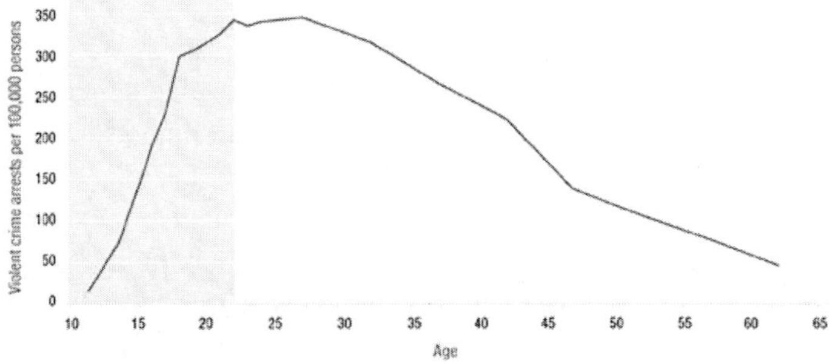

Exhibit 1. Age-specific arrest rates, 2020.

---

[2] NAS, The Promise of Adolescence, 77-94.

[3] National Institute of Justice, Desistance from Crime: Implications for Research, Policy, and Practice, Washington, DC: U.S. Department of Justice, Office of Justice Programs, National Institute of Justice, November 2021, NCJ 301497, https://www.ojp.gov/pdffiles1/nij/301497.pdf.

[4] "Statistical Briefing Book: Law Enforcement & Youth Crime," Office of Juvenile Justice and Delinquency Prevention, posted July 8, 2022, https://ojjdp.ojp.gov/statistical-briefing-book/ crime/faqs/qa05301.

[5] Development Services Group, Inc., Alternatives to Detention and Confinement, literature review (Washington, DC: U.S. Department of Justice, Office of Justice Programs, Office of Juvenile Justice and Delinquency Prevention, 2024 (forthcoming)); National Research Council, Reforming Juvenile Justice: A Developmental Approach (Washington, DC: The National Academies Press, 2012), https://doi.org/10.17226/14685; NAS, The Promise of Adolescence.

3) Only a small percentage of youths are arrested for any crime — even fewer for violent crime.

Less than 1% of youths ages 0 to 17 were arrested for any offense in 2022, and less than a half of 1% were arrested for a violent offense.[6] Research has identified protective factors

- individual, family, peer, school, and community
- that can decrease the likelihood of youths engaging in delinquent behaviors. These factors may protect youths directly
- regardless of other factors
- or indirectly by reducing the negative effects of adverse experiences.[7] Interventions can increase the presence and influence of protective factors and may prevent the onset or continuation of delinquent behaviors. For example, Early Developmental Prevention Programs for At-Risk Youths — which focus on enhancing child, parent-child, or family well-being — are rated effective by CrimeSolutions at reducing future deviance and criminal justice involvement. For youths who have engaged in delinquent behaviors, justice-system interventions that are based on a therapeutic intervention philosophy (e.g., counseling, skills building), focus on high-risk youths, and have high-quality implementation can be effective at reducing recidivism across all levels of system penetration.[8]

For example, Multisystemic Therapy — which is a family- and community- based treatment program targeting youths between the ages of 12 and 17 who present with serious antisocial and problem behavior and with serious criminal offenses — was rated effective by CrimeSolutions for reducing the number of rearrests and the number of days youths were incarcerated.

---

[6] Based on NIBRS arrest estimates available from the FBI's Crime Data Explorer website: https:// cde.ucr.cjis.gov/.

[7] Development Services Group, Inc., Protective Factors Against Delinquency, literature review (Washington, DC: Office of Juvenile Justice and Delinquency Prevention, last updated December 2015), https://www.ojjdp.gov/mpg/litreviews/Protective%20Factors.pdf.

[8] Lipsey, M. W. (2009). The Primary Factors that Characterize Effective Interventions with Juvenile Offenders: A Meta-Analytic Overview. Victims & Offenders, 4(2), 124–147. https://doi. org/10.1080/15564880802612573.

4) Youth arrests for violent offenses have declined from a historic peak in the mid-1990s.

The estimated number of youth arrests for violent crime — which includes murder, robbery, and aggravated assault — declined 67% from 2006 to 2020 (see exhibit 2).[9] By 2020, violent crime arrests involving youths reached a new low: 78% below the 1994 peak. More recent data from the FBI's National Incident-Based Reporting System (NIBRS) indicate that youth arrests for violent crimes increased 17% between 2021 and 2022.[10] Nevertheless, trends show that both the number and rate of youth arrests for violent crime remain well below levels in the mid-1990s and the most recent uptick in youth arrests in the mid-2000s. The one-year increase in arrests should be viewed in this historical context and caution is warranted when predicting future patterns.[11]

Learn More

- OJJDP Model Programs Guide
- OJJDP Statistical Briefing Book
- Five Things About Juvenile Delinquency Intervention and Treatment

5) The youth contribution to violent crime arrests is less than that from other age groups, including young adults.

The youth proportion of violent crime arrests declined from the mid-1990s (19%)[12] through at least 2020 (7%).[13] Based on data from NIBRS, youths

---

[9] Charles Puzzanchera, Trends in Youth Arrests for Violent Crimes, Juvenile Justice Statistics National Report Series Fact Sheet (Washington, DC: U.S. Department of Justice, Office of Justice Programs, Office of Juvenile Justice and Delinquency Prevention, 2022), https://ojjdp.ojp.gov/ publications/trends-in-youth-arrests.pdf.

[10] Arrest estimates post-2020 are not directly comparable to pre-2020 estimates due to the FBI's transition from the Summary Reporting System (SRS) to the National Incident-Based Reporting System (NIBRS).

[11] Jeffrey A. Butts and Howard N. Snyder, Too Soon to Tell: Deciphering Recent Trends in Youth Violence, (Chicago, IL: Chapin Hall Center for Children at the University of Chicago, November 2006), https://ncjj.org/PDF/Howardpubs/CHIB110-YouthCrime.pdf.

[12] Howard N. Snyder, Juvenile Justice Bulletin: Juvenile Arrests 1995 (Washington, DC: U.S. Department of Justice, Office of Justice Programs, Office of Juvenile Justice and Delinquency Prevention, February 1997), https://www.ojp.gov/pdffiles/163813.pdf; and Howard N. Snyder, Juvenile Justice Bulletin: Juvenile Arrests 1996 (Washington, DC: U.S. Department of Justice, Office of Justice Programs, Office of Juvenile Justice and Delinquency Prevention, November 1997), https://www.ojp.gov/pdffiles/arrest96.pdf.

[13] Charles Puzzanchera, Trends in Youth Arrests for Violent Crimes.

accounted for 9.4% and young adults ages 18 to 24 accounted for 19.9% of all arrests for violent crime in 2022.[14] The youth proportion of arrests and their arrest rates for violent crime varied by offense. For example, young adults were arrested at higher rates for murder and aggravated assault; however, older youths (ages 15 to 17) had higher rates for robbery and carjacking.

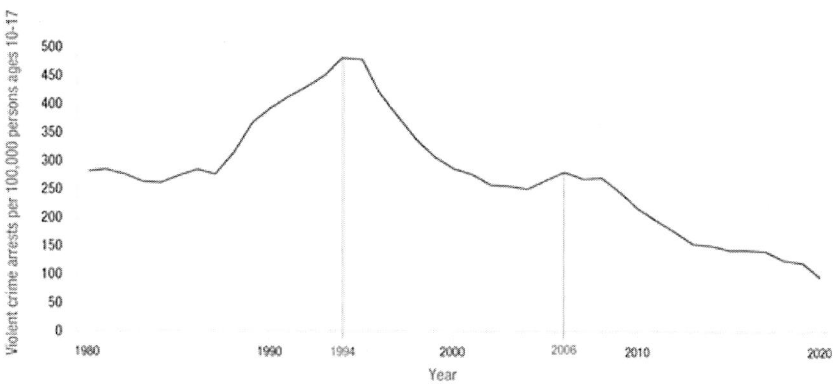

Exhibit 2. Youth arrest rate trends, 1980-2020.

The National Crime Victimization Survey (NCVS), sponsored by the Bureau of Justice Statistics (BJS), collects victims' perceptions of the age of individuals who perpetrate offenses. In 2022, 9.3% of violent incidents were perpetrated by individuals perceived to be ages 12 to 17, which did not differ significantly from this age group's share of the population. Nearly 60% of violent incidents were committed by someone perceived to be age 30 or older and 24% by those ages 18 to 29 — when the age was reported by the victim.[15]

[14] Based on NIBRS arrest estimates available from the FBI's Crime Data Explorer website: https:// cde.ucr.cjis.gov/.

[15] Alexandra Thompson and Susannah N. Tapp, Criminal Victimization, 2022 (Washington, DC: U.S. Department of Justice, Office of Justice Programs, Bureau of Justice Statistics, September 2023), https://bjs.ojp.gov/document/cv22.pdf.

Chapter 3

Crimes Involving Juveniles, 1993–2022*

Susannah N. Tapp
Alexandra Thompson
Erica L. Smith
and Lizabeth Remrey

This statistical brief presents findings on crimes involving juveniles, both as victims and as alleged or perceived offenders. It reports on (1) rates of nonfatal violent victimization of juveniles, (2) the number of deaths of juveniles due to homicide, (3) the percentage of nonfatal violent incidents in which the offender was perceived to be a juvenile, and (4) the percentage of persons arrested who were juveniles.

Data are from the Bureau of Justice Statistics' (BJS) National Crime Victimization Survey (NCVS), the FBI's Supplementary Homicide Reports (SHR), and the FBI's National Incident-Based Reporting System (NIBRS).

For additional information on these data collections and the similarities and differences between the BJS and FBI crime victimization data, including populations and types of crime covered, see Methodology or The Nation's Two Crime Measures, 2011–2020 (NCJ 303385, BJS, February 2022).

---

* This is an edited, reformatted and augmented version of U.S. Department of Justice, Office of Justice, Programs Bureau of Justice Statistics Publication No. NCJ 308554, dated April 2024.

In: Perspectives on Juvenile Justice: Legal, Social, and Policy Issues
Editor: David Y. Reyes
ISBN: 979-8-89530-669-7

Trends in Nonfatal Victimization Rates from 1993 to 2022

- From 1993 to 2022, the rate of nonfatal violent victimization (which includes rape or sexual assault, robbery, aggravated assault, and simple assault) declined for persons ages 12 to 17, persons ages 18 to 24, and persons age 25 or older (figure 1).
- For persons ages 12 to 17, the violent victimization rate declined 85%, from 184.8 per 1,000 in 1993 to 27.4 per 1,000 in 2022.
- The violent victimization rate declined 74% from 1993 to 2022 for persons ages 18 to 24 (from 141.6 per 1,000
- to 36.8 per 1,000) and 62% for persons age 25 or older(from 56.0 per 1,000 to 21.3 per 1,000).

Source: Bureau of Justice Statistics, National Crime Victimization Survey, 1993–2022.

Note: In the National Crime Victimization Survey (NCVS), violent crime includes rape or sexual assault, robbery, aggravated assault, and simple assault. Estimates for 2006 should not be compared to estimates for other years. See Criminal Victimization, 2007 (NCJ 224390, BJS, December 2008) for more information on changes to the 2006 NCVS. Due to a sample increase and redesign in 2016, victimization estimates among persons ages 12 to 17 in 2016 are not comparable to estimates for other years.

See Criminal Victimization, 2016: Revised (NCJ 252121, BJS, October 2018). Population estimates used to calculate rates per 1,000 persons were generated using NCVS data files. See appendix table 1 for estimates and standard errors.

Figure 1. Rate of nonfatal violent victimization, by age of victim, 1993–2022.

The most recent year of data for the NCVS, SHR, and NIBRS is 2022. Juvenile crime victims in the NCVS refers to persons ages 12 to 17 who experienced at least one nonfatal victimization in a given year. Juveniles in NIBRS refers to those age 17 and younger. Estimates for other age groups are also included in this report for reference. For the NCVS, rates are presented as the number of victimizations per 1,000 persons age 12 or older (or more specific age group) living in noninstitutionalized residential settings in the United States. For NIBRS, rates are presented as the number of victimizations or arrests per 100,000 persons in the population (or in a specific age group). For both collections, statistical significance is reported at the 95% confidence level. See figures, tables, and appendix tables for specific findings.

Rates of Nonfatal Victimization from 2018 to 2022

- The rate of nonfatal violent victimization for persons ages 12 to 17 was higher in 2022 (27.4 per 1,000)
- than in 2020 (17.4 per 1,000) and 2021 (13.2 per 1,000) (figure 2). The rate in 2018 was not statistically different from the rate in 2022.
- From 2021 to 2022, the rate of violent victimization also increased for persons ages 18 to 24 (from 23.1 per 1,000 to 36.8 per 1,000) and persons age 25 or older (from 16.0 per 1,000 to 21.3 per 1,000). For both age groups, the 2018 violent victimization rate was not statistically different from the rate in 2022.

Trends in the Number of Homicides from 1993 to 2022

- From 1993 to 2022, the total number of homicides in the United States fluctuated annually, declining from more than 24,520 in 1993 to a low of 14,160 in 2014 before increasing to 23,060 in 2021 (figure 3). There were 21,590 homicides in 2022, which was not significantly different from the number in 2021 (23,060).
- An estimated 710 persons age 11 or younger and 1,410 persons ages 12 to 17 were victims of homicide in 2022. The number of homicides of juveniles in 2022 was not statistically different from the number in 2021.

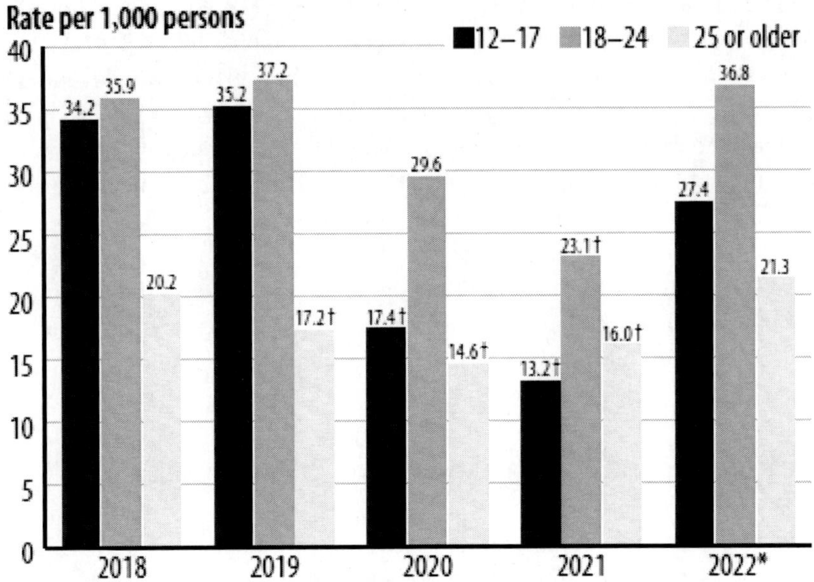

Source: Bureau of Justice Statistics, National Crime Victimization Survey, 2018–2022.

Note: In the National Crime Victimization Survey (NCVS), violent crime includes rape or sexual assault, robbery, aggravated assault, and simple assault. Population estimates used to calculate rates per 1,000 persons were generated using NCVS data files. See appendix table 2 for estimates and standard errors.

* Comparison year.

† Difference with comparison group is significant at the 95% confidence level.

Figure 2. Rate of nonfatal violent victimization, by age of victim, 2018–2022.

Rates of Homicide Victimization from 2018 To 2022

- In 2022, the homicide rate was higher for persons age 18 or older (7.5 per 100,000) than for persons ages 12 to 17 (5.4 per 100,000) and persons age 11 or younger (1.4 per 100,000) (figure 4).
- The homicide rate among persons ages 12 to 17 increased from 2.9 per 100,000 in 2018 to 5.4 per 100,000 in 2022.
- From 2018 to 2022, persons age 11 or younger had a lower homicide rate than persons age 12 or older.

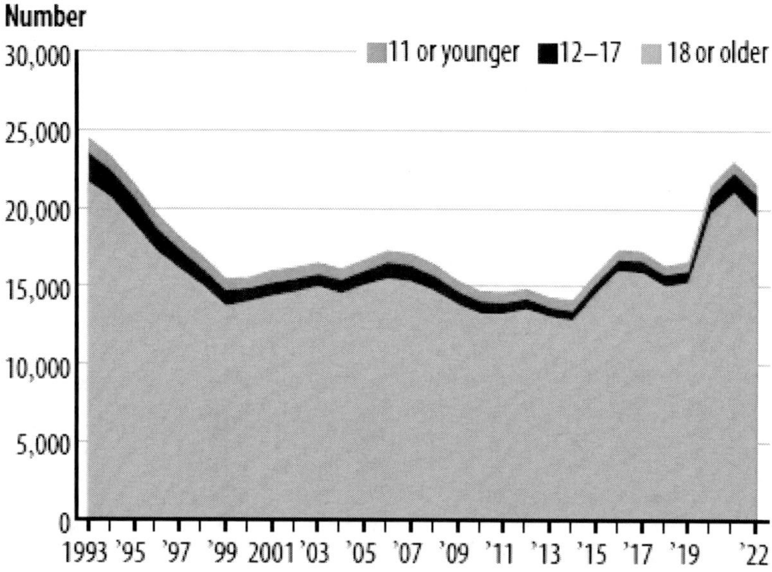

Source: Federal Bureau of Investigation, Uniform Crime Reporting (UCR) Program, UCR Supplementary Homicide Reports Program, 1993–2020, and UCR National Incident-Based Reporting System Estimation Program, 2021 and 2022.

Note: See appendix table 3 for estimates and confidence intervals. Confidence intervals are calculated for 2021 and 2022 because estimates are from the Uniform Crime Reporting Program National Incident-Based Reporting System Estimation Program. They are not applicable for 1993 to 2020.

Figure 3. Number of homicides, by age of victim, 1993–2022.

Nonfatal Violent Incidents, by Offender Age, from 2021 to 2022

- In both 2021 and 2022, less than 10% of nonfatal violent incidents were committed by an offender the victim perceived to be between the ages of 12 and 17, when the offender's age was reported (figure 5).[1] In 2022, the offender was perceived to be in the age range of 12 to 17 years old in 9.3% of violent incidents.

[1] An incident is a specific criminal act involving one or more victims.

- There were no statistically significant differences between 2021 and 2022 in the percentage of nonfatal violent incidents by perceived age of the offender.

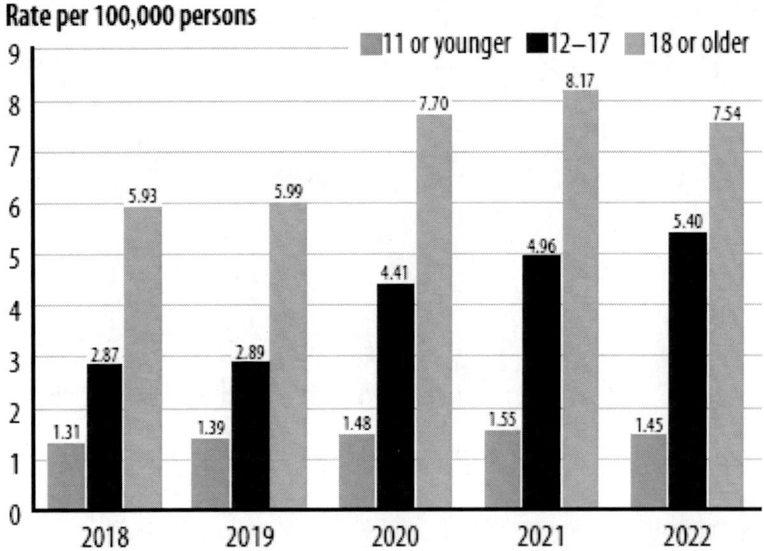

Note: See appendix table 4 for estimates and confidence intervals. Confidence intervals are calculated for 2021 and 2022 because estimates are from the Uniform Crime Reporting Program National Incident-Based Reporting System Estimation Program. They are not applicable for 2018 to 2020.

Source: Federal Bureau of Investigation, Uniform Crime Reporting (UCR) Program, UCR Supplementary Homicide Reports Program, 2018–2020, and UCR National Incident-Based Reporting System Estimation Program, 2021 and 2022; and Office of Juvenile Justice and Delinquency Prevention, Easy Access to Juvenile Populations: 1990–2020, https://www.ojjdp.gov/ojstatbb/ezapop.

Figure 4. Homicide rate per 100,000 persons, by age of victim, 2018–2022.

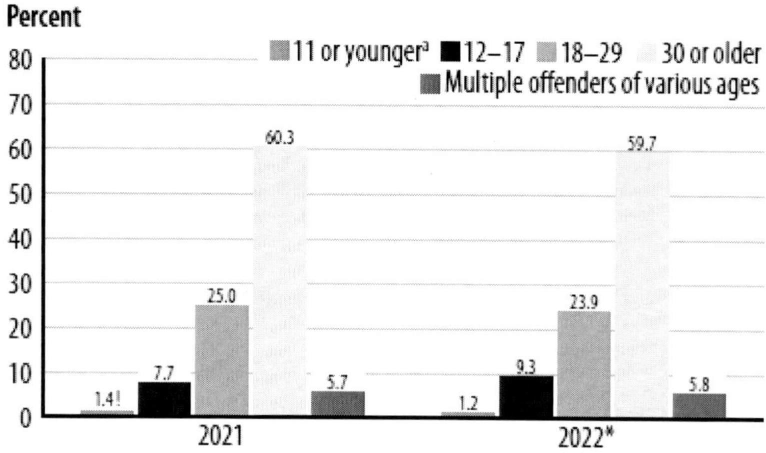

Source: Bureau of Justice Statistics, National Crime Victimization Survey, 2021 and 2022.

Note: In the National Crime Victimization Survey (NCVS), violent crime includes rape or sexual assault, robbery, aggravated assault, and simple assault. Details may not sum to totals due to rounding and missing data for offender characteristics. An incident is a specific criminal act involving one or more victims. Offender characteristics are based on victims' perceptions of offenders. Includes incidents in which the perceived offender characteristics were reported. The age of the offender was unknown in 14% of incidents in 2021 and 17% of incidents in 2022. See appendix table 5 for estimates and standard errors.

* Comparison year. There were no statistically significant differences between 2021 and 2022.

! Interpret with caution. Estimate is based on 10 or fewer sample cases, or coefficient of variation is greater than 50%.

[a] While the NCVS does not survey victims age 11 or younger, victims may report the offender to be age 11 or younger.

Figure 5. Percent of nonfatal violent incidents, by age of offender, 2021 and 2022.

Juvenile Arrests in 2021 and 2022

- In 2022, juveniles accounted for 9.9% of all arrests for violent crime, up from 8.7% in 2021 (figure 6). The FBI defines the aggregate category of violent crime recorded by law enforcement to include homicide, rape, robbery, and aggravated assault.

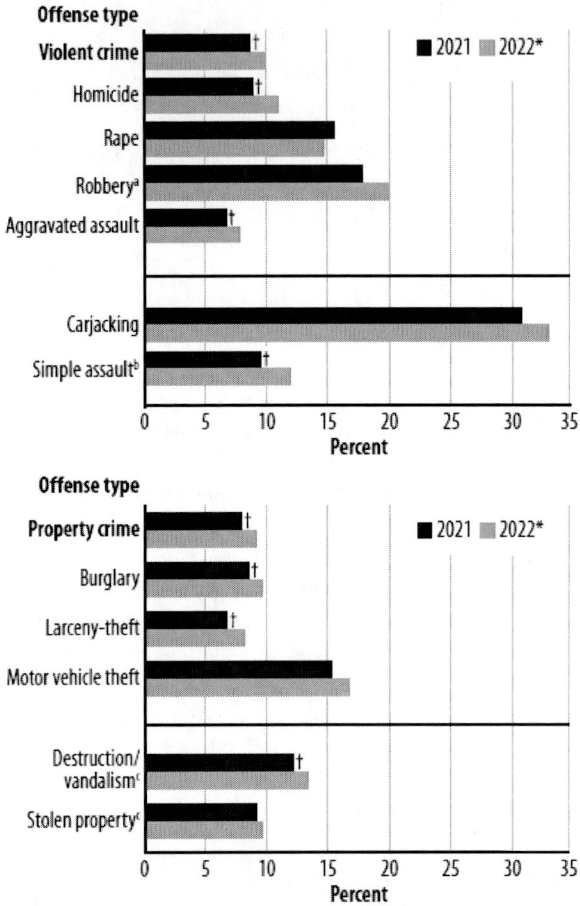

Source: Federal Bureau of Investigation, Uniform Crime Reporting (UCR) Program, UCR National Incident-Based Reporting System Estimation Program, 2021 and 2022.

Note: In the Uniform Crime Reporting Program, violent crime includes homicide, rape, robbery, and aggravated assault. Property crime includes burglary, larceny-theft, and motor vehicle theft. See appendix table 6 for estimates.

* Comparison year.

† Significant difference from comparison group at the 95% confidence level.

[a] Robbery includes carjacking.

[b] Not included in the overall violent crime percentages.

[c] Not included in the overall property crime percentages.

Figure 6. Percent of all arrests that were of persons age 17 or younger, by offense type, 2021 and 2022.

- From 2021 to 2022, the percentage of arrests that were of juveniles increased for multiple violent and property offense categories. Juveniles made up a larger percentage of arrests in 2022 than in 2021 for total violent crime and for the individual categories of homicide, aggravated assault, and simple assault. The percentage of persons arrested who were juveniles also increased from 2021 to 2022 for total property crime and the following property crime types: burglary, larceny-theft, and destruction or vandalism.
- Juveniles made up a larger portion of total arrests (all offense types captured in NIBRS) in 2022 (9.2%) than in 2021 (7.6%), largely due to an increase in the share of total arrests that were arrests of persons ages 12 to 17 from 2021 (7.4%) to 2022 (9.0%) (not shown in figures).
- In both 2021 and 2022, juveniles accounted for a larger percentage of arrests for carjacking than for any other violent crime.

Methodology

About the National Crime Victimization Survey Data

For additional information on the National Crime Victimization Survey, see the Methodology section in Criminal Victimization, 2022 (NCJ 307089, BJS, September 2023).

About the Supplementary Homicide Reports Data

The Supplementary Homicide Reports (SHR) are collected by the FBI's Uniform Crime Reporting (UCR) Program. The SHR provides detailed information on homicide incidents, including data on the reporting agency and its resident population; the sex, age, and race of victims and offenders; and the victim-offender relationship, weapon use, location, and circumstance of the crime.[2] The analyses presented exclude deaths caused by negligence, suicide, or accident; justifiable homicides; attempts to murder; and murders of U.S.

---

[2] See The Nation's Two Measures of Homicide (NCJ 247060, BJS, July 2014).

residents that occurred outside the United States. Deaths from the terrorist attacks of September 11, 2001, are also not included in these analyses.

The data included in the SHR are on homicides known to law enforcement. The determination that a crime was a homicide was made solely based on police investigation rather than the decision of a court, medical examiner, coroner, jury, or other non-law enforcement entity.

The SHR data were weighted to compensate for the average annual 10% of homicides that were not reported to the SHR from 1993 to 2020. The annual weights are calculated using a three-step process. For details on the weighting process, see the Methodology section in Homicide in the U.S. Known to Law Enforcement, 2011 (NCJ 243035, BJS, December 2013).

About the Easy Access to Juvenile Populations Data

The Easy Access to Juvenile Populations (EZAPOP) is a data source published by the Office of Juvenile Justice and Delinquency Prevention. EZAPOP provides national-, state-, and county-level U.S. resident population data by age, race, and sex. The data come from population data originally collected by the U.S. Census Bureau and modified by the National Center for Health Statistics. For more information on the data, see the EZAPOP web page.

Homicide rates for this report were calculated by dividing the estimated number of homicide victims, based on data from the SHR or NIBRS, by estimates of the U.S. resident population for the appropriate age group, generated by the EZAPOP data tool. Rates were per 100,000 U.S. residents.

About the National Incident-Based Reporting System data The National Incident-Based Reporting System (NIBRS) is a data collection system designed and maintained by the FBI through the UCR Program that compiles data on crimes recorded by participating state and local law enforcement agencies. NIBRS captures detailed information on 52 different offenses that can occur within a crime incident and collects arrest-only information for an additional 10 offenses.[3] For more information about the NIBRS data structure and details about the data elements included in the collection, see the Bureau of Justice Statistics' (BJS) National Incident- Based Reporting System page and the FBI's Crime Data Explorer. NIBRS data in this report are for the 2021 and 2022 data years.

[3] Federal agencies submitting data to NIBRS may report an additional 19 offense types and 3 arrest-only offense types that are exclusive to federal crime incidents.

NIBRS Definitions

Violent crime is an aggregate category made up of the offenses of homicide, rape, robbery, and aggravated assault.

Homicide consists of two violent crimes: murder and nonnegligent manslaughter. Murder and nonnegligent manslaughter are defined as "The willful (nonnegligent) killing of one human being by another." Attempted murder is categorized as aggravated assault in NIBRS and is not included in the definition of homicide. Other fatalities, such as accidental deaths, suicides, and traffic-related deaths are not included. "Felony murder," or situations where a victim dies of another cause (such as a heart attack) because of a crime being committed against them, is not classified as murder.

Rape is defined by the FBI UCR Program as "Penetration, no matter how slight, of the vagina or anus with any body part or object, or oral penetration by a sex organ of another person, without the consent of the victim." Rape occurs without the consent of the victim, including instances where the victim is unable to give consent due to their age or their temporary or permanent mental or physical incapacity.

Rape includes attempted but not completed crimes.

It does not include the offenses of statutory rape or incest. For this report, rape is an aggregation of the three NIBRS offense types of rape, sodomy, and sexual assault with an object, defined as:

1. Rape—the carnal knowledge of a person, or the penetration of a person's vagina or anus by the sex organ of another person
2. Sodomy—oral or anal sexual intercourse with another person
3. Sexual assault with an object—to use an object or instrument to unlawfully penetrate, however slightly, the genital or anal opening of the body of another person.

Robbery is "The taking of anything of value from the control, custody, or care of another person by force or threat of force and/or by putting the victim in fear of immediate harm." Assault (the use or threat of force) is a required element of robbery, as is the direct confrontation of the victim by the alleged offender.

Aggravated assault is "An unlawful attack by one person upon another wherein the offender uses a dangerous weapon or displays it in a threatening manner or the victim suffers obvious severe or aggravated bodily injury, or where there was a risk for serious injury/intent to seriously injure." The weapons used or the seriousness of injuries suffered by a victim are factors that determine whether an assault is classified as aggravated.

Carjacking is a specific type of robbery that involves the taking of a vehicle (automobile, truck, bus, or recreational vehicle) from an individual by force or threat of force.

Simple assault is "An unlawful physical attack by one person upon another where neither the offender displays a dangerous weapon, nor the victim suffers obvious severe or aggravated bodily injury involving apparent broken bones, loss of teeth, possible internal injury, severe laceration, or loss of consciousness." The absence of a weapon and the nature of the injuries suffered by a victim are factors that determine whether an assault is classified as simple.

Property crime is an aggregate category consisting of the offenses of burglary, larceny-theft, and motor vehicle theft.

Burglary is "The unlawful entry into a building or some other structure to commit a felony or theft." Larceny-theft is an element of burglary, but it is not considered larceny-theft if it is associated with the unlawful entry of a structure.

Larceny-theft is "The unlawful taking, carrying, leading, or riding away of property from the possession or constructive possession of another person." Motor vehicle theft is not included in the larceny-theft offense category due to the great volume of offenses.

Motor vehicle theft is "The theft of a motor vehicle." A motor vehicle is defined as "a self- propelled vehicle that runs on the surface of the land and not on rails." Motor vehicles include automobiles, buses, recreational vehicles, trucks, and other motorized vehicles (e.g., motorcycles).

Destruction/vandalism is "To willfully or maliciously destroy, damage, deface, or otherwise injure any public or private property without the consent of the owner or the person having custody or control of it."

Stolen property offenses are "Buying, receiving, possessing, selling, concealing, or transporting any property with the knowledge that it has been unlawfully taken, as by burglary, embezzlement, fraud, larceny, robbery, etc."

Persons arrested data are calculated by counting the total number of unique offenses for which an arrest occurred.

For example, if a person was arrested for an incident that involved three different offenses—burglary, stolen property, and destruction/vandalism—each arrest offense would be counted separately, and the demographic characteristics of the arrested person would be connected to each of the three offenses.

For more information, see NIBRS User Manual at https://le.fbi.gov/file-repository/nibrs-user-manual-063023.pdf/view.

Calculating National Estimates of Crime Based on NIBRS

Beginning with the 2021 data year, the FBI began publishing national estimates of crime known to law enforcement based on NIBRS data. To calculate national estimates using NIBRS data, BJS and the FBI, in partnership with RTI International, established a new set of statistical procedures to incorporate the NIBRS data structure and account for agencies that did not report data to the system. In October 2022, the FBI published the first set of national estimates derived from the new methodology. The data tables for the 2021 and 2022 data years are available through the FBI's Crime Data Explorer on the NIBRS Estimates page.

Estimation Procedures to Account for Missing Data and Potential Bias in the Estimates

The transition to NIBRS represents a significant improvement in how reported crime is measured and estimated by the federal government. NIBRS captures detailed data about the characteristics of criminal incidents, including:

- a broad array of offenses
- types and amount of property lost
- demographic information about victims, offenders, and persons arrested
- what type of weapon, if any, was used in the incident.

NIBRS coverage has increased each year, as more law enforcement agencies have submitted data to the system. For the 2021 data year, 11,818 of the 18,924 law enforcement agencies in the United States submitted at least 1 month of data to NIBRS, representing approximately 65% of the U.S. population. For the 2022 data year, 13,293 of the 18,884 agencies in the United States submitted at least 1 month of data to NIBRS, representing approximately 77% of the U.S. population.

The estimation methodology accounts for the number of agencies reporting data, the population covered, and other key issues that must be considered when estimating crime based on NIBRS.

Item Nonresponse

Item missingness refers to instances in which a valid value has not been reported for a critical field within a reported incident needed for estimation, either because the information is missing or because the reporting agency submitted a value of unknown.

For some NIBRS data elements, law enforcement agencies may submit a value of unknown or may simply not provide a value when they submit a crime incident record. These unknown or missing values impact the estimation procedures for key indicators. For instance, when estimating critical indicators like the demographic characteristics (e.g., age, race, sex) of a crime victim, there must be known values to produce rates by those demographic characteristics. To fill in the unknown or missing values, hot deck imputation is used.[4] Imputation is only conducted when the underlying assumption in the imputation process (that the donor agency is similar to the imputed agency) is met. The NIBRS data elements where imputation is employed include age, sex, and race of victims; age, sex, and race of persons arrested; age, sex, and race of alleged offenders among cleared cases (e.g., those crime incidents that resulted in arrest or were cleared by exceptional means); and victim-offender relationship among cleared cases.[5]

Accounting for Partial Reporting Agencies

Agencies are asked to report monthly crime incidents for the data year. Partial reporting agencies are agencies that reported some crime incidents through NIBRS but not for all 12 months of the data year. For partial reporting agencies, the estimation process must first assess the amount of data submitted

---

[4] See page 17 of *Violent Victimization Known to Law Enforcement in the Bakken Oil-Producing Region of Montana and North Dakota, 2006–2012* for a description of hot deck imputation.

[5] In certain situations, elements beyond law enforcement's control prevent the agency from arresting and formally charging the offender. When this occurs, the agency can clear the offense exceptionally. The FBI definition of "cleared by exceptional means" can be found in the Glossary on the Crime Data Explorer website.

by each participating law enforcement agency. This is measured by determining how many months of data were provided. Imputation is conducted for agencies reporting crime incident information for at least 3, but fewer than 12, months of the calendar year.

When accounting for missing crime incident data in NIBRS, the entire incident record must be imputed, which could include missing offense information, victim demographic characteristics, location of the incident, weapon use, and characteristics of persons arrested, among other things. The data structure in NIBRS requires the use of a complex, two-step imputation process. First, a model is specified to predict the total number of incidents in a month. Second, using the estimated number of incidents from that model, hot deck imputation is used to identify an agency that matches on agency characteristics and has the closest number of total incidents among the agencies with matching characteristics. The incidents from the similar agency are used in place of the missing incidents. For agencies that reported some, but not all, months of data in a year, the reported data are eligible for use in this imputation process.

Unit Nonresponse

Nonreporting agencies are law enforcement agencies that do not report any crime incident data to NIBRS. The number of nonreporting agencies has decreased annually, as additional law enforcement agencies complete their transitions to NIBRS reporting. The percentage of eligible law enforcement agencies that were nonreporting agencies was about 30% in 2022, with 70% of law enforcement agencies reporting at least 1 month of data to NIBRS that year.

To account for nonreporting agencies—agencies that have not reported any information through NIBRS during the year—a unit nonresponse weight is applied to the reporting agencies. NIBRS unit nonresponse weights allow reporting agencies to represent both themselves and some portion of the nonreporting agencies with similar agency characteristics, such as agency size and agency type.

Furthermore, different statistical weights are created for different geographic levels of estimation because the distribution of nonreporting agencies throughout the United States varies by state and region. Specifically, a weight is created for estimation at each of the geographic levels for which estimates are produced: (1) national, (2) regional, (3) state, (4) metropolitan statistical area, (5) judicial district, and (6) FBI field office. Having separate weights for different geographic areas helps ensure that the weights accurately reflect the geographic area being estimated.

Confidence Intervals

A confidence interval is a statistical measure of how well the estimated value of an indicator represents the population value, usually expressed as a range. The degree of statistical confidence around estimates derived from NIBRS crime data is partly a function of:

a) the overall population coverage rate each year
b) which agencies are reporting to NIBRS—because agency participation is not random across all potential reporting agencies.

Sixty-five percent of the population was covered by NIBRS-reporting agencies in 2021, and that increased to 77% in 2022, resulting in greater precision for most NIBRS-based crime estimates for 2022. A higher coverage rate increases the amount of statistical confidence in the estimates. These measures of statistical confidence are expressed as confidence intervals around each NIBRS-based estimate, as appropriate. The confidence intervals present the estimated range in which the population value lies, based on a 95% confidence estimate. The wider the range of the confidence interval, the more statistical uncertainty there is in the estimate.

Reliability of the Estimates

The reliability of NIBRS-based crime estimates is affected by several factors, including low agency coverage rates and the rareness of the event or phenomenon being measured (e.g., bias/hate crime), among other factors.

Consistent with standard principles and practices, statistically unreliable estimates—those with a level of statistical uncertainty above an established threshold— are not included in the published data because they may lead to erroneous conclusions or interpretations. Decisions about which estimates to withhold are based on a set of specific and consistent criteria developed as part of the estimation procedures.

For further information about the development of the estimation procedures, including links to technical reports documenting the process, see the BJS NIBRS Estimation Project.

Appendix Table 1. Estimates and standard errors for figure 1: Rate of nonfatal violent victimization, by age of victim, 1993–2022

	12–17			18–24			25 or older		
Year	Rate per 1,000 persons		Standard error	Rate per 1,000 persons		Standard error	Rate per 1,000 persons		Standard error
1993	184.8	†	11.10	141.6	†	9.15	56.0	†	3.02
1994	189.3	†	9.40	144.2	†	7.81	55.3	†	2.52
1995	156.3	†	8.62	135.4	†	7.75	49.3	†	2.42
1996	146.8	†	9.08	122.7	†	8.04	45.0	†	2.50
1997	135.5	†	9.53	110.0	†	8.28	43.7	†	2.68
1998	119.1	†	8.46	112.2	†	8.01	36.7	†	2.32
1999	108.7	†	8.36	88.9	†	7.22	32.6	†	2.20
2000	73.2	†	6.60	75.0	†	6.51	26.9	†	1.97
2001	74.4	†	6.07	59.2	†	5.08	22.9		1.57
2002	62.7	†	6.37	68.5	†	6.56	22.3		1.86
2003	78.3	†	6.78	63.8	†	5.80	21.1		1.63
2004	49.7	†	4.54	55.4	†	4.68	20.7		1.40
2005	59.8	†	5.73	61.0	†	5.59	19.4		1.51
2006	--		--	--		--	--		--
2007	61.8	†	6.09	46.6		4.87	19.8		1.66
2008	54.3	†	5.77	43.2		4.76	19.1		1.54
2009	43.0	†	5.45	38.5		4.82	17.4		1.63
2010	28.1		3.99	33.9		4.27	16.0	†	1.52
2011	37.7	†	4.35	49.1	†	4.86	16.9	†	1.38
2012	48.4	†	4.62	41.0		3.90	21.2		1.40
2013	52.1	†	6.09	33.8		4.31	18.1		1.68
2014	30.1		3.80	26.8	†	3.32	17.9		1.43
2015	31.3		4.08	25.1	†	3.31	16.2	†	1.38
2016	25.1		2.90	29.6		3.03	17.7	†	1.19
2017	33.5		3.48	34.7		3.35	17.2	†	1.15
2018	34.2		3.80	35.9		3.72	20.2		1.43
2019	35.2		3.82	37.2		3.75	17.2	†	1.24
2020	17.4	†	2.46	29.6		3.32	14.6	†	1.14

Year	12–17			18–24			25 or older		
	Rate per 1,000 persons		Standard error	Rate per 1,000 persons		Standard error	Rate per 1,000 persons		Standard error
2021	13.2	†	1.79	23.1	†	2.45	16.0	†	1.05
2022*	27.4		2.95	36.8		3.36	21.3		1.21

Source: Bureau of Justice Statistics, National Crime Victimization Survey, 1993–2022.

Note: In the National Crime Victimization Survey (NCVS), violent crime includes rape or sexual assault, robbery, aggravated assault, and simple assault. Due to a sample increase and redesign in 2016, victimization estimates among persons ages 12 to 17 in 2016 were not comparable to estimates for other years. See Criminal Victimization, 2016: Revised (NCJ 252121, BJS, October 2018). Population estimates used to calculate rates per 1,000 persons were generated using NCVS data files.

* Comparison year.

† Difference with comparison group is significant at the 95% confidence level.

-- Estimates for 2006 should not be compared to estimates for other years. See Criminal Victimization, 2007 (NCJ 224390, BJS, December 2008) for information on changes to the 2006 NCVS.

Appendix Table 2. Estimates and standard errors for figure 2: Rate of nonfatal violent victimization, by age of victim, 2018–2022

Victim age	2018		2019		2020		2021		2022*	
	Rate per 1,000 persons	Standard error	Rate per 1,000 persons	Standard error	Rate per 1,000 persons	Standard error	Rate per 1,000 persons	Standard error	Rate per 1,000 persons	Standard error
12–17	34.2	3.80	35.2	3.82	17.4 †	2.46	13.2 †	1.79	27.4	2.95
18–24	35.9	3.72	37.2	3.75	29.6	3.32	23.1 †	2.45	36.8	3.36
25 or older	20.2	1.43	17.2 †	1.24	14.6 †	1.14	16.0 †	1.05	21.3	1.21

Source: Bureau of Justice Statistics, National Crime Victimization Survey, 2018–2022.

Note: In the National Crime Victimization Survey (NCVS), violent crime includes rape or sexual assault, robbery, aggravated assault, and simple assault. Population estimates used to calculate rates per 1,000 persons were generated using NCVS data files.

* Comparison year.

† Difference with comparison group is significant at the 95% confidence level.

Appendix Table 3. Estimates and confidence intervals for figure 3: Number of homicides, by age of victim, 1993–2022

Year	11 or younger		12–17		18 or older	
	Estimate	95% confidence interval	Estimate	95% confidence interval	Estimate	95% confidence interval
1993	1,034	~	1,852	~	21,641	~
1994	964	~	1,735	~	20,628	~
1995	913	~	1,762	~	18,931	~

Year	11 or younger		12–17		18 or older	
	Estimate	95% confidence interval	Estimate	95% confidence interval	Estimate	95% confidence interval
1996	959	~	1,481	~	17,204	~
1997	865	~	1,230	~	16,113	~
1998	875	~	1,076	~	15,023	~
1999	822	~	1,007	~	13,693	~
2000	756	~	849	~	13,981	~
2001	850	~	835	~	14,352	~
2002	789	~	823	~	14,617	~
2003	790	~	786	~	14,951	~
2004	768	~	858	~	14,523	~
2005	742	~	927	~	15,070	~
2006	782	~	1,036	~	15,491	~
2007	802	~	1,037	~	15,288	~
2008	812	~	955	~	14,698	~
2009	730	~	838	~	13,831	~
2010	708	~	768	~	13,246	~
2011	736	~	672	~	13,253	~
2012	659	~	668	~	13,538	~
2013	678	~	589	~	13,052	~
2014	721	~	597	~	12,846	~
2015	693	~	643	~	14,547	~
2016	683	~	686	~	16,044	~
2017	656	~	758	~	15,880	~
2018	632	~	717	~	15,024	~
2019	667	~	723	~	15,279	~
2020	705	~	1,109	~	19,755	~
2021	761	± 144	1,274	± 283	21,027	± 6,547
2022	710	± 277	1,409	± 213	19,474	± 4,257

Source: Federal Bureau of Investigation, Uniform Crime Reporting Program (UCR), UCR Supplementary Homicide Reports Program, 1993–2020, and UCR National Incident-Based Reporting System Estimation Program, 2021 and 2022.

Note: Confidence intervals are provided for 2021 and 2022 because estimates are from the Uniform Crime Reporting Program National Incident-Based Reporting System Estimation Program. They are not applicable for 1993 to 2020.

~Not applicable.

Appendix Table 4. Estimates and confidence intervals for figure 4: Homicide rate per 100,000 persons, by age of victim, 2018–2022

Year	11 or younger		12–17		18 or older	
	Estimate	95% confidence interval	Estimate	95% confidence interval	Estimate	95% confidence interval
2018	1.31	~	2.87	~	5.93	~
2019	1.39	~	2.89	~	5.99	~

	11 or younger		12–17		18 or older	
Year	Estimate	95% confidence interval	Estimate	95% confidence interval	Estimate	95% confidence interval
2020	1.48	~	4.41	~	7.70	~
2021	1.55	± 0.29	4.96	± 1.1	8.17	± 2.55
2022	1.45	± 0.56	5.40	± 0.81	7.54	± 1.65

Source: Federal Bureau of Investigation, Uniform Crime Reporting Program (UCR), UCR Supplementary Homicide Reports Program, 2018–2020, and UCR National Incident-Based Reporting System Estimation Program, 2021 and 2022; and Office of Juvenile Justice and Delinquency Prevention, Easy Access to Juvenile Populations: 1990–2020, https://www.ojjdp.gov/ojstatbb/ezapop.

Note: Confidence intervals are provided for 2021 and 2022 because estimates are from the Uniform Crime Reporting Program National Incident-Based Reporting System Estimation Program. They are not applicable for 2018 to 2020.

~Not applicable.

Appendix Table 5. Estimates and standard errors for figure 5: Percent of nonfatal violent incidents, by age of offender, 2021 and 2022

	2021				2022*			
Offender age	Estimate		Standard error		Estimate		Standard error	
Total	100	%	~		100	%	~	
11 or younger[a]	1.4	!	0.35	%	1.2		0.36	%
12–17	7.7		1.00		9.3		1.09	
18–29	25.0		1.89		23.9		1.74	
30 or older	60.3		2.37		59.7		2.17	
Multiple offenders of various ages	5.7		0.84		5.8		0.84	

Source: Bureau of Justice Statistics, National Crime Victimization Survey, 2021 and 2022.

Note: In the National Crime Victimization Survey (NCVS), violent crime includes rape or sexual assault, robbery, aggravated assault, and simple assault. Details may not sum to totals due to rounding and missing data for offender characteristics. An incident is a specific criminal act involving one or more victims. Offender characteristics are based on victims' perceptions of offenders. Includes incidents in which the perceived offender characteristics were reported. The age of the offender was unknown in 14% of incidents in 2021 and 17% of incidents in 2022.

*Comparison year. There were no statistically significant differences between 2021 and 2022.

~Not applicable.

! Interpret with caution. Estimate is based on 10 or fewer sample cases, or coefficient of variation is greater than 50%. aWhile the NCVS does not survey victims age 11 or younger, victims may report the offender to be age 11 or younger.

Appendix Table 6. Estimates for figure 6: Percent of all arrests that were of persons age 17 or younger, by offense type, 2021 and 2022

Offense type	2021		2022*	
Violent crime	8.7	% †	9.9	%
Homicide	8.9	†	11.0	
Rape	15.5		14.7	
Robbery[a]	17.9		19.9	
Aggravated assault	6.7	†	7.8	
Carjacking	30.8	%	32.9	%
Simple assault[b]	9.5	% †	11.9	%
Property crime	8.1	% †	9.3	%
Burglary	8.7	†	9.8	
Larceny-theft	6.9	†	8.3	
Motor vehicle theft	15.6		17.0	
Destruction/vandalism[c]	12.4	% †	13.6	%
Stolen property[c]	9.3	%	9.8	%

Source: Federal Bureau of Investigation, Uniform Crime Reporting Program (UCR), UCR National Incident-Based Reporting System Estimation Program, 2021 and 2022.

Note: In the Uniform Crime Reporting Program, violent crime includes homicide, rape, robbery, and aggravated assault. Property crime includes burglary, larceny-theft, and motor vehicle theft.

* Comparison year.

† Significant difference from comparison group at the 95% confidence level.

[a] Robbery includes carjacking.

[b] Not included in the overall violent crime percentages.

[c] Not included in the overall property crime percentages.

DEPARTMENT OF JUSTICE ★ OFFICE OF JUSTICE PROGRAMS ★ QUI PRO DOMINA JUSTITIA SEQUITUR

The Bureau of Justice Statistics of the U.S. Department of Justice is the principal federal agency responsible for measuring crime, criminal victimization, criminal offenders, victims of crime, correlates of crime, and the operation of criminal and civil justice systems at the federal, state, tribal, and local levels. BJS collects, analyzes, and disseminates reliable statistics on crime and justice systems in the United States, supports improvements to state and local criminal justice information systems, and participates with national and international organizations to develop and recommend national standards for justice statistics. Kevin M. Scott, PhD, is the acting director.

This report was written by Susannah N. Tapp, PhD; Alexandra Thompson; Erica L. Smith; and Lizabeth Remrey, PhD. Emilie Coen, Stephanie Mueller, Lizabeth Remrey, and Alexandra Thompson verified the report.

Eric Hendrixson edited the report. Jeffrey Link produced the report. April 2024, NCJ 308554.

Chapter 4

Juveniles Incarcerated in U.S. Adult Jails and Prisons, 2002–2021*

Zhen Zeng
E. Ann Carson
and Rich Kluckow

Juveniles (persons age 17 or younger) arrested or convicted for a criminal offense may be housed in juvenile residential facilities or in adult jails and prisons, depending on state statute, judicial discretion, and federal law. This report details trends for juveniles who are held in adult facilities.

Key Findings

- The number of juveniles incarcerated in all U.S. adult prisons or jails declined from a peak of 10,420 in 2008 to a low of 2,250 in 2021 (figure 1).
- In 2021, local jails had custody of 1,960 juveniles while state and federal adult prisons held 290.
- The percent of the total jail population who were juveniles declined from 0.9% in 2002 to 0.3% in 2021 (figure 2).
- The percent of the total prison population who were juveniles declined from 0.2% in 2002 to 0.02% in 2021.
- In 2021, 87% of juveniles in adult correctional facilities were held in local jails and 13% were held in prisons, compared to 66% in local

* This is an edited, reformatted and augmented version of U.S. Department of Justice, Office of Justice Programs, Publication No. NCJ 306140, dated June 2023.

In: Perspectives on Juvenile Justice: Legal, Social, and Policy Issues
Editor: David Y. Reyes
ISBN: 979-8-89530-669-7

jails and 34% in prisons in 2002, the earliest year for which comparable data are available for both populations (table 1).

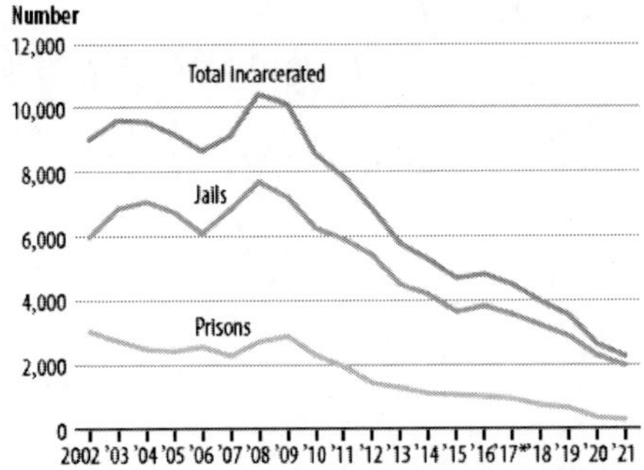

*Prior to 2017, state departments of corrections reported juveniles in their publicly operated facilities only; privately operated facilities were included in state data starting in 2017. The Federal Bureau of Prisons did not report juvenile counts in custody in 2002–2004, 2007, 2008, and 2010. See more details in Measures of Incarcerated Juveniles.

Source: Bureau of Justice Statistics, National Prisoner Statistics program, 2002–2021; Annual Survey of Jails, 2002–2004, 2006–2018, and 2020–2021; and Census of Jails, 2005 and 2019.

Figure 1. Reported number of juveniles held in the custody of adult jails or prisons, 2002–2021.

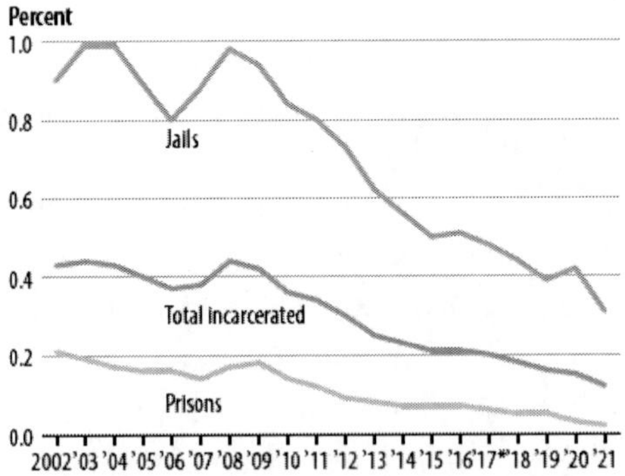

*Prior to 2017, state departments of corrections reported juveniles in their publicly operated facilities only; privately operated facilities were included in state data starting in 2017. The Federal Bureau of Prisons did not report juvenile counts in custody in 2002–2004, 2007, 2008, and 2010. See more details in Measures of Incarcerated Juveniles.

Source: Bureau of Justice Statistics, National Prisoner Statistics program, 2002–2021; Annual Survey of Jails, 2002–2004, 2006–2018, and 2020–2021; and Census of Jails, 2005 and 2019.

Figure 2. Juveniles as a percent of the incarcerated populations of adult jails and prisons, 2002–2021.

Measures of Incarcerated Juveniles

Data for this report come from local jail authorities, prisons through state departments of corrections (DOCs), and the Federal Bureau of Prisons (BOP). Local jail data are based on the jail inmate population confined on the last weekday in June, unless otherwise specified. Prison data are based on persons in the custody of state or federal correctional facilities as of December 31. From 2000 to 2016, the Bureau of Justice Statistics (BJS) asked DOCs and the BOP to report the number of persons age 17 or younger in the custody of their publicly operated adult correctional facilities. Starting in 2017, BJS asked DOCs and the BOP to also include persons age 17 or younger housed in privately operated adult correctional facilities contracted to DOCs and the BOP. Historically, the BOP has only held persons age 17 or younger in adult contract facilities, and these counts were reported to BJS in 2005, 2006, 2009, and 2011 to 2021. BOP data were not submitted to BJS for 2002 to 2004, 2007, 2008, and 2010. More information can be found on the BJS website about the National Prisoners Statistics program, Annual Survey of Jails, and Census of Jails.

Table 1. Juveniles in the custody of adult jails and prisons in the United States, 2002–2021

	Total			Juveniles in adult jails			Juveniles in adult prisons				
	Total	Male	Female	Jail total	Male	Female	Prison total	Federal[a]	State[b]	Male	Female
2002	9,010	8,470	540	5,970	5,540	430	3,040	/	3,040	2,930	110
2003	9,610	8,980	630	6,870	6,350	520	2,740	/	2,740	2,630	110
2004	9,560	8,870	690	7,080	6,500	580	2,480	/	2,480	2,370	110
2005	9,180	8,480	700	6,760	6,150	610	2,420	210	2,210	2,330	90
2006	8,660	8,100	560	6,100	5,650	450	2,560	190	2,360	2,450	110
2007	9,120	8,500	620	6,840	6,310	530	2,280	/	2,280	2,190	90
2008	10,420	9,840	590	7,700	7,210	500	2,720	/	2,720	2,630	90
2009	10,110	9,480	630	7,220	6,690	530	2,890	140	2,740	2,790	100
2010	8,560	7,990	560	6,260	5,770	480	2,300	/	2,300	2,220	80
2011	7,860	7,340	520	5,920	5,470	450	1,940	150	1,790	1,870	70
2012	6,860	6,360	500	5,430	4,980	450	1,430	110	1,330	1,380	50
2013	5,780	5,370	400	4,500	4,140	350	1,280	90	1,190	1,230	50
2014	5,280	4,920	370	4,180	3,850	340	1,100	70	1,040	1,070	30
2015[c]	4,700	4,330	360	3,640	3,310	330	1,060	60	990	1,020	30
2016[c]	4,820	4,390	420	3,810	3,420	390	1,010	50	960	970	30
2017	4,500	4,180	310	3,560	3,290	270	940	40	890	890	40
2018	3,960	3,610	350	3,220	2,900	320	740	40	700	710	30
2019	3,530	3,290	250	2,880	2,660	230	650	30	630	630	20

	Total			Juveniles in adult jails			Juveniles in adult prisons				
	Total	Male	Female	Jail total	Male	Female	Prison total	Federal[a]	State[b]	Male	Female
2020	2,630	2,480	150	2,280	2,140	140	350	10	340	340	10
2021	2,250	2,080	160	1,960	1,800	150	290	20	270	280	10

Source: Bureau of Justice Statistics, National Prisoner Statistics program, 2002–2021; Annual Survey of Jails, 2002–2004, 2006–2018, and 2020–2021; and Census of Jails, 2005 and 2019.

Note: Includes persons age 17 or younger. All data are adjusted for nonresponse and rounded to the nearest 10. Details may not sum to totals due to rounding. Results may differ from previous reports due to updates from jail and prison respondents.

/Did not report.

[a] The Federal Bureau of Prisons reported counts of juveniles held in adult contract facilities to BJS in 2005, 2006, 2009, and 2011–2021.

[b] Prior to 2017, BJS requested state departments of corrections to report juvenile counts in public facilities only. Starting in 2017, BJS requested juvenile data in both publicly or privately operated correctional facilities.

[c] In 2015 and 2016, the Annual Survey of Jails (ASJ) collected jail population data at midyear and yearend but only collected demographic data on the yearend population. Because jails typically hold fewer inmates at yearend than at midyear, the 2015 and 2016 data reported here were adjusted for seasonal variation and represent estimated midyear counts.

Appendix Table 1. Standard errors for jail data in table 1: Juveniles in the custody of adult jails and prisons in the United States, 2002–2021

	Jail total	Male	Female
2002	186	177	27
2003	379	342	57
2004	188	170	33
2005	~	~	~
2006	148	140	22
2007	166	145	36
2008	170	155	29
2009	195	175	37
2010	226	204	47
2011	175	158	36
2012	245	224	34
2013	207	184	47
2014	168	152	30
2015	121	107	30
2016	154	121	54
2017	128	120	20
2018	131	121	25
2019	~	~	~
2020	93	91	9
2021	69	65	17

Source: Bureau of Justice Statistics, Annual Survey of Jails, 2002–2004, 2006–2018, and 2020–2021; and Census of Jails, 2005 and 2019.

~Not applicable. Data represent a complete enumeration based on the Census of Jails.

Appendix Table 2. Estimates for figure 2: Juveniles as a percent of the incarcerated populations of adult jails and prisons, 2002–2021

	Total incarcerated			Jails			Prisons		
	Total population	Juveniles Number	Juveniles Percent	Total population	Juveniles Number	Juveniles Percent	Total population	Juveniles[a] Number	Juveniles[a] Percent
2002	2,105,620	9,010	0.43%	665,480	5,970	0.90%	1,440,140	3,040	0.21%
2003	2,159,900	9,610	0.44	691,300	6,870	0.99	1,468,600	2,740	0.19
2004	2,211,090	9,560	0.43	713,990	7,080	0.99	1,497,100	2,480	0.17
2005	2,286,710	9,180	0.40	760,800	6,760	0.89	1,525,910	2,420	0.16
2006	2,334,490	8,660	0.37	765,820	6,100	0.80	1,568,670	2,560	0.16
2007	2,377,420	9,120	0.38	780,580	6,840	0.88	1,596,840	2,280	0.14
2008	2,393,810	10,420	0.44	785,530	7,700	0.98	1,608,280	2,720	0.17
2009	2,382,920	10,110	0.42	767,430	7,220	0.94	1,615,490	2,890	0.18
2010	2,362,530	8,560	0.36	748,730	6,260	0.84	1,613,800	2,300	0.14
2011	2,334,570	7,860	0.34	735,600	5,920	0.80	1,598,970	1,940	0.12
2012	2,314,920	6,860	0.30	744,520	5,430	0.73	1,570,400	1,430	0.09
2013	2,308,160	5,780	0.25	731,210	4,500	0.62	1,576,950	1,280	0.08
2014	2,306,910	5,280	0.23	744,590	4,180	0.56	1,562,320	1,100	0.07
2015[b]	2,254,010	4,700	0.21	727,410	3,640	0.50	1,526,600	1,060	0.07
2016[b]	2,248,800	4,820	0.21	740,670	3,810	0.51	1,508,130	1,010	0.07
2017	2,234,350	4,500	0.20	745,160	3,560	0.48	1,489,190	940	0.06
2018	2,202,830	3,960	0.18	738,440	3,220	0.44	1,464,390	740	0.05
2019	2,164,640	3,530	0.16	734,470	2,880	0.39	1,430,170	650	0.05
2020	1,770,300	2,630	0.15	549,140	2,280	0.42	1,221,160	350	0.03
2021	1,840,660	2,250	0.12	636,340	1,960	0.31	1,204,320	290	0.02

Source: Bureau of Justice Statistics, National Prisoner Statistics program, 2002–2021; Annual Survey of Jails, 2002–2004, 2006–2018, and 2020–2021; and Census of Jails, 2005 and 2019.

Note: Data are adjusted for nonresponse and rounded to the nearest 10. Details may not sum to totals due to rounding. Results may differ from previous reports due to updates from jail and prison respondents.

[a] The Federal Bureau of Prisons reported counts of juveniles held in adult contract facilities to the Bureau of Justice Statistics (BJS) in 2005, 2006, 2009, and 2011–2021. Prior to 2017, BJS requested state departments of corrections to report juvenile counts in public facilities only. Starting in 2017, BJS requested juvenile data in both publicly or privately operated correctional facilities.

[b] In 2015 and 2016, the Annual Survey of Jails (ASJ) collected jail population data at midyear and yearend but only collected demographic data on the yearend population. Because jails typically hold fewer inmates at yearend than at midyear, the 2015 and 2016 data reported here were adjusted for seasonal variation and represent estimated midyear counts.

The Bureau of Justice Statistics of the U.S. Department of Justice is the principal federal agency responsible for measuring crime, criminal victimization, criminal offenders, victims of crime, correlates of crime, and the operation of criminal and civil justice systems at the federal, state, tribal, and local levels.

BJS collects, analyzes, and disseminates reliable statistics on crime and justice systems in the United States, supports improvements to state and local criminal justice information systems, and participates with national and international organizations to develop and recommend national standards for justice statistics. Alexis R. Piquero, PhD, is the director.

This report was written by Zhen Zeng, PhD; E. Ann Carson, PhD; and Rich Kluckow, DSW. Danielle Kaeble verified the report.

Brigit Baron and Maureen Stuart edited the report. Tina Dorsey and Priscilla Fauntleroy produced the report.

Chapter 5

Gun Control: Juvenile Record Checks for 18- to 21-Year-Olds*

Jordan B. Cohen

On June 25, 2022, President Biden signed into law the Bipartisan Safer Communities Act (BSCA; P.L. 117-159), which includes several firearms-related sections. Section 12001 addresses juvenile access to firearms by

- clarifying that the prohibition on transferring a firearm to a disqualified individual applies to juveniles (18 U.S.C. §922(d)); and
- expanding background check procedures to screen persons 18 to 21 years of age for disqualifying juvenile justice or mental health records (18 U.S.C. §922(t)).

To implement these measures, the law required upgrades to the background check system established by the Brady Handgun Violence Prevention Act (Brady Act, 34 U.S.C. §40901, P.L. 103-159). Prior to P.L. 117-159, it does not appear that such records were routinely queried as part of a federal firearms background check. Prohibited firearm transfers, background checks, and background check system requirements under federal law, as well as the amendments made by P.L. 117-159, are described below.

---

* This is an edited, reformatted and augmented version of Congressional Research Service Publication No. IF12154, updated February 5, 2024.

In: Perspectives on Juvenile Justice: Legal, Social, and Policy Issues
Editor: David Y. Reyes
ISBN: 979-8-89530-669-7

Firearms Receipt, Possession, and Transfer Prohibitions

The Gun Control Act of 1968 (GCA, 18 U.S.C. §§921-931) is one of the two principal federal statutes—along with the National Firearms Act of 1934 (NFA, 26 U.S.C. §53)— regulating firearms in the United States.

The GCA requires all persons engaged in the business of importing, manufacturing, and selling firearms to be federally licensed as federal firearms licensees (FFLs). The law generally prohibits unlicensed persons from transferring any firearm without going through an FFL. The GCA prohibits FFLs from transferring a long gun (i.e., rifle or shotgun) or ammunition to anyone under 18 years of age, and from transferring a handgun or ammunition suitable for a handgun to anyone under 21 years of age (18 U.S.C. §922(b)(1)). The GCA also generally prohibits any person from transferring a handgun or ammunition suitable for a handgun to a juvenile, and juveniles are prohibited from possessing a handgun or ammunition suitable for a handgun, although there are exceptions (e.g., under adult supervision, or for employment, ranching, farming, target practice, and hunting [18 U.S.C. §922(x)]).

The GCA sets forth nine categories of persons prohibited from shipping, transporting, receiving, or possessing firearms or ammunition (18 U.S.C. §922(g)). For example, prohibited persons include individuals under indictment or convicted of a crime punishable by imprisonment for a term over one year; subjected to a court order that restrains them from harassing, stalking, or threatening an intimate partner or child of such intimate partner; convicted of a domestic violence misdemeanor offense; who have renounced U.S. citizenship; addicted to a controlled substance; aliened unlawfully in the United States or admitted to the United States under a nonimmigrant visa; dishonorably discharged from the Armed Forces; "adjudicated as a mental defective"; found guilty by reason of insanity; committed to mental institutions; or who are fugitives from justice.

According to the Bureau of Alcohol, Tobacco, Firearms and Explosives (ATF), persons "adjudicated as a mental defective" include anyone who a court, board, commission, or other lawful authority has determined, as a result of marked subnormal intelligence, mental illness, incompetency, a condition, or a disease,

- is a danger to himself or herself, or others;
- lacks the mental capacity to contract or manage his or her own affairs;
- is found insane by a court in a criminal case; or

- is found incompetent to stand trial, or not guilty by reason of lack of mental responsibility, pursuant to certain provisions of the Uniform Code of Military Justice.

Also, according to ATF, persons "committed to a mental institution" include anyone who has been formally committed to a mental institution by a court, board, commission, or other lawful authority. A commitment includes a commitment to a mental institution involuntarily, for mental defectiveness or mental illness, or for other reasons, such as drug use. A commitment does not include a person admitted to a mental institution for observation or by voluntary admission (27 C.F.R. §478.11).

In addition, under the GCA, persons under felony indictment are prohibited from receiving (but not possessing) any firearm or ammunition (18 U.S.C. §922(n)). It is a felony for any person to transfer, or dispose of, any firearm or ammunition to any person knowing, or having reasonable cause to believe, that the transferee is a prohibited person (18 U.S.C. §922(d)). The nine categories of prohibited persons enumerated under 18 U.S.C. §922(d) are parallel with 18 U.S.C. §§922(g) and (n). Violations of 18 U.S.C. §922(d) are punishable by a fine and up to 10 years' imprisonment (18 U.S.C. §924(a)(2)).

Amended Prohibited Transfers and Juvenile Records

P.L. 117-159 amended the firearms transfer prohibition under 18 U.S.C. §922(d) to include the transfer of any firearm or ammunition to any person the transferor knows or has reasonable cause to believe would fall into at least one of the nine prohibited categories under that provision, "including as a juvenile." It also amended Section 922(d)(4) to include any juvenile who has been "adjudicated as a mental defective" or "committed to any mental institution" at "16 years of age or older."

Federally Required Firearms Background Checks

Pursuant to the Brady Act, the Federal Bureau of Investigation (FBI) established the National Instant Criminal Background Checks System (NICS) in November 1998. NICS queries federal, state, tribal, territorial, and local criminal history and other public records for information that could indicate that an unlicensed, prospective transferee is prohibited from acquiring a firearm under the GCA. Whenever an unlicensed person seeks to acquire a firearm from an FFL, both the FFL and prospective purchaser must complete and sign ATF Form 4473. On this form, the purchaser attests under penalty of law that he or she is not a prohibited person and that he or she is the "actual buyer." The FFL must also verify the purchaser's name, date of birth, and other information by examining government-issued identification (e.g., a driver's license). The signed and completed Form 4473 authorizes the FFL to initiate a background check through NICS on a prospective unlicensed transferee who seeks to acquire a firearm from them through a sale, trade, or redemption of firearms exchanged for collateral (18 U.S.C. §922(t)).

Under the Brady Act, states may opt to handle firearms eligibility determinations or allow the FBI to handle such determinations. States that have opted to handle those determinations themselves are known as Point of Contact (POC) states. In response to a background check, the NICS is to respond to an FFL or POC state official with an NICS Transaction Number (NTN) and one of four outcomes:

1. "proceed" with transfer or permit/license issuance, because a prohibiting record was not found;
2. "denied," indicating a prohibiting record was found;
3. "delayed," indicating that the system produced information suggesting there could be a prohibiting record, such as criminal charges without a final disposition; or
4. "canceled" for insufficient information provided.

In the case of a "proceed," the background check record is purged from NICS within 24 hours; "denied" requests are kept in perpetuity. In the case of a "delayed" transaction, after the passage of three business days, FFLs may proceed with the transaction at their discretion if they have not received a final eligibility determination from the NICS. During this time, NICS examiners, or POC state officials, may attempt to ascertain whether the person is prohibited. If it is learned that a transferee is prohibited after a transfer has occurred, a firearms retrieval referral is to be issued to the ATF and state or local chief law enforcement officer.

Amended NICS Procedures

P.L. 117-159 amended the GCA (18 U.S.C. §922(t)) with a separate procedure for persons under 21 years of age, allowing a firearms transfer to be delayed for an additional 7 days (i.e., up to 10 business days total) for persons under 21 if "cause exists to further investigate a possibly disqualifying juvenile record under" under 18 U.S.C. §922(d). If the investigation is not completed within 10 business days, or if at any point the FBI identifies the "possibly disqualifying juvenile record" to be inaccurate, including for mental health adjudication records that occurred while the intended purchaser was under 16 years of age, P.L. 117-159 requires that the firearm transfer be allowed to occur. Pursuant to the Brady Act, the Attorney General is required to remove these erroneous records from the system with 30 days.

P.L. 117-159 requires any agency that makes accessible the aforementioned possible disqualifying records under 18 U.S.C. §§922(d), (g), or (n) to NICS to report annually to the Senate and House Judiciary Committees and the Senate and House Appropriations Committees on the records removed from NICS, why the records were removed, and the cause for their original submission.

The requirement that NICS contact state authorities expires on September 30, 2032.

NICS-Queried Computer Systems, Files, and Amended System Requirements

Based on the prospective purchaser's name and other identifying information, NICS queries several national data systems for records that could disqualify him or her from receiving and possessing a firearm under federal or state law. These systems include the

- Interstate Identification Index (III) for records on persons convicted or under indictment for felonies and serious misdemeanors;
- National Crime Information Center (NCIC) for files on persons who are subject to civil protection orders and arrest warrants, immigration law violators, and known and suspected terrorists;

- NICS Indices for federal and state record files on persons prohibited from possessing firearms, which would not be included in either III or NCIC; and
- immigration-related databases maintained by the Department of Homeland Security's Immigration and Customs Enforcement for non-U.S. citizens who may have been previously deported or are believed to be residing unlawfully in the United States.

P.L. 117-159 amended Section 103 of the Brady Act to require the Attorney General to upgrade NICS with the capacity to contact immediately, for purposes of 18 U.S.C.§922(d), possible sources of disqualifying juvenile records for persons under 21 years old in the jurisdiction where they reside, including state, tribal, or territorial repositories of criminal history, records, juvenile justice information, and/or mental health adjudication records, as well as local law enforcement agencies.

The FBI was appropriated $100 million in FY2023 to conduct these NICS upgrades. In January 2024, the U.S. Department of Justice reported that 527 gun sales to individuals under the age of 21 have been blocked because of rule changes made by P.L. 117-159.

Chapter 6

Juvenile Justice Funding Trends*

Kristin Finklea

Summary

Although juvenile justice is generally the purview of the states, the federal government has played a role through the administration of grant programs. Congress has influenced states' juvenile justice systems by authorizing and funding grant programs administered by the Department of Justice's (DOJ's) Office of Juvenile Justice and Delinquency Prevention (OJJDP).

The Juvenile Justice and Delinquency Prevention Act (JJDPA; P.L. 93-415), enacted in 1974, was the first comprehensive juvenile justice legislation passed by Congress. The JJDPA authorized a series of grant programs designed to support state juvenile justice systems and prevent juvenile delinquency. Since its enactment, the JJDPA has undergone several key amendments, including a significant reorganization in 2002 (by the 21st Century Department of Justice Appropriations Authorization Act; P.L. 107-273). Its grant programs were most recently amended and reauthorized by the Juvenile Justice Reform Act of 2018 (P.L. 115-385). Funding for programs authorized by the JJDPA, as well as for other non-JJDPA grant programs administered by OJJDP, is provided through the Juvenile Justice Programs account in the annual Commerce, Justice, Science, and Related Agencies appropriations act. After the restructuring of juvenile justice grant programs in 2002, total funding for these programs began to decline. This decline generally continued through FY2007, after which funding for these programs started to increase. For FY2010, Congress provided $424 million for juvenile justice

* This is an edited, reformatted and augmented version of Congressional Research Service Publication No. R44879, dated April 9, 2024.

In: Perspectives on Juvenile Justice: Legal, Social, and Policy Issues
Editor: David Y. Reyes
ISBN: 979-8-89530-669-7

programs—the largest appropriation since FY2003. Juvenile justice funding then generally declined again from FY2010 through FY2017. After appropriating a low of $247 million for juvenile justice programs in FY2017, Congress increased juvenile justice funding annually from FY2018 through FY2023— the largest appropriation since FY2010—before decreasing it for FY2024. The Consolidated Appropriations Act, 2024 (P.L. 118-42), provides $375 million for juvenile justice programs for FY2024.

The federal government has no juvenile justice system of its own. Rather, juvenile justice is administered by the states. The federal government, though, seeks to influence states' juvenile justice systems through the administration of grant programs and the provision of funds.[1]

This report provides a brief overview of funding for the juvenile justice-related grant programs administered by the Department of Justice's (DOJ's) Office of Juvenile Justice and Delinquency Prevention (OJJDP).

Juvenile Justice Legislation and Grant Programs

A number of federally funded juvenile justice grant programs are authorized by the Juvenile Justice and Delinquency Prevention Act of 1974 (JJDPA, P.L. 93-415). Since its enactment, the JJDPA has been revised by several key amendments, including a significant reorganization in 2002 (by the 21st Century Department of Justice Appropriations Authorization Act; P.L. 107-273). Most recently, its grant programs were amended and reauthorized by the Juvenile Justice Reform Act of 2018 (P.L. 115-385).

The JJDPA as originally enacted had three main components: (1) it established OJJDP to coordinate and administer federal juvenile justice efforts; (2) it created grant programs to assist states with their juvenile justice systems; and (3) it promulgated core mandates to which states must adhere in order to be eligible for certain grant funding. Although the JJDPA has been amended several times over the past 40+ years, it continues to feature these three components.

---

[1] For more information on the legislative history of juvenile justice and details on the grant programs outlined in this report, refer to CRS Report RL33947, *Juvenile Justice: Legislative History and Current Legislative Issues*.

The JJDPA has been the primary channel through which the federal government has provided juvenile justice funding to states. However, other programs also administered by OJJDP have contributed to overall federal juvenile justice funding.

The following section outlines various juvenile justice grant programs, including those authorized by the JJDPA. Grant programs noted in this section have been congressionally authorized at some point in time and have received an appropriation at least once in the 10-year period from FY2015 through FY2024. Congress has also provided appropriations for juvenile justice programs that do not have separate authorizations of appropriations; these programs are not discussed in this section, but they are included in Table 1, which outlines funding for juvenile justice programs since FY2015.

State Formula Grant Program

The JJDPA authorizes OJJDP to make formula grants to states[2] for the planning, establishment, operation, coordination, and evaluation of projects that develop more effective juvenile delinquency programs and improve juvenile justice systems.[3] Funds are allocated annually based on each state's relative population of people under age 18. States must adhere to certain core mandates to receive their funding.[4] The Juvenile Justice Reform Act of 2018 (P.L. 115-385) amended the program and reauthorized its funding through FY2023. While its authorization of appropriations has expired, the program has continued to receive funding. For FY2024, this program was appropriated $65 million (P.L. 118-42).

---

[2] In this report, the term *state* includes the 50 states, the District of Columbia, and the territories (American Samoa, Guam, the Northern Mariana Islands, Puerto Rico, and the U.S. Virgin Islands).

[3] 34 U.S.C. §11131.

[4] There are four core mandates with which—unless for specified exceptions—states must generally comply: states must keep status offenders (such as truants) out of secure detention or correctional facilities; states cannot detain or confine juveniles in facilities in which they would have contact with adult inmates; juveniles cannot be detained or confined in any jail or lockup for adults; and states must show that they are working to address racial and ethnic disparities within their juvenile justice systems.

Title V Incentive Youth Promise Grants for Local Delinquency Prevention

The JJDPA authorizes OJJDP to make grants to states, which are then transmitted through subgrants to units of local government (or nonprofits in partnership with units of local government) for delinquency prevention programs for juveniles who have come into contact with, or are at risk to come into contact with, the juvenile justice system.[5] The Juvenile Justice Reform Act of 2018 (P.L. 115-385) amended the program and reauthorized its funding through FY2023. The JJDPA also authorizes OJJDP to make grants to eligible Indian tribes to support delinquency prevention programs for at-risk youth or those who have come into contact with the juvenile justice system. Traditionally, Congress dedicates amounts from the total appropriation for the Title V program for specific programs and purposes areas (e.g., the Tribal Youth program). While its authorization of appropriations has expired, the program has continued to receive funding. For FY2024, this program was appropriated $55 million (P.L. 118-42).

Victims of Child Abuse Act Grants

The Victims of Child Abuse Act of 1990 (Title II of the Crime Control Act of 1990, P.L. 101-647) authorizes several grant programs administered by OJJDP.

Subtitle A authorizes support for regional and local Children's Advocacy Centers (CACs), including state chapters, and for related training and technical assistance (34 U.S.C. §§20301- 20307). The CAC program was most recently reauthorized (through FY2028) via Section 3 of the Respect for Child Survivors Act (P.L. 117-354). For FY2024, it received $41 million (P.L. 118-42).

Subtitle B authorizes support for Court Appointed Special Advocates (CASAs) (34 U.S.C. §§20321-20323) and Subtitle C authorizes training of judicial personnel to improve handling of child abuse and neglect proceedings (34 U.S.C. §§20331-20334). Funding for these activities was most recently reauthorized through FY2027 in the Violence Against Women Act Reauthorization Act of 2022 (Division W of P.L. 117-103). For FY2024,

[5] 34 U.S.C. §11313.

CASA received $14 million and the training program received nearly $5 million (P.L. 118-42).[6]

Juvenile Mentoring Program

The Juvenile Mentoring Program was authorized by the Incentive Grants for Local Delinquency Prevention Programs Act (P.L. 102-586). Grants under this program are awarded to local educational agencies (in partnership with public or private agencies) to establish and support mentoring programs to reduce delinquent behavior, improve scholastic performance, and reduce school dropouts.[7] The program has continued to receive funding even though it was repealed in the 2002 JJDPA reauthorization (P.L. 107-273). For FY2024, this program was appropriated $104 million (P.L. 118-42).

Total Juvenile Justice Appropriations

Congress appropriates funding for programs authorized by the JJDPA as well as for other non-JJDPA juvenile justice grant programs through the Juvenile Justice Programs account in the annual Commerce, Justice, Science, and Related Agencies Appropriations Act. Figure 1 shows total appropriations for juvenile justice programs for the 25-year period from FY2000 through FY2024.

Funding for juvenile justice programs peaked in 2002 at $565 million. From FY2002 to FY2007, however, overall funding fell by 38% to $348 million. The majority of this reduction came from cuts to the Juvenile Accountability Block Grant (JABG) program.[8] From FY2007 to FY2010, total funding for juvenile justice programs increased by almost 22% to $424

---

[6] CASA is funded out of the State and Local Law Enforcement Assistance account rather than the Juvenile Justice Programs account; training for judicial personnel to improve handling of child abuse and neglect proceedings is funded out of the Juvenile Justice Programs account.

[7] For more information on the Juvenile Mentoring Program and youth mentoring, see CRS Report RL34306, *Vulnerable Youth: Federal Mentoring Programs and Issues*.

[8] Although the authorization for the JABG program was not a part of the JJDPA, it nevertheless was administered by OJJDP. The JABG program authorized the Attorney General to make grants to states and units of local government to strengthen their juvenile justice systems, including holding juveniles accountable for their actions. Authorization for this program expired in FY2009, but Congress continued to provide appropriations through FY2013.

million, with funding for JJDPA programs increasing by 27% to $331 million over this same period. This was the largest juvenile justice appropriation since FY2003.

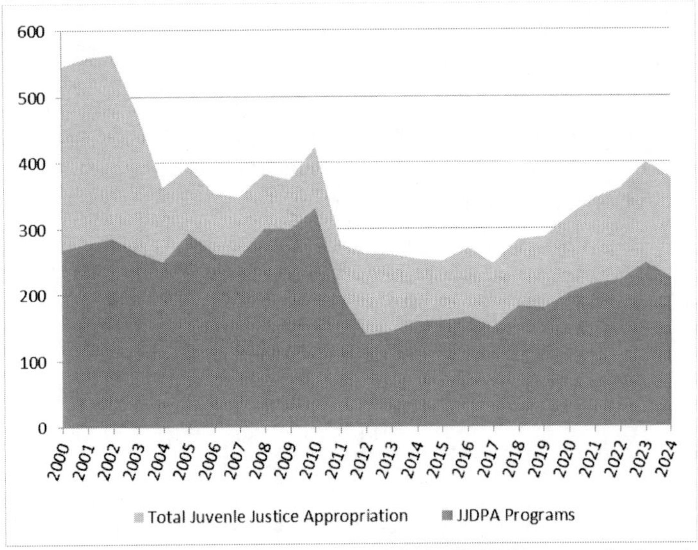

Sources: FY2000 enacted taken from P.L. 106-113. FY2001 enacted taken from P.L. 106-553. FY2002 enacted taken from P.L. 107-77. FY2003 enacted taken from P.L. 108-7. FY2004 taken from P.L. 108-199. FY2005 taken from P.L. 108-447. FY2006 taken from P.L. 109-108. FY2007 appropriation is based on FY2006 enacted minus a 1.28% rescission, as per P.L. 110-5. FY2008 enacted taken from P.L. 110-161. FY2009 enacted taken from P.L. 111-8. FY2010 enacted taken from P.L. 111-117. FY2011 enacted based on a CRS analysis of the text of P.L. 112-10. FY2012 enacted taken from P.L. 112-55. FY2013 amount provided by the U.S. Department of Justice. FY2014 enacted taken from P.L. 113-76. FY2015 enacted taken from P.L. 113-235. FY2016 enacted taken from P.L. 114-113. FY2017 enacted taken from P.L. 115-31. FY2018 enacted taken from P.L. 115-141. FY2019 enacted taken from P.L. 116-6. FY2020 enacted taken from P.L. 116-93. FY2021 enacted taken from P.L. 116-260. FY2022 enacted taken from P.L. 117-103. FY2023 enacted taken from P.L. 117-328. FY2024 enacted taken from P.L. 118- 42.

Notes: Numbers are rounded. Amounts are in nominal dollars. The amounts include all rescissions of current year budget authority. The FY2013 funding level also reflects sequestration pursuant to the Budget Control Act of 2011 (P.L. 112-25). JJDPA = Juvenile Justice and Delinquency Prevention Act (P.L. 93-415).

Figure 1. Total Juvenile Justice Programs Appropriations, FY2000-FY2024. (dollars in millions).

Funding for juvenile justice programs again began to decline in FY2011, and that decline generally continued through FY2017. From FY2010 to FY2017, total funding for juvenile justice programs decreased by nearly 42%, from $424 million to $247 million. Contributing to this drop, Congress eliminated funding for the Challenge Grants[9] in FY2011 and for the JABG program in FY2014. During this time period, Congress also started appropriating funding for programs that had not previously been funded under the Juvenile Justice Programs account, including funding for missing and exploited children programs and child abuse training programs for judicial personnel and practitioners.

After appropriating $247 million for juvenile justice programs in FY2017, Congress increased juvenile justice funding annually from FY2018 through FY2023. Congress increased funding for juvenile justice programs to nearly $283 million for FY2018, which included funds for a new Opioid Affected Youth Initiative. Congress again increased juvenile justice program funding to $287 million in FY2019, and it set aside money for an initiative serving children exposed to violence.[10] Congress then increased funding for juvenile justice programs to $320 million for FY2020 and included a new set-aside from the JJDPA Title V Incentive Grant program for grants to prevent trafficking of girls. Congress continued to increase funding for FY2021 through FY2023, when it appropriated $400 million for juvenile justice programs—the largest appropriation since the $424 million provided in FY2010. Congress most recently decreased funding for juvenile justice programs, appropriating $375 million for FY2024. This included a $10 million reduction in funding for the JJDPA Title II State Formula Grants and a $10 million reduction for the JJDPA Title V Incentive Grants.

Historical Appropriations by Program

Table 1 provides a breakdown of funding for the Juvenile Justice Programs account by program for the 10-year period from FY2015 to FY2024.

---

[9] The Challenge Grants program authorized OJJDP to make discretionary grants to state, local, and tribal governments and private entities to carry out programs to develop, test, or demonstrate promising new initiatives that may prevent, control, or reduce juvenile delinquency. The program last received appropriations in FY2010.

[10] Funding for this purpose was previously provided under the State and Local Law Enforcement Assistance Account from FY2012 to FY2016.

Table 1. Juvenile Justice Appropriations by Program, FY2015-FY2024
(dollars in millions)

Program	FY2015	FY2016	FY2017	FY2018	FY2019	FY2020	FY2021	FY2022	FY2023	FY2024
State Formula Grants	55	58	55	60	60	63	67	70	75	65
Emergency Planning— Juvenile Detention Facilities	(1)	(1)	(1)	(1)	(1)	(1)	(1)	(1)	(1)	(1)
Juvenile Mentoring Program Grant	90	90	80	94	95	97	100	102	107	104
Title V Incentive Grants for Local Delinquency Prevention	15	18	15	28	25	42	49	50	65	55
Tribal Youth Program	(5)	(10)	—	(5)	(5)	(5)	(10)	(14)	(17)	(16)
Gang Prevention	(3)	(5)	(4)	(4)	—	—	—	—	—	—
Community-Based Violence Prevention Initiative	(6)	—	(8)	(8)	—	—	—	—	—	—
National Forum on Youth Violence Prevention	(1)	—	—	—	—	—	—	—	—	—
Children of Incarcerated Parents Web Portal	—	(1)	(1)	(1)	(1)	(1)	(1)	(1)	(1)	—
Girls in the Juvenile Justice System	—	(2)	(2)	(2)	(2)	(2)	(3)	(5)	(6)	(5)
Opioid Affected Youth Initiative	—	—	—	(8)	(9)	(10)	(10)	(12)	(13)	(11)
Children Exposed to Violence Initiative	—	—	—	—	(8)	(8)	(8)	(8)	(10)	(9)
Prevention of Trafficking of Girls	—	—	—	—	—	(2)	(2)	(4)	(5)	(4)
Vulnerable and At-Risk Youth Initiative	—	—	—	—	—	—	—	(3)	(2)	—
Victims of Child Abuse Act	19	20	21	21	23	27	30	33	41	41
Community-Based Violence Prevention Initiative	—[a]	8	—[a]	—[a]	—	—	—	—	—	—
Training for Judicial Personnel	2	2	2	2	3	4	4	4	5	5

Table 1. (Continued)

Program	FY2015	FY2016	FY2017	FY2018	FY2019	FY2020	FY2021	FY2022	FY2023	FY2024
Missing and Exploited Children	68	72	73	76	82	88	94	99	105	103
Competitive Grants Focusing on Girls in the Juvenile Justice System	2	—[b]	—[b]	—[b]	—[b]	—[b]	—[b]	—[b]	—[b]	—[b]
Children of Incarcerated Parents Web Portal	1	—[b]	—[b]	—[b]	—[b]	—[b]	—[b]	—[b]	—[b]	—[b]
Improving Indigent Defense	—	3	2	2	—	—	3	3	3	3
Total Juvenile Justice Appropriation	252	270	247	283	287	320	346	360	400	375

Sources: FY2015 enacted taken from P.L. 113-235. FY2016 enacted taken from P.L. 114-113. FY2017 enacted taken from P.L. 115-31. FY2018 enacted taken from P.L. 115-141. FY2019 enacted taken from P.L. 116-6. FY2020 enacted taken from P.L. 116-93. FY2021 enacted taken from P.L. 116-260. FY2022 enacted taken from P.L. 117-103. FY2023 enacted taken from P.L. 117-328. FY2024 enacted taken from P.L. 118-42.

Notes: Numbers in parentheses are nonadds that have been set aside from other grant programs. Amounts may not add to totals due to rounding. Amounts are in nominal dollars.

[a] For FY2015, FY2017, and FY2018, funding for the Community-Based Violence Prevention Initiative was appropriated as set-aside funding from the Title V Incentive Grants.

[b] For FY2016-FY2024, funding for the Competitive Grants Focusing on Girls in the Juvenile Justice System and the Children of Incarcerated Parents Web Portal was appropriated as set-aside funding from the Title V Incentive Grants.

Appropriations for specific programs in the Juvenile Justice Programs account can vary from year to year. In addition, Congress sometimes provides funding for programs as a specific line item in the Juvenile Justice Programs account, but in other years funding for those programs is provided as a set-aside from another program in the account. For example, the Community-Based Violence Prevention Initiative, Web Portal for Children of Incarcerated Parents, and Competitive Grants Focusing on Girls in the Juvenile Justice System have received line-item appropriations in some fiscal years and have been funded by set-asides from the Title V Incentive Grants program in other years. By contrast, some programs, when funded, have consistently been funded through set-asides from the Title V program (e.g., the Tribal Youth program).

Chapter 7

Investigation of the Texas Juvenile Justice Department*

U.S. Department of Justice

Executive Summary

After an extensive investigation of conditions for children in five secure facilities operated by the Texas Juvenile Justice Department (TJJD), the United States Department of Justice (DOJ) concludes that there is reasonable cause to believe that TJJD violates the Eighth and Fourteenth Amendments of the United States Constitution, the Individuals with Disabilities Education Act (IDEA),[1] and the Americans with Disabilities Act (ADA).[2] Consistent with the Civil Rights of Institutionalized Persons Act (CRIPA),[3] we provide this Report to notify Texas of DOJ's conclusions, the facts supporting those conclusions, and the recommended minimum remedial measures necessary to address the violations identified.

* This is an edited, reformatted and augmented version of the U.S. Department of Justice Civil Rights Division, U.S. Attorney's Offices for the Districts of Texas Publication, dated August 1, 2024.

[1] 20 U.S.C. §§ 1400–1482.

[2] 42 U.S.C. § 12132.

[3] *Id.* § 1997 *et seq*. As discussed below, DOJ conducted this investigation by its authority under both CRIPA and the Violent Crime Control and Law Enforcement Act of 1994, 34 U.S.C. § 12601.

In: Perspectives on Juvenile Justice: Legal, Social, and Policy Issues
Editor: David Y. Reyes
ISBN: 979-8-89530-669-7

Findings

The United States provides notice of the following identified conditions:

- Protection from harm: Children in TJJD's secure facilities are often exposed to excessive physical and chemical force. Children also spend prolonged periods of time in isolation, under stark conditions and without access to adequate mental health and educational services. And children endure sexual abuse by both staff and other children. These conditions cause children serious harm and violate the Constitution.
- Mental health care: Children in TJJD's secure facilities do not receive adequate mental health assessments, treatment planning, and counseling services. TJJD also fails to provide adequate substance use disorder treatment and treatment for children who engage in self-harm or have suicidal thoughts. TJJD's response to children's behavior exposes children to excessive force and isolation. These deficiencies in mental health services violate the Constitution.
- Special education: Children with disabilities in TJJD's secure facilities do not receive a free appropriate public education. Special education services are not individualized to meet learning needs; fail to include specially designed instruction, behavioral supports, related services, and transition services; and are based on outdated information about children's needs. Without appropriate services, children with disabilities cannot access the general education curriculum, preventing meaningful progress. Each of these failures violates the IDEA.
- Discriminating against children with disabilities: Children with disabilities in TJJD's secure facilities do not receive reasonable modifications to complete programs required for their release. Instead, children are expelled from programming due to disability-related behavior and required to repeat it, prolonging their time in TJJD's custody or resulting in their transfer to prison. TJJD also denies children with disabilities an equal opportunity to benefit from education. Both practices violate the ADA.

The negative impact of these violations is mutually exacerbating. Children in TJJD's secure facilities are exposed to conditions that cause serious and lasting physical, mental, and emotional harm. At the same time, they are denied treatment and services they need to cope with their environment, earn release, return to their communities, and become productive citizens. This harmful environment undermines any rehabilitative purpose in their commitment.

Background

TJJD is a centralized statewide agency that includes five secure facilities subject to our investigation: (1) Evins Regional Juvenile Center in Edinburg, Texas; (2) Gainesville State School in Gainesville, Texas; (3) Giddings State School in Giddings, Texas; (4) McClennan County State Juvenile Correctional Facility (Mart) in Mart, Texas; and (5) Ron Jackson State Juvenile Correctional Complex in Brownwood, Texas.[4] TJJD's administration conducts oversight, provides resources, and sets systemwide policies for secure care. Children are often moved between the facilities to access specialized treatment programs housed in specific facilities.[5] TJJD leadership also shifts services from one facility to another.[6]

Hundreds of children are confined in TJJD's secure facilities every year. These facilities house children ages ten to nineteen. A Texas county juvenile court commits children to TJJD's custody when they are found to have committed an act that would be considered a crime if they were an adult or after they have violated the conditions of their probation or parole. Around eighty percent of children in TJJD's secure facilities are Black or Latinx. TJJD considers its secure facilities "the most serious place a [child] can go in Texas within the juvenile justice system." Each facility is surrounded by tall fences topped with barbed wire, has controlled and closely monitored entrances, and relies on locked doors to control and limit children's movement.

Problems have persisted at TJJD's secure facilities for decades. Throughout the early 2000s, repeated allegations of physical and sexual abuse as well as operational and safety concerns—coupled with substantial efforts

---

4 Aside from the five secure facilities, TJJD operates four halfway houses and a probation services division.

5 For a full description of TJJD's specialized programs, see Appendix A.

6 During our investigation, for example, TJJD moved intake services for boys and girls from Ron Jackson to Mart and then later moved intake services for boys back to Ron Jackson.

by high-ranking facility staff to cover up the misconduct—led the agency to be placed under governor-ordered conservatorship.[7] In 2007, DOJ's investigation of the Evins facility found that TJJD failed to keep children safe from violence.[8] In 2011, following reports of sexual abuse and significant operational problems systemwide, the Texas legislature combined TJJD's predecessors—the Texas Youth Commission and the Texas Juvenile Probation Commission—into one agency. In 2017 and 2021, Governor Abbott ordered two separate Texas Ranger investigations of sexual abuse and "potentially illegal behavior" at the facilities.

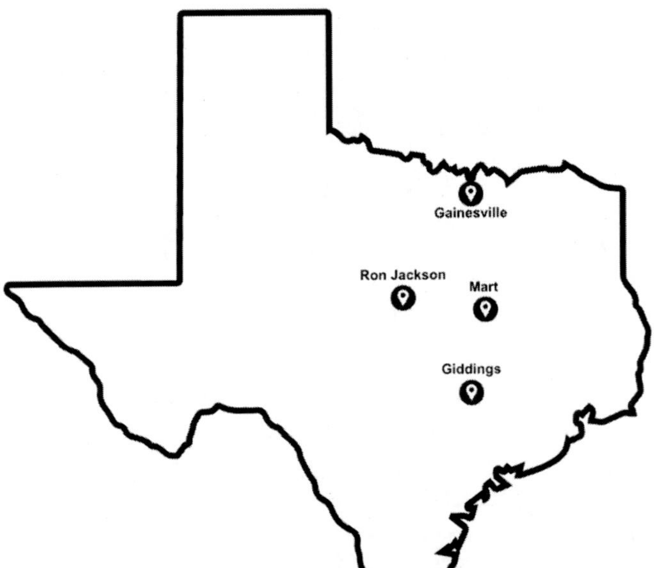

Figure 1. Map of Texas showing the locations of TJJD's five secure facilities.

During the same three decades, the overall population of children in TJJD's secure facilities declined, but the needs of the children that remained in custody intensified. In 2005, there were 4,127 children in secure facilities. As of July 2024, there were about 700 children, an eighty-three percent

---

[7] Sunset Self-Evaluation Report 44–45, Tex. Juv. Just. Dep't (Sept. 1, 2021), https://perma.cc/5883-5K6B.

[8] See Complaint ¶ 18, United States v. Texas, No. 7:08-CV-00038 (S.D. Tex. Feb. 1, 2008), ECF No. 1, https://perma.cc/FU2Z-F46M.

decrease. In 2021, TJJD reported that around sixty-five percent of children in its secure facilities have significant mental health issues, sixty-four percent of boys and eighty-four percent of girls report four or more traumatic events during their childhoods, and ninety-one percent of girls are identified as a clear or possible concern for being a victim of sex trafficking. On average, children are five grade levels behind in reading and six grade levels behind in math, with about thirty percent receiving special education services. According to TJJD, "[t]his is the highest concentration of acute needs . . . in the history of the agency."

Investigation

In October 2021, the Special Litigation Section of DOJ's Civil Rights Division and each of the United States Attorney's Offices in Texas opened a joint investigation of conditions for children confined in TJJD's five secure facilities.[9] At first, our investigation focused on whether TJJD adequately protects children in the facilities from harm and provides adequate mental health care. As new evidence came to light, we expanded our investigation to consider whether TJJD provides children with disabilities appropriate special education services and whether TJJD denies children with disabilities access to programs required for release and an equal opportunity to benefit from education.

Seven expert consultants aided our investigation and provided expertise in areas related to facility operations and practices, including use of force, investigations, and behavior management; mental health services for children and adolescents; special education and related services for children with disabilities; and reasonable modifications for children with disabilities. We engaged these consultants based on their significant collective experience conducting evaluations and providing technical assistance to jurisdictions to improve outcomes for justice-involved children. These expert consultants accompanied us on site visits, conducted interviews, reviewed documents and

---

[9] CRIPA allows DOJ to investigate violations of children's constitutional and federal rights in state or local juvenile justice facilities when such violations are "pursuant to a pattern or practice of resistance to the full enjoyment of such rights." 42 U.S.C. § 1997a(a); *see also id.* § 1997(1)(B)(iv) (defining "institution" to include juvenile justice facilities). Section 12601 of the Violent Crime Control and Law Enforcement Act of 1994 similarly allows DOJ to investigate violations of the Constitution or federal law by those responsible for "the incarceration of juveniles." 34 U.S.C. § 12601(a).

videos, and provided their expert opinions to inform our investigation and conclusions.

Our team inspected all five facilities at least twice, making thirteen in-person visits. Department staff and expert consultants toured the facilities and observed correctional operations and procedures, mental health meetings and reviews, and educational instruction in the schools and on the units. We spoke with hundreds of children in custody, as well as facility leadership, security staff, clinicians, teachers, and other staff.

Over the course of our investigation, DOJ staff and expert consultants reviewed thousands of pages of documents, including incident and use of force reports, policies and regulations, training materials, mental health records, education records, general records, unit logs, grievances, and investigative files. We and our expert consultants also reviewed hundreds of hours of video footage. Finally, our investigation included extensive outreach to families and other stakeholders and community groups.

We thank Texas for the cooperation extended to DOJ and recognize the courtesy and professionalism of all State officials and counsel involved. We also thank the advocates, families, and children across Texas who spoke with us. We are particularly grateful to those whose lives have been impacted by the juvenile justice system for trusting us with their stories.

Failing to Keep Children Safe from Harm

The Constitution protects children in juvenile justice facilities from harm. Unconstitutional harm includes conditions of confinement that demonstrate an "unnecessary and wanton infliction of pain" or officials' deliberate indifference to a serious threat to a person's health or safety.[10] Unconstitutional harm may also include restrictions placed on children that amount to punishment because they are not rationally related to a legitimate government objective or are excessive in relation to that objective.[11]

Texas' rehabilitative goal is relevant to whether the treatment of children who are committed to its secure facilities is constitutional. The overarching

---

[10] *Estelle v. Gamble*, 429 U.S. 97, 102 (1976) (internal quotation marks and citations omitted); *Farmer v. Brennan*, 511 U.S. 825, 834–38 (1994).

[11] *Bell v. Wolfish*, 441 U.S. 520, 535–38 (1979). The United States Supreme Court has not addressed whether the Eighth Amendment or the Fourteenth Amendment provides the proper standard for assessing conditions of confinement for children committed to juvenile justice facilities. Conditions in TJJD's secure facilities violate both constitutional standards.

governmental objective of commitment to TJJD's secure facilities is to rehabilitate children so they return to their communities as law-abiding, productive citizens.[12] This is reflected in the State Juvenile Justice Code's purpose of "provid[ing] treatment, training, and rehabilitation that emphasizes the accountability and responsibility of both the parent and the child for the child's conduct" and "provid[ing] for the care, the protection, and the wholesome moral, mental, and physical development of [the] children."[13] This purpose is also emphasized on TJJD's website:

> While public safety and accountability are certainly considerations for youth, the juvenile correctional system emphasizes treatment and rehabilitation. Even when it is necessary to incarcerate youth, the setting is designed to be protective, not punitive, and the goal is to educate youth about discipline, values, and work ethics, thus guiding them toward becoming productive citizens.[14]

The developmental vulnerability of children is similarly relevant to whether conditions in TJJD's secure facilities are constitutional. Relying on "developments in psychology and brain science [that] continue to show fundamental differences between [child] and adult minds,"[15] the U.S. Supreme Court has recognized several times that "children are constitutionally different from adults."[16] For example, the Court has stated that children "have a lack of maturity and an underdeveloped sense of responsibility," are "more vulnerable . . . to negative influences and outside pressures," and have characters that are not as "well formed" as those of adults.[17] The Court has also made clear that "youth is more than a chronological fact. It is a moment and condition of life when a person may be most susceptible to influence and to psychological

---

[12] Tex. Fam. Code Ann. § 51.01.

[13] *Id.*

[14] Tex. Juv. Just. Dep't, The Juvenile Justice System in Texas (2022), https://perma.cc/QS4G-KSYW.

[15] *Graham v. Florida*, 560 U.S. 48, 68 (2010).

[16] *Miller v. Alabama*, 567 U.S. 460, 476 (2012) (finding mandatory life imprisonment without parole for children is unconstitutional); *see also Graham*, 560 U.S. at 79 (finding that mandatory life imprisonment without parole for children who did not commit homicide is unconstitutional); *Roper v. Simmons*, 543 U.S. 551, 575 (2005) (finding that imposing the death penalty on children is unconstitutional).

[17] *Miller*, 567 U.S. at 471 (quoting *Roper*, 543 U.S. at 569); *see also Graham*, 560 U.S. at 68.

damage."[18] Texas courts agree, long recognizing that children are different than adults and warrant additional protections.[19]

Applying these principles, we find that conditions in TJJD's secure facilities cause children serious harm and violate the Constitution. Children are regularly subjected to force, both physical and chemical. They spend prolonged time in isolation, exposing them to mental health consequences like suicidal ideation. And they are not reasonably safe from sexual abuse by staff and other children.

Several additional factors contribute to TJJD's harmful environment. An underdeveloped behavior management system does not promote positive behavior and results in an overreliance on force to manage children's negative behavior. A lack of structured daily activities and inadequate adult supervision invites misbehavior from children who are bored and lack impulse control and self-regulating skills. A dysfunctional grievance system prevents children from reporting abuse and impedes TJJD's ability to track and correct problems. Inadequate mental health and special education services, along with a lack of reasonable modifications, discussed more fully in later sections of this Report, result in children with disabilities experiencing additional punishment through the use of force and isolation, exclusion from required programs and education, and extended time in TJJD's custody.

1. TJJD Uses Excessive Force on Children

Use of force that causes "the unnecessary and wanton infliction of pain" violates the Constitution.[20] Use of force is also unconstitutional when it is objectively unreasonable, which means the force is not rationally related to a legitimate governmental objective or is excessive in relation to that objective.[21] Factors to consider in determining whether force is unconstitutional include the need for the use of force, the amount of force used in relation to that need, the threat staff reasonably perceive, and any efforts staff make to lessen the severity of the force.[22] The extent of an individual's

---

[18] *Miller*, 567 U.S. at 476 (internal quotation marks and citations omitted).

[19] *See Henderson v. State*, 962 S.W.2d 544, 562 (Tex. Crim. App. 1997) ("[The] State has a legitimate, and in fact compelling, interest in protecting the well-being of its children Children are deemed to warrant protection because of their inexperience, lack of social and intellectual development, moral innocence, and vulnerability.").

[20] *Hudson v. McMillian*, 503 U.S. 1, 5 (1992).

[21] *Kingsley v. Hendrickson*, 576 U.S. 389, 396–98 (2015).

[22] *Hudson*, 503 U.S. at 7; *Kingsley*, 576 U.S. at 396–97.

injury, the severity of the security problem, and whether the individual was actively resisting may also be relevant to whether force is unconstitutional.[23]

Juvenile justice facilities like TJJD should follow a continuum of responses to children's misbehavior, generally beginning with staff making themselves present and providing adult supervision when a potential problem first develops, followed by attempts to de- escalate the situation through verbal prompts and redirects to the child. Staff should use force only after these interventions fail or are impossible due to an immediate threat to other children or staff. Staff should also use only the amount of force necessary to neutralize the threat.[24]

Although TJJD's use of force policy is generally consistent with the standards set forth above, the agency's practice differs. Our review of video footage and incident reports shows that staff routinely use force that causes "the unnecessary and wanton infliction of pain" and is excessive in relation to any legitimate government purpose.[25] This violates children's constitutional rights.

1.1. TJJD Harms Children By Using Pepper Spray Excessively and Without Adequate Decontamination Procedures

Pepper spray (also known as oleoresin capsicum or OC spray) has an intense and immediate effect on those sprayed. It is an oil made from chili pepper compounds. Pepper spray disables individuals by releasing substances within the nerve cells that cause burning, skin and eye irritation, and difficulty breathing. In significant exposures, pepper spray oils may create a rash or blisters on the skin and may damage the cornea, resulting in permanent vision loss. It may also result in death if it creates gagging and shortness of breath that leads to suffocation.

TJJD staff often use far more pepper spray, and deploy it far more frequently, than necessary to meet the threat posed. In the minority of juvenile justice facilities that permit security staff to carry pepper spray,[26] staff are

---

[23] *Kingsley*, 576 U.S. at 397; *see also Fairchild v. Coryell Cnty., Tex.*, 40 F.4th 359, 366 (5th Cir. 2022) (describing the "core of the excessive force inquiry" under *Kingsley* as whether "the amount of force [was] proportional to the need for force").

[24] *Fairchild*, 40 F.4th at 366.

[25] *Kingsley*, 576 U.S. at 396–97; *Hudson*, 503 U.S. at 7.

[26] Most juvenile justice facilities do not permit security staff to carry pepper spray. *Pepper Spray in Juvenile Facilities*, Council of Juv. Just. Adm'rs, (rev. Mar. 2019), https://perma.cc/G35P-UAK9; *see also J.H. v. Edwards*, No. CV 20-293-JWD-EWD, 2020 WL 3448087, at *38 (M.D. La. June 24, 2020) (acknowledging expert testimony that "the use of pepper spray [in juvenile justice facilities] is disfavored").

typically issued canisters containing 1.5-3 ounces of pepper spray (known as MK-3 or MK-4), which are intended for staff to wear on a duty belt for individual use. When the use of pepper spray is considered necessary, staff should release one short burst of pepper spray. At TJJD, however, security staff and supervisors are armed with MK-9 canisters, which contain 13.4 ounces of pepper spray, are intended for use when managing large crowds, and discharge more pepper spray over a greater area than individual-sized canisters. TJJD staff often discharge these MK-9 canisters directly into a child's face at very close range and for excessive lengths of time. In many incidents, multiple staff discharge pepper spray at the same time, resulting in copious amounts of pepper spray throughout the unit. In some cases, this results in staff and children becoming physically incapacitated to the point of vomiting.

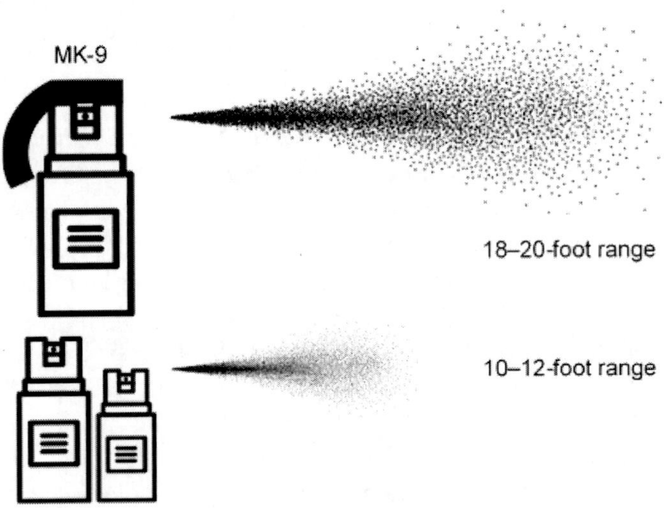

Figure 2. MK-9 canisters of pepper spray—intended for large crowd control—reach roughly twice the distance of MK-4 or MK-3 canisters.

TJJD staff also routinely use pepper spray as a first response to children's misbehavior, rarely making any attempt to verbally defuse a situation. Verbal interventions, if attempted at all, typically consist of yelling at the child to "stop" or "chill," threatening to use pepper spray, or at times using abusive language.

Below are examples that illustrate TJJD's pattern of misuse and overuse of pepper spray:

- In September 2022, Jose[27] was being disruptive at Gainesville, jumping on furniture and banging his head. Video shows staff pepper sprayed him after placing him in handcuffs. Staff made no effort to verbally engage with Jose before resorting to pepper spray.
- In September 2022, Emily reportedly made threats at school. The responding staff can be heard on video inciting Emily by calling her derogatory names ("ho" and "bitch") and swearing at her. At one point, the staff dares Emily to do something in response. Ultimately, the staff tells Emily to "shut up," pepper sprays her, and then says, "That's what's up, ho."
- In August 2022, a Mart staff member pepper sprayed Isabella while escorting her to the Regulation & Safety Unit (RSU)[28] in handcuffs. Staff made no attempt to engage with her verbally before spraying her.
- In July 2022, staff on a mental health unit at Giddings used excessive pepper spray on Jacob. Video footage shows one staff member intentionally discharging a MK-9 canister of pepper spray directly into Jacob's face at very close range. Staff also made minimal attempts to verbally de-escalate before resorting to pepper spray.
- In July 2022, a staff member pepper sprayed Daniel at Giddings for slamming the washing machine door. The staff can be heard warning Daniel, "Do it one more time and I'll [pepper spray] you. I'm not playing games." When Daniel slammed the door again, the staff sprayed him directly in the face at close range.

Accounts we heard directly from children at TJJD support this pattern: "Staff don't care and will use the whole can of [pepper] spray."

Untimely and inadequate decontamination procedures exacerbate the harmful effects of TJJD's overuse of pepper spray. As soon as the threat is

---

[27] To protect the identities of the children at TJJD, we have used pseudonyms based on the Social Security Administration's list of most popular boys' and girls' names for children born in Texas in 2008. *See Popular Baby Names, Popular Names by State, Popularity for top 100 names in Tex. for births in 2008*, Soc. Sec. Online, https://www.ssa.gov/cgi-bin/namesbystate.cgi (last visited July 11, 2024).

[28] Formally known as the Security Unit, the RSU is a self-contained unit at all five facilities used to "temporarily remove youth who engage in certain dangerous or disruptive behaviors from the general campus population." According to TJJD policy, children must be released from the RSU within 1–2 hours unless specific criteria for admission are met. Those who meet the admission criteria may be admitted to the RSU for up to twenty-four hours, with additional 24-hour extensions granted.

over, individuals should flush their eyes with cool water to alleviate the burning sensation, wash affected skin with mild soap, and receive a medical evaluation. Consistent with these standards, TJJD's policy states that any child "affected by [pepper] spray must be decontaminated with cool water as soon as the purpose of the restraint has been achieved." But most units are not equipped with cool water showers. As a result, children who are pepper sprayed are generally not decontaminated until after transport to the RSU, causing them to suffer the effects of pepper spray long after the purpose of restraint has been achieved. Because the RSU at Mart does not have a dedicated decontamination shower, children there may wait even longer. At the time of our site visit, Mart staff were using a garden hose over the top of a shower enclosure to decontaminate children, but for Isabella, they could not locate the hose, which significantly delayed her decontamination.

> "I ain't got time to deal with that[,] so soon as [the child's] shirt come off, I'm spraying her fat ass."
>
> Mart staff member

Bystanders who are exposed to pepper spray in TJJD facilities must decontaminate, if they can, in showers, sinks, or water fountains using lukewarm water. We reviewed many incidents where children who faced secondary exposure were sent to their cells without any opportunity to decontaminate. In April 2022, a Ron Jackson staff member discharged an excessively long blast from an MK-9 canister of pepper spray to stop a fight in a unit's dayroom. The staff made no attempts to verbally intervene before resorting to force and appeared to wait until the fight escalated to a physical level before taking any action at all. She gave no warning that she was about to discharge pepper spray. Multiple children were exposed and observed coughing and breathing in a distressed manner. In light of the unnecessarily long blast, the entire dayroom should have been decontaminated, but there is no evidence that this occurred.

Finally, for children with preexisting respiratory conditions—such as emphysema and asthma—or other health problems, exposure to pepper spray may pose a heightened risk of harm. TJJD policy appropriately prohibits the use of pepper spray on children with "chronic, serious respiratory problem[s] or other serious health condition[s] identified by TJJD ([for example], significant eye problems, known history of severe allergic reaction to [pepper spray], or severe dermatological problems)," except when "necessary to prevent loss of life or serious bodily injury." In practice, however, the only condition TJJD considers a contraindication is a severe allergy to pepper spray. In this way, TJJD violates its own policy and exposes children with respiratory and other health conditions to an increased risk of harm.

1.2. TJJD Harms Children by Using Excessive Physical Force and Dangerous Restraint Techniques

TJJD staff use more physical force than necessary, including restraints that can restrict a child's ability to breathe. Additionally, TJJD's limited supervisory review of uses of physical force undermines staff accountability.

Investigations conducted by TJJD's Office of Inspector General highlight the pattern of TJJD's use of excessive physical force. The Office of the Inspector General is a law enforcement agency responsible for conducting investigations of allegations involving "abuse, neglect, or exploitation of children" in TJJD's secure facilities.[29] At times, these investigations result in criminal charges against TJJD staff. For example:

- In October 2023, a former Ron Jackson staff member was charged with assault after both overhead surveillance and body-worn camera video reportedly showed him lift a child up and slam him to the floor, causing a laceration above the child's eye and a concussion. A grand jury indicted the staff member on the charge of official oppression in February 2024.
- In June 2022, two Evins staff were charged with criminal offenses after both overhead surveillance and body-worn camera video reportedly showed one of the staff slamming a child's head into a brick pillar, knocking him unconscious. The boy allegedly was handcuffed with his hands and arms behind his back throughout this ordeal.[30] One of the staff members then reportedly turned off his body camera, after which one of the staff members allegedly spat on the unconscious boy before dragging him to the RSU, causing additional injuries to the child. In May 2024, one of the two staff members accepted a plea agreement on the charge of official oppression.
- In March 2022, a former TJJD staff member was criminally charged for alleged conduct stemming from an incident at Mart's RSU.

---

[29] Tex. Hum. Res. Code Ann. § 242.102(a)(2).

[30] *See Hudson*, 503 U.S. at 7 (noting that in determining whether a use of force was "wanton and unnecessary," courts should consider "the threat 'reasonably perceived by the responsible officials'") (internal citation omitted).

> According to the Office of Inspector General, the staff responded to an assault by a child by "intentionally punching the [child] in the head, face, and body." The staff then allegedly "forcefully slammed the [child] to the floor while handcuffed."

Our document and video review shows additional dangerous physical restraint practices at TJJD that present a serious risk of restricting children's breathing. Some TJJD staff use unsafe techniques such as placing children face down on the floor and kneeling on their back or torso. In April 2022, a Ron Jackson staff member pepper sprayed two girls fighting in a dayroom. A large male staff then used his full body weight to lie on top of one of the girls while she was face down on the floor.

As with pepper spray, we observed TJJD staff resorting to physical force without making meaningful attempts to use nonphysical interventions. Surveillance videos show children sitting or pacing idly in the unit dayrooms, with minimal or no staff interaction. When children then engage in misbehavior, staff physically intervene without first trying to redirect the child or de-escalate the child through verbal prompts, regardless of the severity of the child's misbehavior.

Uses of physical force are also not consistently reviewed by supervisors, undermining staff accountability. In some cases, we found that staff failed to complete use of force reports. For example, while on site at Evins, a boy reported to us that a staff member had slammed him to the ground. We confirmed through video review that the incident the boy described had occurred. In the video, the staff can be seen slamming the boy to the floor and using his full body weight to pin the boy down while others placed him in restraints. But no staff filed a use of force or incident report.

Even where staff complete use of force reports, the supervisory review section was left blank in most of the reports we examined, suggesting that use of force reports are not regularly reviewed by a supervisor or review board. The Sunset Commission's[31] June 2023 review of site visit reports by the

---

[31] The Texas legislature created the Sunset process in 1977 to regularly examine the effectiveness of and need for state agencies. During an agency's review, the Sunset Commission seeks comment from agencies, stakeholders, and the public to identify problems and brainstorm opportunities for improvement. The Sunset Commission's recommendations and proposed bills regarding the agency are then considered during the legislative session. The Sunset Commission's review of TJJD took place during the 2022-2023 review cycle as part of the 88th Legislative Session. After finding that TJJD "remains caught in [a] long- standing cycle of instability," the Sunset Commission recommended about fifty changes to TJJD's funding and operations. TJJD praised the Sunset Commission's review, describing it as a

Office of Independent Ombudsman reflects our findings, noting ongoing problems with "[l]ate, incomplete, inaccurate, or nonexistent documentation from TJJD staff[,] including serious incident reports, records regarding youth housed in isolation units, and responses to [Office of Independent Ombudsman's] requests for follow-up action."

> An internal audit found that 63 percent of staff turned off their body-worn cameras while conducting cell checks, talking to or supervising children, or talking to each other.

TJJD staff's failure to comply with body-worn camera policies likewise limitssupervisory review. The Sunset Commission found that as of May 2022, TJJD still had not addressed problems identified during an August 2021 internal audit relating to violations of body-worn camera policies. That audit found that sixty-three percent of staff audited "turned off their body-worn cameras while conducting cell checks, talking to or supervising youth, or talking to each other" in violation of TJJD policy. Without adequate oversight of use of force and accountability for body-worn camera policies, excessive force will continue to occur with impunity.

1.3. TJJD's Inadequate Behavior Management System and Lack of Structured Programming Harm Children by Contributing to Unnecessary Uses of Force

TJJD's behavior management policy generally includes key principles of effective behavior management systems in juvenile justice facilities. Such systems: (1) provide incentives to promote positive behaviors and encourage engagement in education, treatment, and programming; (2) include skill-development training aimed at helping children control their behaviors; and (3) ground staff training and policies and procedures in principles of adolescent development. But we found little evidence that TJJD's behavior management policy is operationalized systemwide. The lack of a functional behavior management system hinders children's motivation to follow the rules and contributes to unnecessary force.

"fair assessment" that "really grasped [TJJD's] issues." In May 2023, the Texas legislature adopted ninety-five percent of the Sunset Commission's recommendations related to twenty-one entities, including TJJD. *See* Tex. Sunset Advisory Comm'n, 2022-23 88th Leg., *Final Results of Sunset Reviews 2022–23*, at 1 (June 2023), https://perma.cc/DJW9-KFW8.

We saw little evidence that TJJD staff use incentives effectively to promote positive behaviors in most of the facilities. For example, although most of the facilities had a game room as a reward for children who behaved well, there was not a well- understood system for earning that reward. There were also few signs or descriptions of the behavior program posted on most of the units. Staff generally did not mention the program during discussions of behavior management. Most children did not appear to understand the elements of the behavior management program, except to say that if they went to school and behaved, they earned points.[32]

On-site observations and video review also show that staff's interactions with children are typically minimal and reactive. Staff are largely disengaged until a child's behavior reaches a "boiling point," at which time staff respond with significant force. Sometimes, staff's initial interventions lead to an escalation of the child's behavior, resulting in violence and the use of force to regain control.

Along with an inadequate behavior management system, a lack of structured programming similarly leads to unnecessary force. Idle time for children throughout TJJD's secure facilities is extraordinarily high. On-site observations and video review show that children have very few opportunities for constructive activities to fill their day, with the lack of structured programming being even more pronounced on weekends.

When children are out of their cells, the atmosphere within the dayrooms is unstructured and chaotic. This inevitably leads to incidents of violence, as children sit around and annoy each other until frustrations result in fights, assaults, and destruction of property. As one child put it, "[S]taff think this dorm is bad, but we're just bored." Another child added, "They're setting kids up for failure."

2. TJJD Harms Children Through Excessive Use of Isolation

The Constitution protects children in juvenile justice facilities from excessive isolation (that is, time spent alone in a space from which they cannot leave).

---

32 The behavior program appeared to be more systemically applied and better understood at Gainesville than at the other facilities. The Gainesville behavior program includes a reward room called the "Main Event," where children can spend time—including overnight—as a reward for good behavior. We observed (in person and through video review) many positive interactions between staff and children on this unit, including playing games together, laughing, smiling, talking, and eating.

Isolation of children violates the Constitution when imposed under conditions that present a serious threat to the child's health, including mental health, and officials are deliberately indifferent to that threat.[33] Officials are deliberately indifferent when they are aware of the threat of harm (or the threat is obvious) and fail to take reasonable measures to decrease the risk of harm.[34] Excessive isolation of children can also violate the Constitution when it amounts to punishment.[35] This occurs if isolation is not rationally related to a legitimate government objective or it is excessive in relation to that objective.[36]

Excessive isolation poses a serious risk of harm to all human beings. But that threat is particularly severe for children. Because children's brains are still developing, "their time spent in solitary confinement [is] even more difficult and the developmental, psychological, and physical damage more comprehensive and lasting."[37] Children also "experience time differently—-a day for a child feels longer than a day to an adult—-and have a greater need for social stimulation."[38] As a result, exposure to stressful conditions such as isolation can result in long-term negative changes in children's bodies and brains. Children placed in isolation are at high risk of harmful psychiatric effects, including hallucinations, paranoia, depression, anxiety, self-harm, and suicide. Recognizing the growing body of research about isolation's harmful effects, courts in recent cases consider children's particular vulnerability to serious harm when assessing whether the isolation at issue is constitutional.[39]

---

[33] *Hope v. Harris*, 861 Fed. App'x 571, 582–83 (5th Cir. 2021); *Cleveland v. Bell*, 938 F.3d 672, 676 (5th Cir. 2019).

[34] *Farmer*, 511 U.S. at 837–43; *Cleveland*, 938 F.3d at 676.

[35] Bell, 441 U.S. at 561.

[36] *Id.*

[37] *Solitary Confinement (Isolation) Position Statement*, Nat'l Comm'n on Corr. Health Care (Apr. 2016), https://perma.cc/RE6L-RA76.

[38] *Id.*

[39] *See, e.g.*, *Alex A. v. Edwards*, No. CV 22-573-SDD-RLB, 2023 WL 5984280, at *18 (M.D. La. Sept. 14, 2023), *order vacated on other grounds, appeal dismissed as moot sub nom. Smith v. Edwards,* No. 23- 30634, 2023 WL 8747492 (5th Cir. Dec. 19, 2023) ("There is no dispute that solitary confinement has a very negative affect [sic] on the developing brain of adolescents; it exacerbates already existing mental health problems, it can exacerbate or cause the onset of mental illness and depression, and it causes an increased risk of suicide."); *see also J.H. v. Williamson Cnty.*, 951 F.3d 709, 718 (6th Cir. 2020) ("A growing chorus of courts have recognized the unique harms that are inflicted on juveniles when they are placed in solitary confinement."); *C.P.X. v. Garcia*, 450 F. Supp. 3d 854, 909 (S.D. Iowa 2020) ("Due to their traumatic backgrounds and mental health issues, juveniles in detention facilities are 'exquisitely vulnerable to psychiatric and behavioral decompensation when housed in solitary confinement.'") (internal citation omitted); *G.H. v. Marstiller*, 424 F. Supp. 3d 1109, 1116 (N.D. Fla. 2019) (finding that plaintiffs had alleged sufficient facts to show that the practice of isolating children "violates

TJJD's isolation practices expose children to a significant risk of harm and violate the Constitution. TJJD imposes excessive periods of disciplinary isolation on children in the RSU, secure units at each facility where TJJD temporarily places children when they "engage in certain dangerous or disruptive behaviors." Children in the general campus population are also locked alone in their cells for excessive periods of time for reasons unrelated to their behavior.

> "A kid in a room for 22 hours is a like a shaken bottle of soda. And you open that door[,] and you open that lid[,] and you hope that you have enough people there to keep the situation safe."
>
> Sunset Advisory Commission Testimony from Shandra Carter, TJJD Executive Director

Texas knows that children in TJJD's secure facilities spend too much time in isolation and that "[i]solation . . . has tremendous negative consequences."[40] In fact, the Executive Director has made repeated appeals to Texas officials regarding TJJD's need to address the excessive time children in TJJD's secure facilities spend in lockdown.[41]

2.1. Children Spend Excessively Long Periods of Time in the RSU Under Unnecessarily Restrictive Conditions

Although TJJD policy appropriately limits most initial RSU admissions to one to two hours, we found many instances where children spent days or weeks in the RSU. In some cases, TJJD placed children there for non-behavioral reasons. For example, Abigail spent eight days in Mart's RSU in October 2022 pending transfer to a halfway house.[42]

While in the RSU, children typically spend 22–23 hours a day in their cells, with some children spending twenty-four hours a day there. Out-of-cell

---

contemporary standards of decency" due to "children's heightened vulnerability and continued physical, psychological, and social development").

[40] See Hearing Before Tex. House Comm'n on Juv. Just. & Fam. Issues, 88th Leg., R.S. (Aug. 9, 2022) (testimony by Exec. Interim Dir., Tex. Juv. Just. Dep't, Shandra Carter at 27:19-27:39), https://tlchouse.granicus.com/MediaPlayer.php?view_id=46&clip_id=23404 (last visited June 27, 2024).

[41] *Farmer*, 511 U.S. at 837–43 (explaining that officials are deliberately indifferent when they are aware of the threat of harm and fail to take reasonable measures to decrease the risk of harm).

[42] We also found several children who TJJD held in the RSU for weeks prior to transfer to Evins. For example, Ethan was confined in Mart's RSU for about fourteen days. Angel was confined for about thirteen days. Juan was confined for about eleven days.

time is generally limited to about fifteen minutes for a shower, one hour of large muscle exercise (which typically consists of walking around the dayroom alone), and sometimes a short visit to the medical unit. In some cases, RSU logs reflect that TJJD "offers" children large muscle exercise inside the child's cell. The only education services that children in the RSU receive are daily packets that teachers pass out with minimal interaction, generally spending about five minutes on the RSU. All meals are served to children inside their cells. Based on unit logs, counselors typically visit children for about one minute and talk to children through their doors. This type of isolation exposes children to a significant risk of harm.

2.2. Children Are Isolated for Excessively Long Periods of Time in the General Population Units

Children across TJJD's secure facilities also experience excessive amounts of time alone in their cells under "operational lockdowns" and security practices unrelated to their behavior. While in their cells, children have virtually nothing to do to pass the time. Most children are permitted minimal or no property in their cells. Regardless of what it is called or why it is imposed, excessive time that children spend locked alone in their cells poses a serious risk of harm.[43]

Children regularly spend 17–22 hours per day locked alone in their cells.

Security video and cell check logs show that children in all five of TJJD's facilities regularly spend about 17–22 hours a day alone in their cells. Children are routinely locked in their cells during shower and bathroom time,[44] shift change, medication pass, and many mealtimes.

Although TJJD administrators state that bedtime for children is around 8:00-9:00 p.m., we found that children are often locked in their cells for the night much earlier. At Mart, for example, our consultants' review of randomly selected security video showed that children in all units were locked in their

---

[43] *See Hearing Before Tex. House Comm'n on Juv. Just. & Fam. Issues*, 88th Leg., R.S. (Aug. 9, 2022) (testimony by Exec. Interim Dir., Tex. Juv. Just. Dep't, Shandra Carter at 27:19-27:39), https://tlchouse.granicus.com/MediaPlayer.php?view_id=46&clip_id=23404 (last visited June 27, 2024) (stating that "[i]solation, we know, has tremendous negative consequences" and acknowledging that "operational room confinement . . . has the same impact as isolation").

[44] The cells in TJJD's general population units do not have plumbing. Staff must let children out to use the toilet and take a shower.

cells for the night before 7:00 p.m.[45] At Evins, where staff and children referred to the practice as "racking up," we observed children on one unit locked down for the night at 4:39 p.m.[46] At Giddings, we observed some children locked down for the night at 5:25 p.m. In general, once in their cells for thenight, children do not come back out until the next day around 6:00 a.m. at the earliest. But in many cases, children remained in their cells later, often eating breakfast there. Indeed, throughout our visits, children reported that they would be locked in their cells if we were not on site.

In many cases we reviewed, use of force occurs after children become upset about having to rack up. For example, in December 2022 at Evins around 4:45 pm, Michael refused to rack up for the day, instead running into the dorm's shower area. A staff member followed him, physically pulled him out, and restrained him by pulling his arms behind his back. Michael was then handcuffed and escorted to his cell by two staff.

Once in his cell, right after removing Michael's handcuffs, one staff pushed him to the ground. From there, the child covered his head. While in that position, another staff pepper sprayed him. He was then re-cuffed and taken to the RSU, where he spent several days.

On a Saturday in December 2022 at Evins, Anthony also became upset because he could not make his telephone call before staff directed the unit to rack up. The resulting use of physical force by staff left Anthony with a cut on his chin that required a trip to the infirmary. It was 11:30 a.m. when staff ordered children to rack up.

Consistent with our observations, the Sunset Commission found that "[y]outh will go to great—and at times, dangerous—lengths to avoid all-day lockdowns." The Commission's Report describes an example of one child who "timed the tying of a ligature around his neck to ensure staff performing routine door checks would pull him out of isolation before he was critically injured." Children in TJJD's custody supported this finding, telling us that at times: "You gotta get yourself in trouble to get attention."

Because of the high risk of harm whenever children are locked alone in their cells, staff should regularly conduct safety checks of each child at random intervals, something TJJD staff fail to do. Review of surveillance video and security check logs shows that staff often fail to look in the child's cell to confirm their safety. There were also several times when staff did not conduct

[45] TJJD released children from their rooms in the morning as early as 5:45 a.m. in some facilities to as late as 10:00 a.m. in others.

[46] We observed six staff on the unit at the time, suggesting that low staffing levels were not the cause of the lockdown.

cell checks at random intervals, which increases the chances that children will engage in self-harm and suicide since they can anticipate when staff will check on them. At one facility, our consultants' review of almost 130 hours of surveillance video showed that only about twenty percent of cell checks complied with TJJD's policy. Consistent with our observations, TJJD's Office of Inspector General found that in February 2023, a staff member at Evins falsified records by documenting that he had conducted five-minute cell checks—which are required for children on suicide alert[47] status—when, in fact, he neglected to check on them for nearly an hour. Failing to perform timely cell checks for children on suicide alert status exposes them to a serious risk of harm, including death. Our conversations with children echoed this concern: "If I'm behind a door, I feel like I could kill myself.

They don't check on us there."

3. TJJD Fails to Adequately Protect Children from Sexual Abuse

Children in juvenile justice facilities have a constitutional right to be free from sexual abuse by staff.[48] State officials also have a constitutional duty to protect children from assaults by other children.[49] The State must take reasonable steps to protect the children in its care from sexual abuse whenever the threat is known or should have been apparent.[50] Widespread sexual abuse, "coupled with[ ] inadequate supervision, creates a constant threat to [children's] safety" that violates the Constitution.[51]

When determining whether conditions are incompatible with contemporary standards of decency (and therefore violate the Constitution), courts consider "objective indicia of society's standards, as expressed in legislative enactments and state practice."[52] Texas family law defines "abuse," in relevant part, as "sexual conduct harmful to a child's mental, emotional, or

---

47 Children on suicide alert status are supposed to receive a heightened level of monitoring by staff to ensure their safety.

48 *See Alberti v. Klevenhagen*, 790 F.2d 1220, 1223–24 (5th Cir. 1986) (holding that pattern of sexual violence among both pretrial and convicted adults violates the Eighth Amendment).

49 *Johnson v. Johnson*, 385 F.3d 503, 524 (5th Cir. 2004) (citing *Farmer*, 511 U.S. at 833–34) ("Being violently assaulted in prison is simply not part of the penalty that criminal offenders pay for their offenses against society.") (alterations omitted).

50 *Farmer*, 511 U.S. at 834; *Stokes v. Delcambre*, 710 F.2d 1120, 1125–26 (5th Cir.1983) (finding that officials have a duty to not confine an individual under conditions that make it "likely he would be beaten and sexually assaulted").

51 *Alberti*, 790 F.2d at 1226.

52 *Graham*, 560 U.S. at 61 (quoting *Roper*, 543 U.S. at 572).

physical welfare," including conduct that constitutes criminal offenses under the Texas penal code.[53] Texas' penal code criminalizes a range of child sexual misconduct, including "sexual assault,"[54] "improper sexual activity with a person in custody or under supervision,"[55] "indecency with a minor,"[56] and "official oppression."[57]

Reports of sexual abuse have plagued TJJD for decades. In 2007, "[t]he agency was placed under conservatorship by the governor" and state agencies "investigated thousands of complaints and allegations [of sexual misconduct,] work[ing] with prosecutors to address the criminal violations found."[58] In 2011, following reports of sexual abuse and significant operational problems systemwide, the Texas legislature combined TJJD's predecessors—the Texas Youth Commission and the Texas Juvenile Probation Commission—into one agency. In 2017, allegations of sexual misconduct prompted Governor Abbott to request that the Texas Rangers investigate "a significant number of sexual misconduct allegations."[59] This resulted in several more staff arrests.

A December 2019 report from the Bureau of Justice Statistics provided TJJD with additional notice of a pattern of abuse in its secure facilities. The Bureau of Justice Statistics found that, in three of the five TJJD secure facilities, children reported some of the highest rates of sexual victimization in the country.[60] At Ron Jackson, fourteen percent of the children reported

---

[53] Tex. Fam. Code Ann. § 261.001(1)(E).

[54] Tex. Penal Code Ann. § 22.011 (criminalizing a range of sexual contact with children regardless of knowledge of the victim's age and specifying that there is no consent where the perpetrator is "an employee of a facility where the other person is a resident").

[55] *Id.* § 39.04 (criminalizing a range of sexual contact, as well as the inducement to engage in a range of sexual contact, with an individual in the custody of TJJD).

[56] *Id.* § 21.11 (criminalizing a range of child sexual misconduct, including where the perpetrator exposes, or causes the child to expose, the anus or any genitals "with intent to arouse or gratify the sexual desire of any person").

[57] *Id.* § 39.03(c) (criminalizing a public servant's "sexual harassment," including the "unwelcome sexual advances, requests for sexual favors, or other verbal or physical conduct of a sexual nature, submission to which is made a term or condition of a person's exercise or enjoyment of any right, privilege, power, or immunity, either explicitly or implicitly").

[58] *Sunset Self-Evaluation Report* 44–45, Tex. Juv. Just. Dep't (Sept. 1, 2021), https://perma.cc/5883- 5K6B.

[59] *Id.*

[60] U.S. Dep't of Just., Off. of Just. Programs, Bureau of Just. Stats., *Special Report on Sexual Victimization in Juvenile Facilities Reported by Youth, 2018*, at 28–30 (Dec. 2019), https://perma.cc/4FP2- 9JZX [hereinafter BJS Report].

being sexually victimized by staff or other children.[61] The rate was even higher at Gainesville and Mart, where one in six children reported abuse.[62]

Despite ample notice over two decades, TJJD has failed to implement measures to prevent this pattern of sexual abuse from continuing. Instead, following another Texas Rangers' investigation of sexual misconduct in 2021 that resulted in more staff arrests, TJJD issued a statement narrowly focusing on the Rangers' conclusion that its investigation uncovered no "anomalies, trends, or patterns (e.g., the same suspect committing multiple offenses, crimes committed at a specific time of day, crimes at a particular facility, etc.)." TJJD's response ignored obvious problems with staff training, oversight, supervision, and accountability. It also disregarded the serious and often irreparable harm that sexual abuse causes children. Indeed, the Office of Inspector General's investigation reports show that this pattern of abuse continues.

3.1. TJJD Fails to Prevent Staff From Sexually Abusing Children

Our review of hundreds of investigation reports from the Office of Inspector General shows a pervasive atmosphere of sexual abuse, grooming, and lack of staff accountability and training at TJJD. This atmosphere undermines the treatment and rehabilitation of children—many of whom already have been victims of sexual abuse and trafficking—and causes children serious and often lasting harm. Below are examples that illustrate TJJD's pattern of abuse:

- In December 2022, the Office of Inspector General concluded that a Mart staff member had abused a child. According to its report, video surveillance footage shows that the staff walked into a unit closet, turned off the light, and waited for a child to enter the closet. The video further shows the staff and child "lean forward and kiss each other on the lips," after which they exited the closet.
- In October 2022, the Office of Inspector General concluded that an Evins staff member had abused a child by engaging in an "inappropriate relationship" with him. The Office of Inspector General found that the staff had mailed the child inappropriate letters and engaged in inappropriate phone calls with the child. The staff also

---

[61] The BJS Report defines sexual victimization as "any forced or coerced sexual activity with another youth or any sexual activity with facility staff that takes place in a juvenile correctional facility." *Id.* at 1.

[62] *Id.*

mailed the child about fifty pictures of herself, two of which were nude pictures. Both the staff and the child had tattooed each other's names on their wrists.

"You gonna give it to him or he gonna take it. Knock the n****rs out, you wake up with a dick in your ass."
Mart staff member

- In September 2022, the Office of Inspector General concluded that a Mart staff member had committed abuse after body camera footage revealed that he appeared to "have an overly friendlydemeanor" with a child that "bordered on an inappropriate relationship" and had engaged in overtly sexual conversations with a child about "female genitalia, oral sex, and other sexual acts," mentioning "'hickies, breasts, fingering,' and other sexual acts." Transcripts from his body-worn camera reflect the use of violent, sexually graphic, and obviously inappropriate language about the children in his care, including advising that children should be on guard or they may "wake up with a dick in [their] ass."[63]
- In July 2022, the Office of Inspector General concluded that a Ron Jackson staff member had abused a child by soliciting and enticing her to "play with herself" in her cell. This incident was reported after another staff found the child's notebook containing detailed notes "of when [the staff] watched her masturbate." Investigators determined that the staff had turned off his body camera over a dozen times during his shift on that day and that he had engaged in inappropriate conversation right before turning off his camera.[64]
- In March 2022, a contractor who was not to have any direct contact with children engaged in conversations that were sexually explicit and emotionally harmful to a child. The Office of Inspector General

[63] The Office of Inspector General also concluded that the staff had violated TJJD policy requiring 15- minute room checks at random intervals.

[64] The Office of Inspector General also found that the staff member "failed to conduct door log checks on the required interval numerous times" throughout his shift. The staff member was responsible for "two offenders who were on [suicide alert] status at this time, both of whom he failed to conduct appropriate checks based on the [suicide alert] precautions outlined on their paperwork (10-minute intervals)." The Office of Inspector General found that the staff member "often completed four entries at one time while doing door logs to make it appear as though the intervals had been maintained although the entries were incorrect."

determined that this contractor "exhibited grooming and predatory behaviors" that were targeted at specific children.

- In July 2021, the Office of Inspector General concluded that an Evins staff member committed the criminal offenses of indecency with a child and improper sexual activity with person in custody and referred the case for prosecution. According to its report, the staff was found by a coworker in the unit shower area performing oral sex on a child. The staff turned their body-worn camera off just before the incident. In April 2024, the staff was indicted on charges of indecency with a child, improper sexual activity with a person in custody, and violation of the civil rights of a person in custody.

Our on-site observations are consistent with the Office of Inspector General's findings about inappropriate relationships between staff and children. We witnessed a staff member holding hands with a girl, referring to her as "baby," and playfully grabbing another child's shoulders. This type of conduct—coupled with the problems identified above regarding staff reporting, oversight, and compliance with body-worn camera policies—fosters an environment where sexual abuse by staff can occur without detection.

3.2. TJJD Fails to Prevent Children from Sexually Abusing Other Children

Aside from abuse by staff, we found a pattern of sexual victimization and misconduct among children that reflects a lack of adequate staff supervision. In August 2022, the Office of Inspector General sustained allegations that a boy at Gainesville forced another to perform oral and anal sex. In May 2021, the Office of Inspector General referred for criminal prosecution allegations that a boy at Giddings forced his penis on a younger boy's forehead. In an example from Ron Jackson, two children were found to have been together in one of the children's cells for thirty minutes unsupervised.

Many Office of Inspector General investigations sustained allegations involving sexual misconduct in unit bathrooms, dayrooms, classrooms, and workshops. All these areas should have been under the direct supervision of staff. Yet the activity went undetected until surveillance video later revealed it.

Our own review of hundreds of hours of surveillance video confirms that TJJD staff do not provide adequate supervision to the children in their care.

Staff generally appear complacent and disengaged. In many cases, staff ignore behaviors that could jeopardize the safety of children. We observed multiple situations where staff left children unsupervised. This lack of supervision, coupled with significant periods of unstructured time, invites incidents of violence and victimization.

4. TJJD's Dysfunctional Grievance System Contributes to TJJD's Harmful Environment

Interviews of staff and children and a review of over 500 grievances show deficiencies in TJJD's grievance system. These deficiencies contribute to the dangerous and harmful environment in several ways.

TJJD's grievance procedures do not provide children with an adequate method of reporting abuse and harm. Children should be able to obtain a grievance form without having to request it from someone and submit it themselves via secure boxes on every unit and in other facility common areas. At TJJD, however, a child on each unit is given the responsibility to distribute and collect grievance forms upon request from other children. Children on the RSU must request a grievance form from staff and then submit it through staff. These practices inhibit children's ability to submit grievances confidentially and without fear of retaliation.

TJJD also operates an Incident Reporting Center Hotline for children to submit grievances, but it is not effective. Children can only use this phone in the unit dayrooms at limited times and the phone does not always work. The grievance reports staff generate from calls made to this hotline often do not provide the date of the call, making it difficult to track response times.

Where dates are available, we found many grievances where TJJD did not respond promptly to complaints children raised. Several grievances that TJJD should have treated as emergency grievances and addressed immediately were instead assigned TJJD's standard ten-day response time for non-emergencies.

We also reviewed many grievances that TJJD categorized as resolved because the child received a response, even though the response did not meaningfully address the child's complaint. In April 2022, Jayden filed a grievance at Evins stating, "Everyday [sic] I feel like committing suicide because [another boy] is taking my trays! I don't feel safe in the pod because he's there." TJJD responded by placing the child on constant suicide precautions because of his "suicidal thoughts due to a peer taking your food."

After noting that mental health staff would follow up with Jayden, the response stated that the grievance "is now considered resolved." There is no mention of any follow up conducted or planned for the child's complaint about another child stealing his food.

Finally, TJJD does not assign grievance outcomes in a consistent manner. For example, a child at Mart submitted a grievance claiming he had been in TJJD for four months and his Minimum Length of Stay was being extended because he had not yet begun a required six-month treatment program. The grievance response states that staff explained to the child that he is on the waitlist to begin the program and he would begin it as soon as possible. The grievance was then marked as resolved, even though his request to start treatment was denied.[65] In yet another grievance, a girl at Mart complained that she was placed in the RSU for several days without adequate justification. TJJD's response to this grievance was that she was being held in the RSU pending an opening in the Behavior Stabilization Unit.[66] Her grievance was denied.

There is no discernable reason that some grievances are considered resolved, while others are denied or approved. This inconsistency hinders oversight and quality assurance reviews.

Failing to Provide Adequate Mental Health Care

The Eighth Amendment protects children from TJJD's deliberate indifference to their medical needs,[67] including mental health care.[68] TJJD officials are deliberately indifferent to children's mental health needs when they know of a substantial risk of serious harm and disregard that risk by failing to take

---

[65] We reviewed several additional grievances from children complaining about not receiving required treatments in time to complete them before their Minimum Length of Stay deadlines. TJJD's response to these grievances generally acknowledges the delay and references waitlists for these treatments, subsequently marking the grievances as resolved.

[66] This self-contained unit is for up to four children with "immediate and significant mental health issues that engage in frequent aggressive event[s]." The Behavior Stabilization Unit is located at Mart. TJJD conducts weekly treatment team meetings for children in this unit and provides "increased psychiatric oversight."

[67] *Farmer*, 511 U.S. at 834; *Gates v. Cook*, 376 F.3d 323, 343 (5th Cir. 2004).

[68] *Gates*, 376 F.3d at 343 ("[I]t is important to remember that mental health needs are no less serious than physical needs.") (citation omitted); *see also Partridge v. Two Unknown Police Officers of Hous., Tex.*, 791 F.2d 1182, 1187 (5th Cir. 1986) ("A psychological or psychiatric condition can be as serious as any physical pathology or injury, especially when it results in suicidal tendencies.").

reasonable measures to decrease it.[69] The risk of serious harm can arise from a series of individual failures or a combination of conditions that mutually reinforce one another to produce a single serious harm.[70] Officials' knowledge of a substantial risk can be inferred from the risk being obvious.[71]

Systemic deficiencies in mental health care in TJJD's secure facilities severely harm children. TJJD fails to accurately assess and diagnose children's mental health disorders, create adequate treatment plans, and provide counseling. TJJD also automatically suspends mental health services except medication for children whose mental health disorders cause disruptive or violent behaviors. TJJD similarly fails to provide adequate mental health services to children who are dually diagnosed with mental health and substance use disorders or engage in acts of self-harm or suffer from suicidal thoughts. These systemic deficiencies effectively deny children access to adequate care, causing suffering and often interfering with their ability to complete programs required for their release.

Texas is aware of the longstanding nature of its inadequate mental health services and the obvious harms that result. Because State officials have consistently failed to act despite this knowledge, they are deliberately indifferent to children's mental health needs.

1. Most Children in TJJD's Secure Facilities Have Serious Mental Health Needs, Including Histories of Trauma, Requiring Treatment

The percentage of children with serious mental health needs in TJJD's custody has grown at a staggering rate. In January 2020, then Executive Director Camille Cain reported to TJJD's Board of Directors: "In 2014, at the point of intake, we identified 21% of our youth as having moderate to severe mental health needs. In 2019, we were at 53%."[72] When current TJJD Executive Director Shandra Carter testified in August 2022 before a committee of the Texas legislature, she informed lawmakers that "85% of our kids have high or moderate mental health needs."[73] According to the Sunset Advisory

---

[69] *Farmer*, 511 U.S. at 847; *Gates*, 376 F.3d at 333.
[70] *Gates*, 376 F.3d at 333.
[71] *Farmer*, 511 U.S. at 842.
[72] Tex. Juv. Just. Dep't, *Board Meeting Minutes* 2 (Jan. 24, 2020), https://perma.cc/UY8P-PJPD.
[73] *See Hearing Before Tex. House Comm'n on Juv. Just. & Fam. Issues*, 88th Leg., R.S. (Aug. 9, 2022) (testimony by Exec. Interim Dir., Tex. Juv. Just. Dep't, Shandra Carter at 26:32), https://tlchouse.granicus.com/MediaPlayer.php?view_id=46&clip_id=23404 (last visited June 27, 2024).

Commission, over a similar timeframe, "the proportion of youth entering TJJD facilities with moderate or high mental health needs nearly quadrupled."

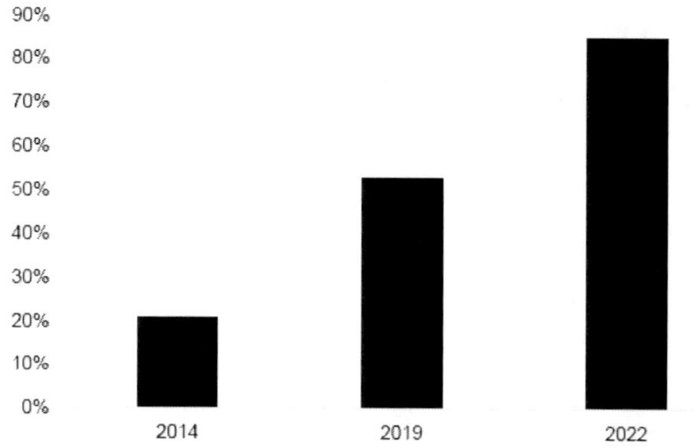

Figure 3. Increase in children with moderate or severe mental health needs in TJJD's custody.

Trauma is one of the most common causes of mental health issues for children in the juvenile justice system. It is an emotional response that results from living through a highly stressful experience, such as physical or sexual abuse, crime, death of a loved one, or exposure to family and other violence. Trauma can produce serious and debilitating symptoms, including flashbacks, repeated intrusive thoughts,[74] physical reactions to reminders of trauma, unpredictable emotions, irritability, angry outbursts, reckless or self-destructive behavior, hypervigilance,[75] problems with concentration, and sleep disturbance.

The effect of trauma on children, whose brains are still developing, can be particularly severe and lasting. In children, repeated episodes of stress and the accompanying excessive, repeated stimulation of the body's production of stress hormones impacts brain development and eventually impairs the child's ability to regulate their response to stressors. Instead of a stress response being a temporary reaction to danger, it becomes a constant, uncontrollable physiological warning of danger that persists, even when no danger is present. As a result, a child who is exposed to repeated trauma has more difficulty

---

[74] Intrusive thoughts are uninvited and usually unwanted ideas and images that come to one's mind.

[75] Hypervigilance refers to a state of watchfulness, where a person is constantly on guard and on the lookout for danger, even when there is little or no risk of something bad happening.

differentiating between safe and dangerous situations, is hyperresponsive to situations they perceive as frightening, and has more difficulty calming down once triggered.[76]

> "This is the highest concentration of acute needs . . . in the history of the agency."
>
> Texas House of Representatives Testimony from Shandra Carter, TJJD Executive Director

According to TJJD, most children in its secure facilities have experienced trauma. TJJD estimates that around sixty-four percent of boys and eighty-four percent of girls have been exposed to four or more potentially traumatic events during their childhood, with ninety-one percent of girls identified as vulnerable to child sex trafficking. As TJJD reports, "[t]his is the highest concentration of acute needs . . . in the history of the agency."

During our investigation, we met many children with intense mental health needs who have cycled through TJJD's facilities and programs, yet their conditions have not improved and their mental health symptoms have not stabilized. Many continue to engage in serious self-harm and exhibit behaviors related to their mental health difficulties that expose them to disciplinary sanctions. William, for example, entered TJJD's custody at eleven years old. His mental health quickly deteriorated, resulting in over 1,000 suicide risk assessments and over eighty acts of suicidal behavior while in TJJD's custody. As soon as William turned sixteen, TJJD transferred him to adult prison for allegedly hitting TJJD staff during an incident. William died by suicide six months later. As set forth below, TJJD's mental health care systematically fails to meet children's needs.

2. Children at TJJD Face Serious Harm and the Substantial Risk of Serious Harm Because of Inadequate Mental Health Care

We found several deficiencies in TJJD's mental health services, which have a cumulative effect of subjecting children to serious harm or the substantial risk of serious harm. Mental health staff do not properly assess children and therefore fail to identify their mental health care needs. Clinicians make little

---

[76] These difficulties are more likely if the child does not have the type of family nurture and support that would help them calm down and, eventually, learn to calm the hormonal response on their own.

effort to coordinate across disciplines, resulting in different clinicians making different diagnoses for the same child, without any meaningful effort to develop an integrated approach to a child's care. Clinicians similarly do not create treatment plans for many children and do not meet with children with sufficient frequency, including discontinuing mental health treatment altogether for children placed in specialized programs. TJJD's clinicians likewise fail to provide effective substance use disorder treatment for children with trauma-related and other mental health problems. Finally, children experience TJJD's overly restrictive response to suicidal ideation or acts of self-harm as punishment.

Although TJJD claims to adhere to a trauma-informed philosophy of care in which trained professionals help children "feel physically and emotionally safe, build[] appropriate trusting relationships, and [learn] . . . self-regulation," we found that TJJD's mental health services do not reflect a trauma-informed approach. On top of its other deficiencies, TJJD's failure to identify, assess, and treat trauma impacts every aspect of mental health services children receive, from assessments to treatment plans to counseling to substance use disorder treatment to suicide prevention.

2.1. TJJD Fails to Provide Adequate Mental Health Assessments and Treatment Plans

To provide adequate mental health care, juvenile justice facilities should have "a systematic program for screening and evaluating [incarcerated people] in order to identify those who require mental health treatment."[77] Individualized mental health assessments and accurate diagnoses that lead to a proposed approach to treatment are essential components.

Most of TJJD's psychological assessments we reviewed are inadequate. They fail to examine family, social, and developmental histories—including traumatic experiences—that are often critical to understanding the context for the child's behavioral functioning. They also fail to meaningfully consider children's extensive histories of past mental health assessments and interventions. They similarly fail to connect a history of mental health

---

[77] *Ruiz v. Estelle*, 503 F. Supp. 1265, 1339 (S.D. Tex. 1980), *aff'd in part, rev'd in part on other grounds*, 679 F.2d 1115 (5th Cir. 1982), *opinion amended in part and vacated in part*, 688 F.2d 266 (5th Cir. 1982); *see also Gates*, 376 F.3d at 336 (affirming district court injunction requiring that incarcerated people in an adult correctional facility be provided "a comprehensive mental health examination").

problems and trauma with specific behaviors.[78] Screening tools—which are intended to flag conditions for further assessment or intervention—are also not used appropriately or consistently. Clinicians do not, for example, conduct follow-up clinical interviews with children flagged for trauma to assess symptoms of any trauma-related disorders. Instead, clinicians list problematic behaviors that resulted in the child's commitment to TJJD, prior diagnoses, and cognitive testing results without attempting to integrate all this information into a cohesive, current clinical plan. Even once a psychological assessment is completed, it is rarely updated to reflect changes in the child's symptoms or circumstances.[79]

TJJD's diagnostic conclusions from this assessment process do not provide meaningful guidance for treatment. Assessments typically conclude with a long list of diagnoses, many of which are repetitive and nonspecific. For example, many children at TJJD are given multiple diagnoses of behavior-related disorders (conduct disorder and oppositional defiant disorder), which largely describe the same set of problems. Often, the only impairments identified about a child's ability to function are their law- breaking behaviors. Because assessments are rarely updated, TJJD's diagnoses for children remain stagnant too.

Treatment plans resulting from TJJD's ineffective diagnoses are also inadequate. The content is generic and could apply to any child, including goals such as "improve anger management" or "decrease aggression," which do not provide a meaningful plan for intervention. Some children receive treatment plans too late. One clinician created a child's treatment plan about a year after their admission to TJJD, while another clinician created the plan four days before the child's release. Moreover, many children who should have treatment plans do not. In a random sampling of mental health records from all five facilities, only about half of the children identified with moderate or severe mental health needs had treatment plans.

Similar problems exist with TJJD's psychiatric process. Off-site psychiatrists with the University of Texas Medical Branch provide psychiatric services at TJJD. Their psychiatric assessments, which are conducted remotely over a virtual platform, are even less rigorous than the psychological assessments and generally default to behavior-related disorders without

---

[78] Because of the disconnect between mental health and behavior, TJJD staff consistently view challenging behaviors as within the child's control, rather than a symptom of trauma or mental health disorder.

[79] Assessments for the children on the mental health units at Giddings are updated upon referral and intake to the unit.

adequate exploration of other mental health issues. They often reach different diagnostic conclusions than the psychological assessments. We found no evidence that TJJD's clinicians seek to address these inconsistencies or develop an integrated treatment plan. In fact, when asked, TJJD staff stated that weekly virtual treatment team meetings enable clinicians to collaborate and ensure consistency. But only a few minutes are devoted to each child's case during these weekly meetings, which is not enough time to develop an integrated treatment plan, and inconsistencies remain unresolved.

Emma's experience illustrates TJJD's failure to provide adequate mental health assessments and treatment plans for children, especially those who have experienced trauma. She has a significant history of trauma—including family violence and sex trafficking—as well as both inpatient and outpatient psychiatric treatment. But TJJD's mental health assessment of Emma does not reflect this traumatic history and her treatment plan does not identify mental health care to cope with it. TJJD's clinicians did not schedule any counseling sessions with Emma until four months after her admission, despite her being recommended for counseling during intake. They then met with her sporadically, with breaks in between sessions lasting a month or more.

Even then, there is no evidence that TJJD ever addressed her mental health symptoms or trauma, instead focusing on her law-breaking behavior. In the meantime, Emma experienced depression and feelings of anger and distress.

Without accurate and thorough mental health assessments and treatment planning, TJJD fails to protect children from serious harm and death. For example, two children died by suicide when TJJD failed to adequately consider critical information in assessing their needs. One child died by suicide after arriving at TJJD from a psychiatric hospital, where he had been hospitalized following a suicide attempt. Even though he was still on suicide alert status when released from the hospital, TJJD failed to consider whether he needed a safety plan or other suicide precautions. Another child died by suicide after TJJD failed to meaningfully consider the extensive information available about the child's mental health difficulties and instead classified the child as having "low mental health treatment needs."

2.2. TJJD Does Not Provide Adequate Counseling Services

Given both the absence and inadequacy of treatment plans, it is no surprise that TJJD does not provide adequate counseling services.[80] We received

[80] *Ruiz*, 503 F. Supp. at 1339 (explaining that minimally adequate mental health care requires individualized treatment by trained mental health professionals).

differing reports regarding the required frequency of counseling services for children of varying mental health needs. Some of the facility clinical directors reported that children with moderate mental health needs should receive one counseling session every other week. Another facility clinical director stated that he could not respond and directed us to the TJJD mental health director. A third facility clinical director conceded that there were insufficient clinical staff to meet the children's counseling needs.

> 9 out of 10 children with mental health needs experience breaks between counseling sessions lasting two months or more.

As a result, the number of counseling sessions children receive is inadequate. After reviewing a random sample of mental health records from all five facilities, we found that children receive an average of 1.04 counseling sessions per month. Almost ninety percent of them have breaks in counseling sessions of two months or longer with no documented clinical reason as to why.

In many other cases, children go months without any counseling. For example, we found several children who were identified as having moderate or high mental health treatment needs who went anywhere from six weeks to thirteen months without counseling after admission. Even when children received counseling, notes from those sessions show little indication that trauma is regularly addressed with children who have trauma histories and diagnoses.

Alexander's experience highlights TJJD's failure to provide counseling services. His mother died by suicide five months before his admission to TJJD. Although his intake assessment identified this event as traumatic for Alexander and concluded he had a moderate need for counseling, he received no counseling for fifteen months. When he finally met with a counselor, the session lasted only fifteen minutes. Although both Alexander and his unit staff expressed concern about his mental health functioning— specifically his distress, anger, and self-harm—nearly a month passed before his next session. He then waited another 3.5 months for his third session. When TJJD transferred Alexander to the Violence Intervention Continuum[81] at Evins,

[81] The Violence Intervention Continuum is a specialized program operated by security staff designed to help children develop skills to reduce risk factors related to violent or aggressive behavior. It includes the Intensive Intervention Program, Redirect program, and Phoenix program. The Intensive Intervention Program is the lowest level of intervention available at Evins, Mart, and Gainesville. It provides a 30-day program to twelve children

TJJD terminated his counseling.[82] Alexander reported that by the time he saw any counselor regularly—about 1.5 years into his commitment—he had become frustrated and began acting out. Alexander's mental health struggles, left largely untreated, likely contributed to the behaviors that became the basis for TJJD moving Alexander to the Violence Intervention Continuum.

For most children like Alexander who TJJD knows have significant mental health difficulties, TJJD's promise of counseling is illusory, leaving them to manage their own symptoms while coping with the conditions of secure confinement. Children we spoke with recognized this, observing: "Sometimes, I think I'd rather be dead than be in here" because "[t]his place ain't made to rehab you."

2.3. TJJD Denies Mental Health Treatment to Children in Its Violence Intervention Continuum

TJJD's policy of automatically withholding most mental health treatment for children sent to the Violence Intervention Continuum conflicts with minimum constitutional standards of care.[83] The Violence Intervention Continuum—a specialized program for children who exhibit violent and aggressive behavior run by security staff—is not a substitute for mental health treatment, which involves care by trained mental health clinicians for mental health disorders. TJJD's practice of pausing mental health treatment while children complete this program ignores that a child's violent or aggressive behavior may result from untreated mental health issues. In some cases, these behaviors can be an indirect consequence of a symptom, such as poor impulse control in a child with attention deficit hyperactivity disorder or fatigue and irritability in a child who is not sleeping due to nightmares or anxiety. In other cases, violence or aggression can reflect general problems that occur alongside—and are worsened by— a mental health disorder, such as challenges in peer interactions or general problems managing stress. For other children, violent

per housing unit. Children in the Intensive Intervention Program are typically allowed to leave their unit for school and other essential services. Redirect is the next level of intervention and is available at Evins. It provides a 30-day program on self-contained units, meaning that children cannot leave their units. Phoenix is the most restrictive program and is available at Evins. It provides a 45- day program on self-contained units, ranging from six to ten children.

[82] We discuss the systemic problems with TJJD's practice of discontinuing mental health services for children in the Violence Intervention Continuum below.

[83] Children in the Violence Intervention Continuum continue to receive prescribed psychiatric medications. But without a clinician's individualized assessment and judgment, medication generally should not be employed as a stand-alone mental health treatment.

or aggressive behavior can be a symptom of trauma that the child previously experienced. In any of these circumstances, withholding mental health treatment as a consequence is both counterproductive, since adequate treatment may be important to addressing the behavior, and punitive, since it effectively punishes the child for symptoms of a mental health disorder.[84]

TJJD offered two justifications for this practice, neither of which addresses the harm of suspending mental health treatment for children who need it. First, one facility clinical director stated that children may request to meet with a mental health professional while in the Violence Intervention Continuum. But reports from children and the mental health professionals assigned to those units—as well as records we reviewed—show that this rarely occurs. In fact, many children we spoke with were not even aware that they could make such a request. Second, TJJD's policy requires monitoring of children's mental health while they are in the Violence Intervention Continuum. But this is not a reason to pause mental health care. To the contrary, the fact that these children require monitoring by mental health clinicians supports continued treatment from those same clinicians.[85]

2.4. TJJD Does Not Provide Effective Substance Use Disorder Treatment for Children with Trauma and Other Mental Health Problems

Because substance use as self-medication is extremely common with children who suffer from trauma and other mental health difficulties, treatment of these children requires an individualized approach to understanding the child's reasons for substance use.[86] For example, a child with a history of trauma and depression may be using substances to cope with overwhelming emotions,

---

[84] TJJD takes a similar approach to children in its Capital Offender Group, a 6- to 9-month program designed to address risk factors for children with violent or aggressive offenses. Like children in the Violence Intervention Continuum, "individual therapy is paused" for these children.

[85] One facility clinical director explained that mental health treatment is suspended as a way to help children focus on better managing their behavior, which has become the primary concern. Others who offered a justification for the practice echoed that view. But this approach largely neglects the causes of the behavior and fails to recognize the interconnectedness between trauma and other mental health problems, substance use, and the behavior that TJJD seeks to "correct."

[86] While maintaining boundaries between therapeutic disciplines may be appropriate, an integrated approach to treatment requires the disciplines to work together to develop a comprehensive assessment and integrated treatment plan for each child. This is not the case at TJJD, where substance use treatment is provided without regard to any co-occurring mental health difficulties and mental health treatment is provided without addressing co-occurring substance use difficulties.

while another child may simply lack the skills needed to avoid peer pressure. Effective substance use disorder treatment counselors must be knowledgeable in substance use disorder intervention methods, adolescent development, mental health disorders, and the influence that trauma can have on a child's behavior.

Contrary to this principle, TJJD's substance use disorder treatment program reflects a one-size-fits-all approach destined to fail for many children. Substance use treatment counselors explicitly confirmed that interventions are identical for all children, regardless of diagnosis or individual reasons for use. Because some children must complete substance use disorder treatment to earn release, TJJD's failure to provide an effective substance use treatment program for children with trauma and mental health problems may create an insurmountable obstacle to going home.

2.5. TJJD's One-Size-Fits-All Suicide Prevention Program Increases the Risk of Harm to Children

Some of the children with mental health problems in TJJD's secure facilities express their anger and pain through suicidal ideation and self-harm. We talked to several children who had been cutting themselves and using materials they found to create and tie ligatures around their necks or otherwise harm themselves. Some of their efforts were intended to cause death, some were expressions of anger and frustration, and some were attempts to get attention when less drastic measures had failed.

While restrictions in response to suicidality may be unavoidable, limitations on movement, access to personal property, or placement in isolation should be imposed only after individualized assessments and only to the minimum extent necessary. Our experts found that TJJD's practices fail to meet this standard. Their responses are often severely restrictive and implemented in a one-size-fits-all fashion, occurring without adequate consideration of the actual imminent risk, the context of threat or ideation, or the individualized treatment needs.[87] Children who engage in suicidal behavior are sometimes restrained, subjected to pepper spray, and sent to the RSU. If not sent to the RSU, their cells are stripped of their bedding, clothes, and all personal possessions. Restrictions of this magnitude should not be

---

[87] For example, in our Failing to Keep Children Safe from Harm Section above, we describe a child who filed a grievance about another child stealing his food trays. In the grievance, the child stated that this made him "feel like committing suicide." TJJD's response was to place the child on "constant" suicide precautions, rather than to address his complaint about his food being stolen.

routine, but used only when a heightened level of risk makes these practices necessary.

Imposing unnecessarily severe levels of restriction causes harm without any incremental increase in safety. In fact, TJJD's overly restrictive approach is experienced by the child as punishment. As a result, children report that they are reluctant to share their suicidal thoughts with TJJD staff.

Madison's experience shows TJJD's overly restrictive and generic approach to suicide precautions. Madison was on suicide alert status when security staff asked her to change her clothes, purportedly concerned that her current clothing could be used for self-harm. Surveillance video shows that, as Madison stood in her cell, she refused to change and threatened to spit in the staff's face. Staff responded, "Please. Please do it," in what looked like an attempt to escalate the situation.[88] As Madison continued to stand in her doorway without moving, one of the staff whispered, "I'm going to spray," and another staff responded sarcastically, "I feel threatened. I feel terrified."

> "Intervention is needed (possible [pepper] spray) if youth is engaging in self-harm and not responding to prompts to stop."
>
> TJJD mental health counselor's note

When Madison did not move, staff pepper sprayed her. In the subsequent incident report, staff justified their use of pepper spray by alleging they feared for Madison's safety.

On top of its overly restrictive approach, TJJD fails to provide children who exhibit self-harm or suicidal thoughts with adequate clinical interventions. At most, mental health counselors make periodic visits to assess any immediate danger, but there is no effort to understand the meaning behind the child's behavior, update (or create) the child's treatment plan, or work with the child to constructively manage these thoughts and feelings. The thoughts and feelings that lead children to such desperate and harmful actions are left untreated. Although suicidal behavior or ideation should be a considered a signal that more clinical intervention is needed, at TJJD, it leads to less.

---

[88] We also discuss Madison's experiences in TJJD custody on page 42.

Failing To Provide Appropriate Special Education and Related Services

TJJD operates a year-round school district for children committed to its secure facilities. Each facility has a high school in a stand-alone building where children are assigned to classes based on their dorms, rather than their grade, educational needs, or disability. Instruction is provided almost exclusively through an online curriculum called Apex Learning, which is intended to be used for first-time credit, as a credit recovery system for students who have failed a middle or high school course, and expanded course access. Apex offers both core subjects (English, math, science, and social studies) as well as electives (Spanish, business law, and art appreciation).[89] It requires children to independently review content and answer multiple-choice or fill-in-the-blank questions to demonstrate mastery. TJJD's teachers act as facilitators only, answering questions when asked by children on whatever course they are completing but providing no direct instruction.[90] TJJD's school district provides education to children with disabilities.

The IDEA offers federal funds to States to help educate children with disabilities. In exchange for those funds, States must comply with several requirements.[91] Among them, States must ensure that all children suspected of having a disability are properly evaluated for eligibility for special education and related services. Once eligible, States must provide a free appropriate public education to all children. Each child receives an individualized education program, or IEP, which must include both specially designed instruction tailored to meet that child's unique needs and related services to permit them to benefit from that instruction. States must also ensure that all children's needs are re-evaluated at least once every three years. Once children turn sixteen, States must provide transition services to plan for each child's post-school activities. Finally, States must establish and follow procedures designed to protect children with behavioral challenges from repeated

---

[89] Some students also participate in career and technical education classes, including culinary arts, welding, woodshop, horticulture, auto repair, construction, and graphic arts. These courses are designed to teach practical skills, but TJJD does not always offer hands-on instruction.

[90] Direct instruction involves: (a) breaking down complex skills; (b) using modeling and thinking aloud to draw children's attention to important features; (c) systematically decreasing supports as children become proficient at demonstrating the skill or concept; and (d) creating purposeful practice opportunities with timely corrective feedback.

[91] Texas receives IDEA funds. *See* Tex. Educ. Agency, *Annual State Application under IDEA Part B & IDEA Eligibility Documentation*, https://perma.cc/F5HE-GVGW.

classroom removals and ensure parents' right to meaningfully participate in the IEP process. The IDEA applies to "all political subdivisions of the State that are involved in the education of children with disabilities," including "[s]tate and local juvenile and adult correctional facilities."[92] Yet TJJD does not comply with its requirements.

1. TJJD Fails to Properly Evaluate All Children Suspected of Having Disabilities

The IDEA requires States to develop and implement an effective system to identify, locate, and evaluate all children—regardless of the severity of their disability—who may be eligible for special education and related services.[93] This is known as a "child find" system. TJJD violates this IDEA requirement.

Typically, school districts engage in organized activities throughout each academic year to identify eligible children. These activities can include a screening process to determine whether children should be referred for initial evaluations because they are struggling academically or behaviorally. Child find activities can also include public awareness campaigns to provide information to families in the languages they speak about the child find process. Finally, these activities may include tracking targeted supports and interventions provided to children for effectiveness.

TJJD's schools fail to engage in any organized activities to identify eligible children. We found no evidence that TJJD has a screening process at intake or during a child's time in custody to identify those struggling academically or behaviorally. The only standardized assessment TJJD uses is the Test of Adult Basic Education, which is limited to math and reading.[94] But TJJD does not use it to flag children with potential disabilities.[95] We also found no evidence of public awareness campaigns to explain the child find process on TJJD's website or anywhere on-site at the facilities. Although the youth handbook shares the process, it is confusing and inaccurate. For example, it accurately explains that a request for initial evaluations can be made at any time and that the school will respond to written requests within

---

[92] 34 C.F.R. § 300.2(a), (b)(1)(iv).

[93] 20 U.S.C. § 1412(a)(3); 34 C.F.R. § 300.111(a)(1)(i).

[94] TJJD uses untrained individuals to administer the Test of Adult Basic Education, casting doubt on the validity of any results.

[95] TJJD policy also indicates that the Test of Word Reading Efficiency (TOWRE) is used as another standardized assessment, but we found no evidence to confirm its use.

fifteen school days, but falsely suggests that requests can be made to any staff (when requests must go to certain staff, such as the director of special education or school principal). Finally, there is no system in place to track academic and behavioral interventions to identify children for referral who continue to struggle after intake. Without these organized activities, TJJD's child find system is ineffective.

TJJD identified and referred only 1 out of 575 children (less than one percent) for initial special education evaluations.

During a random 20-month review period, TJJD identified and referred for initial evaluation only one child out of 575 children—less than one percent. At Mart, the diagnostician[96] reported that they had not conducted a single initial evaluation in the last five years. That is not because most children in custody who may be eligible already receive special education and related services. Only about thirty-three percent of children have IEPs, even though eighty-five percent have high or moderate mental health needs and are, on average, five or six grade levels behind.

This suggests that TJJD fails to identify and refer other eligible children for initial evaluations. That failure includes Madison, who TJJD never referred for initial evaluations, despite her behavior leading her to spend one-quarter of her time in TJJD's custody (115 out of 458 days) in the RSU.[97]

2. TJJD Systematically Reduces, Changes, or Eliminates Special Education and Related Services, Ignoring Children's Individualized Needs

The IEP is "'the centerpiece of the [IDEA's] education delivery system for . . . children [with disabilities].'"[98] It is a comprehensive plan developed by the child's IEP team— including teachers, school officials, and the child's

---

[96] A diagnostician is a special educator who provides assessments and evaluations to determine children's eligibility for special education services. See 19 Tex. Admin. Code Ann. § 239.80. At TJJD's schools, they cover all suspected areas of disability except emotional disturbance.

[97] We also discuss Madison's experiences in TJJD custody on pages 38.

[98] *Endrew F. v. Douglas Cnty. Sch. Dist. RE-1*, 580 U.S. 386, 391 (2017) (quoting *Honig v. Doe*, 484 U.S. 305, 311 (1988)); *see also Fry v. Napoleon Cmty. Schs.*, 580 U.S. 154, 158 (2017) (explaining that the IEP "serves as the 'primary vehicle' for providing each child with the promised FAPE").

parent—following a detailed set of procedures.[99] These procedures emphasize collaboration among parents and educators and require careful consideration of each child's individual circumstances.[100]

The IDEA requires that every IEP include: (1) "a statement of the child's present levels of academic achievement and functional performance;" (2) "how the child's disability affects the child's involvement and progress in the general education curriculum;" (3) "measurable annual goals, including academic and functional goals;" and (4) a "description of how the child's progress toward meeting" those goals will be monitored.[101] The IEP must also describe the "special education and related services. . . that will be provided" so that the child may "advance appropriately toward [achieving] the[ir] annual goals" and "make progress in the general education curriculum."[102] For children who may not otherwise be able to achieve on grade level, IEPs must be appropriately ambitious and include challenging objectives to ensure they make progress that is appropriate in light of their circumstances.[103]

The IDEA similarly requires the IEP team to determine each child's placement on a continuum of educational placement options[104] after considering which services and supports that child needs to be successful and where and how those services and supports can be provided effectively. This is known as the IDEA's least restrictive environment principle, which requires that children with disabilities receive special education and related services in the same classroom as children without disabilities to the maximum extent appropriate.[105]

TJJD consistently reduces, changes, or eliminates children's special education and related services, regardless of their "present levels of achievement, disability, and potential for growth."[106] Of the 74 IEPs we reviewed where the child's IEP from their prior school was available, 73 revealed that TJJD made significant changes. These changes de-individualize children's IEPs in violation of their right to a free appropriate public education under the IDEA.

---

[99] *Endrew F.*, 580 U.S. at 391; 20 U.S.C. § 1414(d)(1)(B). In Texas, the IEP team is called the Admissions, Review, and Dismissal Committee.

[100] *Endrew F.*, 580 U.S. at 391 (citing 20 U.S.C. § 1414).

[101] 20 U.S.C. § 1414(d)(1)(A)(i)(I)-(III).

[102] *Id.* § 1414(d)(1)(A)(i)(IV).

[103] *Endrew F.*, 580 U.S. at 402–03.

[104] To comply with the IDEA, school districts must offer a continuum that includes, among others, general education classes, special education classes, and specialized schools. 34 C.F.R § 300.115.

[105] *Id.* § 300.114(a)(2).

[106] *Endrew F.*, 580 U.S. at 400.

Comparison of IEPs at TJJD vs. Prior Schools

- In nearly 70 percent of IEPs, TJJD recommends the bare minimum special education supports, even though many of these same children received substantially more support in their prior schools.
- In nearly 85 percent of IEPs, TJJD reduces special education and related services by an average of nearly 5 hours per week.
- In every IEP, TJJD uses generic, boilerplate annual goals.
- In nearly every IEP, TJJD eliminates children's behavior intervention plans.

TJJD almost uniformly recommends minimal, if any, specialized programs or services for children with disabilities, disregarding the intensity of their needs in favor of the only supports that TJJD has available. Indeed, nearly seventy percent of the IEPs we reviewed recommended the bare minimum supports for children with disabilities in TJJD's custody, even though most of those children had previously received substantially more support in their prior schools. TJJD explained these changes by claiming to provide all special education supports in an inclusive setting. But TJJD's general education classes are not inclusive. Although special educators enter the classroom for brief periods to work with students, they do not provide any specialized instruction to children with disabilities and do not collaborate with general educators to plan or deliver lessons, both hallmarks of inclusion. We also found no evidence that TJJD offers supplementary aids and services to help children progress in general education, such as providing small group instruction outside the classroom for some portion of the day (known as "resource room"). Without resource room, TJJD fails to properly implement at least twenty children's IEPs that require it. TJJD's failure to consider individualized needs prevents children who require more intensive supports from making meaningful progress.

TJJD also dramatically reduces the amount of support children receive from a special educator or related service provider once in general education classes. Nearly eighty- five percent of IEPs we reviewed reflect a reduction in services by an average of nearly five hours per week. For example, TJJD reduced Sophia's special education services from 300 minutes daily to zero. TJJD also reduced Christian's special education services from 240 minutes daily to forty-five minutes every two weeks. TJJD's systematic reduction of services is not based on children's individualized needs.

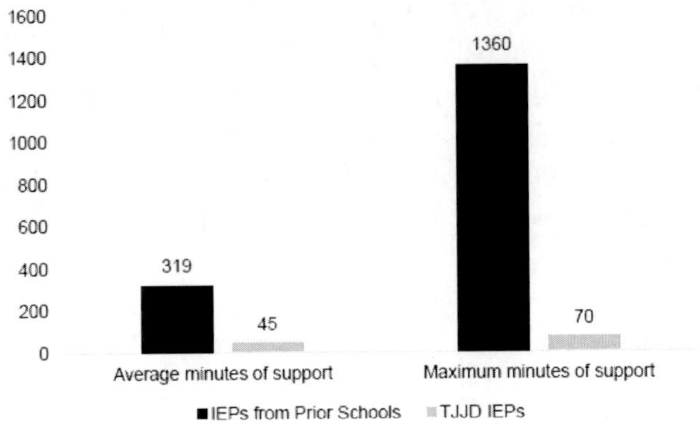

Figure 4. TJJD's reduction in children's special education support per week.

In addition, TJJD-created IEP goals are generic, including the same measure of success and boilerplate language from Texas' state learning standards that all children are expected to achieve. Matthew's IEP is one example of TJJD's inappropriate alteration of IEP goals. Matthew is a 17-year-old with an intellectual disability and "severe cognitive deficits" who requires explicit instruction in functional skills, reads on a third-grade level, and has failed multiple state assessments. Matthew is in the ninth grade for the second academic year. Given his intellectual disability, TJJD should have created individualized goals that modified the ninth-grade curriculum with adapted texts, reduced complexity of assignments, and a slower pace. Instead, TJJD rewrote his individualized goals to reflect the language of sixth and seventh grade state standards, two grades he already completed.

Finally, TJJD automatically eliminates behavior intervention plans from children's IEPs without considering their individualized needs. Behavior intervention plans should outline strategies for school staff to prevent problematic behaviors and teach skills designed to promote positive behaviors. Half of the IEPs we reviewed from prior school districts included a behavior intervention plan. TJJD eliminated nearly all of them after admission to its secure facilities. This includes Mia's, despite her being housed in the Behavior Stabilization Unit at the time of our visit and receiving 163 incident reports and sixty-six referrals to the RSU in a single year. In the rare times where TJJD retains the child's behavior intervention plan, it does not update that plan to reflect the child's placement in TJJD. For example, Andrew's behavior intervention plan from his prior school district includes interventions such as sending him to the office, calling his family, or giving him detention, none of which are available at TJJD.

Sophia's IEP illustrates the deficiencies we found in TJJD's IEPs. At her prior school, she received all academic instruction in a class taught by a special educator for children with IEPs only. She also had a behavior intervention plan that noted that she "will get herself involved when she sees peers that are becoming escalated," but can be "easily redirected." Sophia succeeded in school with those supports.

Once at TJJD, the IEP team overhauled her IEP. TJJD placed Sophia in the general education classroom full-time without explaining how it met her individualized needs. TJJD removed all services provided by a special educator, noting they were "not needed at this time" with no explanation. TJJD also changed her IEP to reflect that her behavior no longer impeded learning, without providing any evidence, and replaced her behavior intervention plan with generic language.

Without these individualized supports and services, Sophia earned failing grades in each of her classes at Ron Jackson and began exhibiting problematic behaviors. Yet when the IEP team convened to discuss her struggles, it made no changes to her IEP. In fact, in every record we reviewed where an IEP team convened to discuss children failing one or more classes, the IEP team made no changes to the child's special education and related services, despite TJJD's obligation under the IDEA to do so to ensure a child's meaningful progress. Instead, TJJD blamed children's poor academic performance on their "lack of effort and lack of completion of assignments."

3. Children Whose Behavior Impedes Learning Do Not Receive Required Behavioral Supports

TJJD violates the IDEA's requirement that it "consider the use of positive behavioral interventions and supports[] and other strategies" when a child's behavior impedes learning.[107] The first step in this process is typically to conduct a functional behavioral assessment, which gathers information to identify which behavioral challenges need to be addressed and their possible causes. The IEP team should use that assessment to create or update a behavior intervention plan. Over a nineteen-month period, TJJD did not conduct any functional behavioral assessments or create a single behavior intervention plan for children who exhibited ongoing, intense emotional or behavioral

[107] 20 U.S.C. § 1414(d)(3)(B)(i).

challenges in the classroom, even when specifically requested to do so by advocates.[108]

TJJD special education staff are not adequately trained about the IDEA's requirements related to positive behavioral supports. None of the special educators we interviewed could identify any formal training they have received on how to conduct a functional behavioral assessment or create and implement a behavior intervention plan.

Teachers' lack of training contributes to TJJD's failure to provide children with disabilities appropriate behavioral supports.

Rather than providing these supports, TJJD disproportionately subjects children with disabilities to disciplinary practices. These children receive almost twice as many incident reports as children without disabilities. Children classified with emotional disturbance on their IEPs receive 2.6 times more incident reports than any other children in TJJD's secure facilities. Children with disabilities also experience about twice as many referrals and admissions to the RSU. Those numbers are even higher for children with emotional disturbance, who experience nearly three times as many referrals and admissions. Once admitted, children with disabilities stay twice as long too, averaging over twelve days or 288 hours. Again, the numbers are higher for children with emotional disturbance, whose stays are three times as long, averaging nearly seventeen days or nearly 400 hours. TJJD's use of disciplinary practices in lieu of appropriate behavioral supports violates the IDEA.

4. TJJD's Special Educators Do Not Provide any Specially Designed Instruction

The IDEA requires that children with IEPs receive specially designed instruction. Specially designed instruction involves special educators changing—based on a child's individualized learning needs—the "content, methodology, or delivery of instruction" to ensure that the child can achieve

---

108 School districts need not conduct functional behavioral assessments if the child's IEP "adequately identifies [their] behavioral impediments and implements strategies to address that behavior." *B. S. v. Waxahachie Indep. Sch. Dist.*, No. 22-10443, 2023 WL 2609320, at *6 (5th Cir. Mar. 23, 2023) (per curiam) (unpublished) (citing *M.W. v. N.Y.C. Dep't of Educ.*, 725 F.3d 131, 140 (2d Cir. 2013)). As discussed above, TJJD-created IEPs systematically eliminate behavior intervention plans and de- individualize behavioral goals once children enter its secure facilities.

their annual goals and master grade-level concepts.[109] Specially designed instruction can address any area of individual need, including academic, behavioral, social, communication, health, and functional.

Examples include intensive small group or one-on-one instruction for children who lack core mathematics skills, explicit instruction in using supports such as a self-monitoring checklist for a child who exhibits executive functioning deficits, or implementing a schedule to reinforce on-task behaviors and ignore verbal outbursts from a child with emotional and behavioral disabilities. The delivery of specially designed instruction must be closely monitored to ensure it achieves the desired results.

TJJD provides no specially designed instruction to children with disabilities. Instead, its special educators enter classrooms, ask if anyone needs help, provide 1:1 assistance to children who request it, and document in logs that they provide special education services if they happen to assist children with disabilities. But this 1:1 assistance does not include direct, explicit instruction tailored to any child's unique learning needs. It includes no changes to content, methodology, or delivery of instruction. And it does not address any child's IEP goals. Instead, the special educators' 1:1 assistance is limited to, for example, helping children locate answers to questions for Apex's online curriculum. Children with disabilities at all five facilities unsurprisingly express frustration with their inability to understand what they are learning.

A typical example of TJJD's lack of specially designed instruction occurred during our observations of a Ron Jackson classroom. While a child struggled to answer questions on Apex, a special educator sat next to him for nearly twenty minutes. At one point, the child remarked, "I don't even know what it's asking me." The special educator did not provide any direct instruction tailored to the child's individualized needs, nor adjust his methodology or delivery to facilitate the child's learning. Instead, the special educator's assistance included generic suggestions to read the question aloud and look in Apexfor the answer. Without specially designed instruction, the child failed to complete the assignment.

The lack of specially designed instruction is especially problematic in reading, given that forty percent of children with disabilities in TJJD's secure facilities read below the third-grade level and more than half of children with disabilities read below the fifth- grade level, even though most are in high school. All the IEPs we reviewed included no specially designed instruction

---

[109] 34 C.F.R. § 300.39(b)(3).

in reading. These IEPs also excluded any IEP goals related to reading, preventing the use of such goals to guide instruction and monitor progress. When asked which reading supports they provide to children with disabilities, TJJD's special educators responded that they "encourage them to read," "read to them," and let Apex read to them "if they'll let it." None of these activities qualify as specially designed instruction.

5. TJJD Fails to Provide Related Services to Eligible Children Due to a Lack of Qualified Related Service Providers on Staff

The IDEA requires States to provide related services to children with disabilities who need them to benefit from special education.[110] Related services can include speech- language pathology and audiology services, physical and occupational therapy, social work, psychological services, and counseling.[111] A child's evaluations determine whether they are eligible for a particular related service.[112] Once the child is eligible, the related service provider should work with the IEP team to create an annual goal that supports the child's individualized needs. Specific details about the related service—such as how it will be delivered, how often, for how long, and where—should all be in the child's IEP.[113] The related service must be implemented by qualified or licensed related service providers as set forth in the IDEA.[114] Any failure to deliver related services not only leads to children with disabilities struggling academically, but may also impact their ability to execute essential life tasks, like navigating social settings, regulating their emotions, or adequately expressing themselves.

Despite the importance of related services, none of TJJD's schools have qualified related service providers on staff. We could not identify any such providers during our site visits to each facility's high school. TJJD also failed to identify any providers when asked, providing a list of teachers who also serve as academic counselors. But it is unclear whether these teachers are qualified under the IDEA to provide related services like counseling or psychological services.

---

[110] 20 U.S.C. § 1414(d)(1)(A)(i)IV); 34 C.F.R. § 300.1.
[111] 20 U.S.C. § 1401(26)(A); 34 C.F.R. § 300.34.
[112] 20 U.S.C. § 1414(a)-(b).
[113] *Id.* § 1414(d)(1)(A)(IV).
[114] 34 C.F.R. § 300.34.

> None of TJJD's five schools have qualified related service providers on staff. None of the schools provide related services.

TJJD's lack of qualified providers prevents eligible children from receiving related services. For example, of the IEPs we reviewed at Ron Jackson, twenty-one include related services, specifically counseling or psychological services.

The frequency and duration of services children are entitled to receive ranges from twenty minutes per semester to fifteen minutes every two weeks. Without a qualified provider, these children miss out on 40–360 minutes of related services each academic year. Ron Jackson's school principal confirmed this IDEA failure, stating that no related services are delivered at that facility. We observed a similar pattern of failing to provide related services—including counseling, psychological services, and speech-language pathology services—to children at TJJD's other four secure facilities. Without related services from qualified providers, children cannot receive a free appropriate public education under the IDEA.

6. TJJD Fails to Conduct Required Evaluations for Children with Disabilities at Least Once Every Three Years

School districts like TJJD's must conduct an evaluation of each child with an IEP "at least once every [three] years, unless the parent and the [school district] agree that [it] is unnecessary."[115] This is called a triennial evaluation. The triennial evaluation provides an objective look at how each child is doing in each area of disability. It also confirms whether a child remains eligible for special education services and identifies appropriate services for their new IEP. Despite the importance of these evaluations, TJJD routinely fails to provide them.

> TJJD has not conducted a single triennial evaluation for children with disabilities. Instead, staff rely upon prior evaluations, even when they are six years old or date back to elementary school.

---

[115] 20 U.S.C. § 1414(a)(2)(B); *see also* 34 C.F.R. § 300.303. Although the IDEA provides a mechanism for waiving the triennial evaluation, it is almost always a bad idea to do so, as children can change significantly in three years. We found no evidence that TJJD asks parents to waive this requirement.

From June 2021 until June 2023, TJJD conducted no triennial evaluations for children with disabilities. At Mart, the diagnostician reported that they had conducted a triennial only once: "It doesn't happen very often." Diagnosticians at Gainesville and Evins reported they had never conducted a triennial whileworking for TJJD. A diagnostician at Ron Jackson remarked that they would not conduct a triennial evaluation unless the prior evaluations were at least six years old. Instead, TJJD's IEP teams review prior evaluations to make recommendations for services, even where those evaluations date back to elementary school for high school students or a child's current performance suggests that they may need additional or different support. TJJD's failure to provide triennial evaluations leaves IEP teams without essential information to ensure a free appropriate public education under the IDEA.

7. TJJD Fails to Provide Transition Planning and Services

Once children with disabilities turn sixteen years old, the IDEA requires their IEPs to include transition planning that is "designed to . . . facilitate the child's movement from school to post-school activities, including post-secondary education, vocational education, integrated employment (including supported employment), continuing and adult education, adult services, independent living, or community participation."[116] Their IEPs must include "appropriate measurable postsecondary goals . . . related to training, education, employment, and . . . independent living skills" and "transition services (including courses of study) needed to assist the child in reaching those goals."[117] Their IEPs must also include measurable annual goals that each child is expected to achieve by the end of the year.[118] Transition planning is particularly important for children with disabilities in juvenile justice facilities, as they typically have poor post-release education and employment outcomes. Yet TJJD fails to prepare children with disabilities for this transition.

---

[116] 34 C.F.R. § 300.43(a)(1); *see also Leigh Ann H. v. Riesel Indep. Sch. Dist.*, 18 F.4th 788, 798 (5th Cir. 2021) (explaining that the IDEA requires that schools provide older children "a transition plan and transition services to help th[em] emerge from high school into the real world of postgraduation life"). In Texas, this planning must start two years earlier than the IDEA requires, when children turn fourteen years old. Tex.Educ. Code Ann. § 29.0111.

[117] 20 U.S.C. § 1414(d)(1)(A)(i)(VIII).

[118] *Id.* § 1414(d)(1)(A)(i)(II).

Many IEPs we reviewed include transition goals only (with poorly developed or missing transition plans), but these goals are largely inappropriate. For example, Aiden's transition goal states that he "will attend a 1-2-year technical school with emphasis in airplane mechanics, and upon completion of that certification, Aiden will be employed as an airplane mechanic." While this may be an appropriate postsecondary goal for Aiden, it is not an appropriate annual goal for his IEP, given that there is no evidence he can leave TJJD's secure facilities to achieve it. Instead, TJJD should have created an annual goal that would bring Aiden one step closer to becoming an airplane mechanic post-release, such as comparing the admission requirements for airplane mechanic programs at different technical schools or completing applications for admission and financial aid.

None of the IEPs we reviewed identify the transition services—including courses of study, related services, or preparation for post-school experiences—that TJJD will provide to children while in custody. Nor can TJJD staff identify who is responsible for providing transition services. Some special educators told us that vocational teachers provide these services, yet vocational teachers denied playing any role.[119] Other special educators reported that the re-entry specialist provides these services, but we found no evidence that this is true. Without any special education staff responsible for coordinating transition services, there is no one to ensure that children work on their transition goals and receive such services.

8. TJJD Fails to Hold Manifestation Determination Reviews Designed to Protect Children with Behavior-Related Disabilities from Repeated Classroom Removals

If a school seeks to remove a child with disabilities from their current placement for more than ten days in a school year, the IDEA requires that an

[119] Even if vocational teachers provided transition services, TJJD's career and technical education programming is inadequate. These courses are not offered as part of the daily school schedule, resulting in children being pulled from their general education classes to attend. The same vocational courses are also not available at all five facilities. When a child with a disability transfers between facilities, their progress in any course stops. This is particularly true at Ron Jackson, where only computer technology is available, and at Evins, where no hands-on instruction is possible because of staffing shortages.

educational team conduct a manifestation determination review.[120] This review involves an evaluation of all relevant information from the child's IEP, teacher observations, and their parent to answer two questions: (1) whether the conduct was caused by, or had a direct and substantial relationship to, the child's disability; or (2) whether the conduct directly resulted from a failure to implement the child's IEP.[121] If the team answers yes to either question, then it must conduct a functional behavioral assessment, develop or modify the child's behavior intervention plan, and return the child to their original educational placement.[122] TJJD fails to conduct manifestation determination reviews for children who have been repeatedly removed from class for behavior-related reasons.

TJJD does not track the amount of instructional time lost through classroom removals, making it impossible to determine when a child has been removed for more than ten school days and a manifestation determination review must be held. TJJD sends children who disrupt learning to a dedicated room at each high school intended as short-term breaks and to the RSU, neither of which TJJD classifies as removals from the child's current placement. But any instance in which a child with a disability is removed from their current placement counts toward the need for a manifestation determination review.[123]

Between June 1, 2021, and January 10, 2023, TJJD reported conducting zero manifestation determination reviews in any of its five secure facilities. Because it fails to hold these reviews, TJJD also does not conduct or review functional behavioral assessments and create or update children's behavior intervention plans.

This prevents children who exhibit challenging behavior from receiving appropriate behavioral supports "designed to address the behavior violation so it does not recur."[124]

---

[120] 20 U.S.C. § 1415(k)(1)(B), (E). The IDEA specifies that "the [school district], the parent, and relevant members of the IEP Team (as determined by the parent and the [district])" must conduct the manifestation determination review. *Id.* § 1415(k)(1)(E)(i).

[121] *Id.* § 1415(k)(1)(E).

[122] *Id.* § 1415(k)(1)(F), (G); *see also* Tex. Educ. Code Ann. § 37.004. There are limited special circumstances in which the school may remove a child from their educational placement for more than ten school days regardless of disability, including possession of weapon or illegal drugs on school property or where the child causes "serious bodily injury" that involves "a substantial risk of death," "extreme physical pain," "protracted and obvious disfigurement," or "protected loss or impairment of the function of a bodily member, organ, or mental faculty." 20 U.S.C. § 1415(k)(7)(D); 18 U.S.C. § 1365(h)(3).

[123] 34 C.F.R. §§ 300.530, 300.536.

[124] 20 U.S.C. § 1415(k)(1)(D).

Over approximately 18 months, TJJD did not hold a single manifestation determination review in any of its five schools.

Natalie's experience highlights why manifestation determination reviews are necessary. During her first month in TJJD's custody in August 2022, Natalie received eight RSU referrals, where she spent nearly 150 hours. Even though Natalie has an IEP for behavior-related disabilities, TJJD removed her behavior intervention plan from her prior school's IEP at her initial IEP meeting in September 2022. For the next three months, Natalie spent over 500 hours in the RSU. From May through July 2023, she spent over 600 hours in the RSU. Since then, TJJD staff continued to refer Natalie to the RSU, but stopped documenting the time, dates of admission, or rationales. During this year-plus span, TJJD staff did not hold a single manifestation determination review for Natalie, despite her classroom removals far exceeding ten school days in an academic year. To explain this decision, a special educator at Mart remarked: "Like a male animal, they have to take some time to adjust to their new setting."

TJJD's failure to hold manifestation determination reviews means that it routinely changes children's educational placements for disciplinary reasons without following the IDEA's procedural requirements. For example, although parents must participate in any IEP meeting that makes decisions about the educational placement of their child,[125] we found no evidence that TJJD ever convenes these meetings when changes we found no evidence that TJJD ever convenes these meetings when changes in placement occur. We also found no evidence that TJJD revises children's IEPs to reflect changes in placement to self-contained units, such as when TJJD admitted Natalie to the Behavior Stabilization Unit in early 2023. Instead, children's IEPs continue to state that their educational program is general education, suggesting they attend school with all other children.

TJJD similarly ignores the IDEA's requirement that children with disabilities removed from their educational placements for disciplinary reasons—whether justified or not— still receive educational services necessary "to participate in the general education curriculum" and "progress toward meeting the[ir IEP] goals."[126] Indeed, children in the RSU at TJJD's

---

[125] *Id.* § 1414(e); 34 C.F.R. § 300.501(c).

[126] 20 U.S.C. § 1415(k)(1)(D)(i). These IDEA "protections apply regardless of whether a [child] who violates a code of student conduct is subject to discipline in the facility or removed to restricted settings, such as confinement to the [child's] cell or 'lockdown' units." Letter from Melody Musgrove, Dir., Off. of Special Educ. Programs, & Michael K. Yudin, Acting

secure facilities do not receive any general or special education services. Children in self-contained housing units—like the Violence Intervention Continuum, Behavior Stabilization Unit, and Crisis Stabilization Unit[127]—also fail to receive general and special education services consistent with their individualized needs or with those provided in TJJD's general education classrooms. In some cases, staffing shortages have meant that they do not receive instruction at all.

9. TJJD Routinely Excludes Parents from the IEP Process

The IDEA requires that parents have a chance to play "a significant role" in the development of their child's IEP.[128] Parents must provide consent for initial evaluations and for special education services.[129] Parents also serve as members of the team that develops the IEP,[130] where their "concerns" about how to "enhanc[e]" their child's education must be considered.[131] The IEP team must likewise ensure that parents "are members of any group that makes decisions on the educational placement of the child"and revise the IEP to address information parents provide.[132] To protect parents' informed involvement, the IDEA includes several procedural safeguards. For example, States must ensure that one or both parents are present at all IEP meetings or

---

Assistant Sec'y, Off. of Special Educ. & Rehab. Servs., to Colleague 5, U.S. Dep't of Educ., Off. of Special Educ. & Rehab. Servs. (Dec. 5, 2014), https://perma.cc/F95R-GWS4; *see also V.W. v. Conway*, 236 F. Supp. 3d 554, 587 (N.D.N.Y. 2017) (finding plaintiffs demonstrated they are substantially likely to succeed on the merits of their IDEA claims where they alleged that "the routine use of solitary confinement . . . in response to behavioral issues" violates the manifestation hearing requirement of the IDEA and that the distribution of work packets to children with disabilities in solitary confinement violates the requirement that "the education provider must continue to provide the services necessary to 'enable the child to continue to participate in the general education curriculum, although in another setting, and to progress toward meeting the goals set out in the child's IEP'") (internal citations omitted).

[127] This self-contained unit is for up to eight children with "immediate and significant mental health issues that threaten the safety of themselves or others." The Crisis Stabilization Unit exists at Giddings only. It is designed to "[p]sychiatrically stabilize youth experiencing a behavioral health crisis" through "[i]ncreased psychiatric oversight" and "onsite unit support from nurses." According to TJJD policy, children must be transferred out of the Crisis Stabilization Unit within ninety days after the admission hearing, unless an extension is granted.

[128] *Schaffer v. Weast*, 546 U.S. 49, 53 (2005).

[129] 20 U.S.C.§ 1414(a)(1)(D).

[130] *Id.* § 1414(d)(1)(B).

[131] *Id.* § 1414(d)(3)(A)(ii).

[132] *Id.* § 1414(d)(4)(A), (e).

given the opportunity to participate.[133] States must also provide an opportunity for parents to examine all records,[134] send prior written notice to parents in their native language any time they propose to initiate or change (or refuse to initiate or change) evaluations or IEP recommendations,[135] and create an opportunity for mediation or to present a complaint when parents disagrees with their child's special education services.[136] "A central purpose of the parental protections [under the IDEA] is to facilitate the provision of a free appropriate public education, which must be made available to the child in conformity with the [IEP]."[137]

TJJD staff do not adequately ensure that parents are equal participants in the IEP decision-making process. Although TJJD must provide written notice of an IEP meeting to all parents five school days before the meeting and reschedule if the date, time, and location does not work for the parent, staff routinely request that parents waive their right to this five-day notification period. Once waived, TJJD staff provide insufficient notice to permit parents to attend. For example, TJJD's first attempt to contact Andrew's mother about his IEP meeting was via email on June 1, 2023, the same day the meeting took place. Christian reported that TJJD tried calling his mother once as his IEP meeting began. When she did not answer, the IEP team held the meeting without her. She had not attended any IEP meetings since Christian's admission to TJJD in October 2022, despite regularly attending all his IEP meetings at his prior school. TJJD's exclusionary practices cause the IEP team to lose a key perspective from parents about how to support their child's unique needs.

Nor does TJJD comply with the IDEA's procedural safeguards related to challenging recommended services, which protects parents' informed involvement in the process. Although TJJD includes a notice of these safeguards and a "Parent's Guide to the Admission, Review, and Dismissal Process" on its website, TJJD's exclusion of parents from IEP meetings makes it less likely that parents will challenge the IEP team's recommendations, as evidenced by no parents exercising their right to request mediation or file a due process complaint from June 2021 through September 2023.

---

[133] 34 C.F.R. § 300.322.
[134] 20 U.S.C. § 1415(b)(3)–(4).
[135] *Id.* § 1415(b)(5)–(6).
[136] *Id.*
[137] *Winkelman v. Parma City Sch. Dist.*, 550 U.S. 516, 524 (2007) (citing 20 U.S.C. § 1401(9)) (internal quotation marks omitted).

Without parents' continued presence throughout the IEP process, children with disabilities may lose their best and most knowledgeable advocate to ensure that their IEP results in a free appropriate public education.

10. TJJD's Reliance on the Online Apex Curriculum, Combined with Lost Instructional Time, Compounds TJJD's IDEA Failures

Apex's online curriculum—the main method of teaching new material in TJJD's schools—sets up children with disabilities for failure. To be successful using Apex, students need solid reading and test- taking skills, the ability to work independently, and prior knowledge of the material. But TJJD expects Apex to teach children new, unfamiliar information. With few exceptions, teachers outsource to Apex the content of all lesson plans, the sequence in which children learn new information, how that information is presented, and how children must show mastery. TJJD provides no direct teacher-led instruction.[138] Instead, TJJD expects children to use Apex to teach themselves. For children who are already multiple grade levels behind, especially those with disabilities, that is impossible.

TJJD's reliance on Apex is particularly concerning with respect to reading instruction. To earn their release, children who are behind in reading must complete a reading program that complies with Texas law.[139] TJJD purports to provide this required reading program through Apex-based courses: Reading Horizons, Foundations in English I, or Foundations in English II. Despite Texas law requiring individualized instruction, none of these courses provide it.[140] Given the inadequacies of TJJD's reading program, it is hard to imagine how any child—including one several grades behind or with a reading

---

[138] TJJD's reliance on Apex also means that its general educators do not offer any differentiated instruction, a hallmark of effective teaching. This type of instruction involves adapting lesson plans to respond to children's different learning styles. Examples include pulling small groups to re-teach an idea to struggling learners or extend the knowledge or skills of advanced learners, offering manipulatives, allowing children to work alone or with a buddy, and making sure there are places to work in the classroom quietly and without distraction. We observed no evidence of differentiated instruction at any of TJJD's schools.

[139] Texas law requires TJJD to provide at least sixty minutes of individualized reading instruction to all children who demonstrate deficits in reading, even if those children are not eligible for special education services. *See* Tex. Educ. Code Ann. § 30.106.

[140] *Id.* TJJD acknowledges that these three courses are insufficient, noting in its Reading Program Curriculum that "students still needing direct phonics instruction may have this need addressed during one-on-one/small group time." But we found no evidence that children received this instruction.

disability—can meaningfully complete it. Indeed, Ashley struggled to meet this requirement, contributing to two separate extensions of one month each to her time in TJJD's custody.

Figure 5. TJJD classroom seating arrangement for Apex instruction.

An example from a Mart classroom highlights the problems with TJJD's use of Apex. We observed a general educator direct children to log into Apex at the start of the class period. She then sat at her desk and logged into her own computer. For about forty-five minutes, security staff engaged several students in a loud discussion of non-academic topics, including smoking marijuana and cigarettes, what prisons are like in Russia and Mexico, being like DeShaun Watson (an NFL player accused of multiple sexual assaults), and why a high school diploma is better than a GED. During this time, Jonathan, a child with disabilities, attempted multiple quizzes on Apex. He completed the first quiz within two minutes, faster than we could read the quiz's questions.

Jonathan received a score of twenty percent. Immediately after, he started another quiz, answering about seventeen questions within sixty seconds.

Jonathan failed that quiz. He then started another quiz, answering about thirty questions within sixty seconds. Jonathan failed that one too. He continued this pattern with three other quizzes before signing out of Apex and joining the conversation happening in the room. At no point did a general or special educator offer Jonathan any instructional support. Instead, the only interaction the general educator had with the children in her classroom was to threaten them once that they would have to go back to working on Apex if they did not stop cursing.

TJJD's daily school schedule also does not allow for adequate instructional time, impacting the potential of children with disabilities to make meaningful progress. Even if TJJD complies with its own school schedule, children receive only sixty percent of the instructional minutes that Texas law requires. Lengthy transitions and transportation issues further decrease instructional time. At Mart, for example, the different dorms of female students arrived between fifteen and forty-five minutes late on three separate days during our site visit. At Ron Jackson, the girls began school almost twenty-five minutes late and transitioned to lunch over thirty minutes early on two separate days during our site visit. The total amount of lost instructional time for the Ron Jackson girls equaled twenty-five percent of their school day. When instructional time is lost or never offered at all, TJJD compounds its IDEA failures.

Discriminating Against Children with Disabilities

Title II of the ADA provides that "no qualified individual with a disability shall, by reason of such disability, be excluded from participation in or be denied the benefits of the services, programs, or activities of a public entity, or be subjected to discrimination by any such entity."[141] The ADA's protections extend to individuals with physical and mental impairments that substantially limit one or more major life activities. To establish a Title II claim, an individual must demonstrate: (1) that they are a qualified individual within the meaning of the ADA; (2) that they are being excluded from participation in, or being denied benefits of, services, programs, or activities for which the public entity is responsible, or are otherwise being discriminated against by the public entity; and (3) that such exclusion, denial of benefits, or

[141] 42 U.S.C. § 12132.

discrimination is by reason of their disability. Title II covers state correctional institutions, including those for children.

TJJD discriminates against children with disabilities in two ways. First, by failing to provide reasonable modifications, TJJD denies children with disability-related behavioral needs access to programs required for their release. Second, TJJD denies the same children equal opportunity to benefit from education once placed in TJJD's self-contained programs. Both failures violate the ADA and undermine any rehabilitative purpose in their commitment to TJJD.

1. TJJD's Disability Discrimination Prevents Children from Earning Their Release and Creates a Pipeline to Prison

The ADA imposes an affirmative obligation on public entities like TJJD to make reasonable modifications to ensure children with disabilities can access programs, unless such modifications "fundamentally alter the nature of the service, program, or activity."[142] TJJD's decision to refer children with known disability-related behavioral needs to the Violence Intervention Continuum, where they cannot access programs required for their release, results in disability discrimination. This discrimination prolongs some children's time in TJJD's custody and results in other children's transfer to prison as early as their sixteenth birthday.[143]

When children exhibit challenging disability-related behaviors, TJJD often refers them to one of its Violence Intervention Continuum programs: the Intensive Intervention Program, Redirect, Phoenix, or Phoenix Max. These programs mainly focus on managing violent and aggressive behavior through graduated levels of restrictions.

Once it admits children to the Violence Intervention Continuum, TJJD denies them access to programs necessary to demonstrate their eligibility for release. Children lose credit for any progress they have made in required treatment programs, including those that target children with offenses

---

[142] 28 C.F.R. § 35.130(b)(1)(i), (ii), (7).

[143] Most children in TJJD's secure facilities receive indeterminate sentences, meaning they are given a minimum length of stay (from 3–24 months) based on their offense and risk level. A smaller group of children receives determinate sentences, meaning that they are given a minimum period of confinement (from 1–10 years) based on their offense. All children must complete this time before demonstrating their eligibility for release.

involving sexual behavior[144] or violence and aggression[145] as well as children with confirmed or suspected substance use disorder.[146] As discussed in the next section, access to education is significantly limited. Yet children are still expected to complete two statutorily required programs offered exclusively at school: positive behavior support system (all children) and reading improvement (struggling readers only). If placed in Redirect or Phoenix, children likewise lose their current stage and their ability to earn additional stages in TJJD's behavior management system for at least twenty-one-days and often longer.[147] But they must achieve the highest stage for release.

Although TJJD refers children to the Violence Intervention Continuum because of their challenging behavior, it fails to provide behavioral and mental health supports to prevent that behavior from reoccurring once they are there. TJJD purports to offer behavioral support plans to a small subset of children and update all children's individual case plans. But its behavioral support plans consist of generic strategies that could apply to any child in any setting (such as "be consistent" and "remind him of his strengths/goals") and are not tracked for effectiveness. And its individual case plans list problematic behaviors without identifying specific behavioral interventions staff will implement. TJJD also halts all mental health services, except psychotropic medication. But adequate treatment can be key to addressing challenging behavior. The lack of behavioral and mental health supports sets children with disabilities up to fail— remaining stuck in the Violence Intervention Continuum without access to programs necessary to earn release—when they cannot manage their complex behavioral needs on their own.

---

144 The Sexual Behavior Treatment Program is unit-based and offered at Gainesville only. A licensed sex offender treatment provider manages the program, which offers individual, group, and family counseling.

145 The Capital & Serious Violent Offender Program includes three levels of intervention: Aggression Replacement Therapy, Power Source, and Capital Offender Group. Aggression Replacement Therapy is a 12-week program. Power Source is a 12- to 16-week program. Capital Offender Group is a 6- to 9-month program. Aggression Replacement Therapy and Power Source are offered at all five facilities, while Capital Offender Group is offered at Gainesville and Giddings only.

146 The Alcohol & Other Drug treatment program includes individual and group counseling, life skills training, and Aggression Replacement Therapy. It is offered at all five facilities.

147 In Redirect, children are demoted at least one stage and are ineligible for promotion until they earn their way to the fourth level of Redirect programming, which takes at least twenty-one days. In Phoenix, children are demoted to the lowest stage and are ineligible for promotion until they earn their way back to Redirect (including the fourth level of Redirect programming once there) or general programming.

> Over a 13-month period, TJJD's Review & Release Panel voted to extend 100 percent of sentences for children with disabilities at least once and 93 percent of their sentences at least twice. On average, TJJD added eight months to their sentences.

Languishing in the Violence Intervention Continuum results in significant extensions to children's time in TJJD's custody. TJJD's Review & Release Panel examines the files of children with indeterminate sentences once their Minimum Lengths of Stay approach and recommends releasing them to the community or extending their sentence. Of the sample we reviewed over a 13-month period, the Review & Release Panel voted to extend one hundred percent of children with disabilities at least once and ninety-three percent of children with disabilities at least twice, all of whom spent time in the Violence Intervention Continuum. On average, TJJD extended these children's sentences by eight months—1.6 times longer than their prior Minimum Lengths of Stay and a roughly sixty percent increase in their time in TJJD's custody. The Review & Release Panel most often votes to extend children's sentences because they fail to complete required treatment programming or continue to exhibit challenging behaviors. But the Review & Release Panel does not consider children's disabilities and their resulting limitations when making recommendations, nor does it assess whether TJJD's programming meets children's needs. Instead, TJJD continues to blame children for their failure to make progress toward rehabilitative goals, no matter how children's disabilities impact their ability to do so.

Luis' experience illustrates how TJJD's use of the Violence Intervention Continuum impacts children with indeterminate sentences. Luis is eligible for special education services based on Other Health Impairment, a disability category that covers his attention deficit hyperactivity disorder. He has also been diagnosed with conduct disorder, oppositional defiant disorder, and several substance use disorders. From October 2022 to October 2023, nearly all of 370 incidents that described his rule violations involved disability-related behavior, such as being non-compliant, disruptive, and aggressive.[148] TJJD admitted him to the RSU nearly 80 times during this period. Rather than

---

[148] Children with attention deficit hyperactivity disorder demonstrate difficulty listening, focusing, and staying on task; fidget and move about constantly; and act without thinking or have difficulty with self- control. Children with conduct disorder or oppositional defiance disorder typically exhibit an inability to follow rules. Finally, children experiencing withdrawal from substance use often display anger, irritability, and depression.

considering whether Luis' behavior is a limitation related to one of his disabilities and providing reasonable modifications like behavioral supports to address the underlying behaviors, TJJD cycled Luis through the Intensive Intervention Program (twice), Redirect, Phoenix, the Behavior Stabilization Unit, and the Crisis Stabilization Unit. The Review & Release Panel reviewed his file five separate times. Each time, the Review & Release Panel noted that he had not completed his required treatment programs, either because he was in the Violence Intervention Continuum (where he could not enroll in those programs) or because his disability-related behavior (which could be prevented with behavioral supports) interfered with treatment. In the last extension we reviewed, the Review & Release Panel justified adding more time to Luis' sentence in part because his treatment team needed to "create a viable treatment plan," something TJJD should have done to address his complex needs from the start.

> Over the same 13- month period, TJJD recommended transfer to prison for 100 percent of children with disabilities in the Violence Intervention Continuum.

Cycling through the Violence Intervention Continuum also creates a pipeline to prison for children with determinate sentences. TJJD central office staff conduct program completion reviews to recommend to juvenile courts whether children should be released, transferred to parole with the Texas Department of Criminal Justice, or transferred to prison. Children can earn release or parole if they meet certain criteria, including completing required treatment programs. But placement in the Violence Intervention Continuum prevents children from meeting half of these criteria and worsens their disability- related behaviors, which TJJD then relies on to recommend their transfer to prison. Indeed, of the sample we reviewed over a 13-month period, TJJD recommended transfer to prison for every child with a disability in the Violence Intervention Continuum. TJJD compounds its failure to meet children's disability-related needs by pushing them into the adult criminal justice system.

Noah's experience illustrates TJJD's pipeline to prison for children with determinate sentences. Noah is eligible for special education services based on Emotional Disturbance.[149] He has also been diagnosed with attention

[149] Children with emotional disturbance have a range of characteristics that lead them to struggle academically, socially, and behaviorally. Common behaviors include fighting, an inability to control their temper, an inability to avoid trouble, and arguing with others.

deficit hyperactivity disorder, conduct disorder, disruptive mood dysregulation disorder, posttraumatic stress disorder, and several substance use disorders.[150] After 2.5 months in general programming without reasonable modifications like behavioral supports, TJJD referred Noah to the Violence Intervention Continuum. TJJD first placed him in Redirect, where he remained for three months, before TJJD placed him in Phoenix and then Phoenix Max. TJJD notes in its recommendation for transfer to prison a "significant uptick" in challenging behaviors once Noah joined the Violence Intervention Continuum, increasing from one incident per week in general programming to four incidents per week in Redirect to over six incidents per week in Phoenix. But TJJD never considered whether the Violence Intervention Continuum's lack of behavioral and mental health supports was to blame for Noah's worsening behavior. Instead, TJJD recommended prison because Noah had not completed his required treatment programs (which were unavailable in the Violence Intervention Continuum), remained on the lowest stage of TJJD's behavior management system (when he had been largely ineligible for promotion), and continued to exhibit behavior related to his disabilities (such as non- compliance, disrupting activities, not getting along with his peers, fighting, and aggression). Noah had only been in TJJD's custody for roughly nine months for a probation violation before TJJD abandoned attempts at rehabilitation and recommended transfer to the adult criminal justice system.

TJJD's disability discrimination occurs despite children's disabilities and related limitations being "open, obvious, and apparent" to TJJD.[151] In fact, TJJD collects and creates detailed information in children's education, mental health, and disciplinary records about their diagnoses and symptoms throughout their time in TJJD's custody. For example, TJJD's intake process requests children's educational records from their prior schools. These records can identify a child's disability that qualifies them for special education services, highlight areas of struggle, describe individualized behavioral supports for the child's disability, and discuss how the child's disability affects their academic progress. TJJD's intake process also collects and reviews children's prior mental health assessments or conducts new ones. These assessments evaluate a child's mental health symptoms and ability to function,

---

[150] Children with posttraumatic stress disorder can exhibit several symptoms, including emotional distress and physical reactivity when exposed to traumatic reminders, negative affect, decreased interest in activities, irritability or aggression, heightened startle reactions, and difficulty concentrating or sleeping.

[151] *Windham v. Harris Cnty., Tex.*, 875 F.3d 229, 237 (5th Cir. 2017) (internal quotation marks and citation omitted).

leading to mental health diagnoses commonly associated with specific characteristics or behaviors.

TJJD's incident reports and admissions to the RSU likewise provide ongoing data on patterns of challenging behavior for each child. Together, these records establish that children's disabilities and their resulting limitations are readily apparent to TJJD.

Yet TJJD fails to act on this knowledge when it refers children to the Violence Intervention Continuum. Each referral packet includes an explanation of how the child meets TJJD's criteria for placement, information about the related incident (which must have been proven true at a disciplinary hearing for Redirect and Phoenix), and a brief checklist of the child's mental state at the time of the referral. Central office staff review these referrals, but rarely consider information TJJD already has about children's disabilities and their related limitations as part of that review. Despite receiving over 1,000 referrals in twelve months, central office staff also do not assess whether TJJD's programming requires modifications to meet the needs of children with disabilities.

Instead, TJJD often blames children for their lack of success.

To avoid disability discrimination, TJJD must provide reasonable modifications so children with disabilities can receive support to manage their disability-related behaviors, avoid referral to the Violence Intervention Continuum, and maintain access to services required for their release. TJJD could provide evidence-based behavioral supports that effectively prevent or reduce disability-related behaviors, increasing safety in TJJD's programs and supporting TJJD's goal of rehabilitation. For example, TJJD could conduct functional behavioral assessments that identify and define each child's behavioral challenges that need addressing, identify the possible factors that cause the behavior, and collect information about which conditions trigger the behavior to identify the behavior's purpose. TJJD could then use those assessments to develop individualized behavior intervention plans. These plans should outline specific steps TJJD staff will take to prevent triggers of each child's challenging behavior, provide strategies to support the child in building short-term skills to manage that behavior, explain in detail how staff will respond to triggers and the behavior (including de- escalation and appropriate consequences), and provide a schedule to measure the plan's effectiveness. Together with behavioral supports, TJJD staff could consider information about children's disabilities and their related limitations when making placement decisions in programs and recommendations for release, extension, parole, or transfer to prison. Finally, TJJD could provide training for staff on effective behavioral interventions for children with disabilities to improve their ability to manage challenging behavior.

These modifications will not fundamentally alter TJJD's programs but instead will support the purpose of children's confinement to TJJD: ensuring their rehabilitation while promoting safety. The IDEA already requires TJJD to conduct functional behavioral assessments and create behavior intervention plans for children with IEPs. Information about children's disabilities and their related limitations is also in TJJD's possession and sometimes included in Violence Intervention Continuum referral packets. TJJD similarly provides at least some training to staff on behavior management strategies. Although TJJD may create safety requirements for its programs, such requirements must be based on actual risks, not speculation or stereotypes about children's disabilities.[152] Moreover, TJJD cannot transfer children with disabilities to the Violence Intervention Continuum based on a safety risk without conducting an individualized assessment first, including deciding whether modifications or services could mitigate that risk.[153] We found no evidence that TJJD does so. Because these modifications are reasonable, TJJD is "liable simply by denying [them]."[154]

1. TJJD Denies Children with Disabilities an Equal Opportunity to Benefit from Education

The ADA also prohibits public entities like TJJD from providing benefits, services, or programs to individuals with disabilities that are "not equal to that afforded others" or "not as effective in affording equal opportunity . . . as that provided to others."[155] To prevent this type of disability discrimination, the ADA imposes an affirmative obligation on public entities to reasonably modify their policies and procedures.[156] TJJD's specialized programs on self-contained units do not ensure an equal opportunity to benefit from education for children with disabilities.

---

[152] 28 C.F.R. § 35.130(h).
[153] *Id.* § 35.139.
[154] *Bennett-Nelson v. La. Bd. of Regents*, 431 F.3d 448, 455 (5th Cir. 2005).
[155] 28 C.F.R. § 35.130(b)(1)(ii), (iii).
[156] *Id.* § 35.130(b)(7).

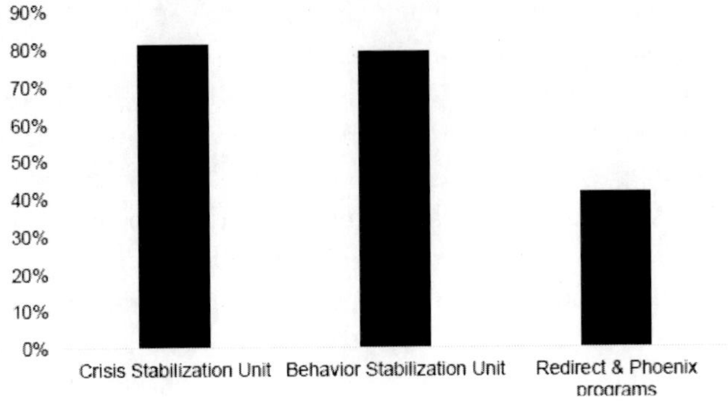

Figure 6. Percentage of children with IEPs or Section 504 plans in TJJD's specialized programs.

Most of the children that TJJD admits to its self-contained programs (Behavior Stabilization Unit, Crisis Stabilization Unit, Intensive Intervention Program at Mart, Redirect, and Phoenix) have disabilities that qualify them for additional support to meet their learning needs.[157] From October 2022 through November 2023, over eighty percent of children in the Crisis Stabilization Unit, nearly eighty percent of children in the Behavior Stabilization Unit, and over forty percent of children in the Violence Intervention Continuum's Redirect and Phoenix programs had disabilities.[158]

Once admitted to these programs, children receive significantly less education than their peers. Education is provided exclusively on the units, yet most of the dorms do not have designated classroom spaces. Most children also cannot access computers, so they cannot work on Apex's online curriculum. Instead, TJJD provides children with worksheets to complete independently. In theory, teachers are supposed to be available to answer questions. But teachers spend significantly less time with children in TJJD's self-contained programs. The assigned teacher in the girls' Behavior Stabilization Unit at Mart estimates that she spends about forty minutes per day on the unit. This is just twenty percent of the yearly instructional minutes children receive in TJJD's high schools. Our review of education logs in the

---

[157] This group of children includes those with IEPs or Section 504 plans. Section 504 of the Rehabilitation Act of 1973 makes it illegal for schools receiving federal funds to discriminate against children with disabilities. Section 504 also requires schools to provide reasonable accommodations and services to allow children with disabilities to participate in and benefit from school programs and activities. *See generally* 29 U.S.C. § 794.

[158] Some of the children experienced multiple admissions to these units, increasing the amount of time TJJD denied them an equal opportunity to benefit from education.

Crisis Stabilization Unit at Giddings demonstrate a similar pattern. From March through July 2023, Andrew received instruction for only three hours total. In each case we observed, children receive far less instructional minutes than their peers who attend the facilities' high schools.

The limited educational opportunity provided in TJJD's specialized programs—often chaotic and uncontrolled environments—is not equal to the educational opportunity provided to other children at TJJD. In the Redirect and Phoenix dorms at Evins, children stopped and started work repeatedly, talked to peers and staff, left the classroom (where one existed) or table, wandered around, stood on furniture, banged on doors, performed cartwheels and flips, shadowboxed, and sang. At any given time, only two or three children completed worksheets. We did not observe any teachers or security staff explaining expectations for learning or behavior during this time.

By admitting children with disabilities to its specialized programs and then providing limited access to education, TJJD "actively undercut[s] the ability of [its] public program to benefit those with disabilities."[159] Without an equal opportunity to benefit from education, children who are already multiple grade levels behind fall behind even further. TJJD also considers each child's educational progress when assessing their eligibility for release, potentially prolonging children's time in custody. But this disability discrimination can be prevented. TJJD could modify its specialized programs to ensure that children receive the minimum number of instructional minutes that Texas law requires.

Recommended Minimum Remedial Measures

To remedy the constitutional and statutory violations identified in this Report, we recommend that TJJD implement, at minimum, the remedial measures listed below.

Use of Force

1. Implement a use of force continuum that:
   a) Requires non-force interventions, such as verbal redirection and de- escalation techniques, to be utilized whenever possible;

---

[159] *Van Velzor v. City of Burleson*, 43 F. Supp. 3d 746, 752 (N.D. Tex. 2014).

   b) Limits physical and chemical force to only when non-force interventions have been tried or are impossible because of exigent circumstances;
   c) Requires restraint techniques safe for use with children; and
   d) Ensures that only the amount of force necessary to neutralize the immediate threat is used.
2. Eliminate the use of MK-9 canisters of pepper spray.
3. Ensure adequate and timely decontamination of all children exposed to pepper spray (including secondarily exposed children) via timely access to cold-water decontamination showers.
4. Ensure adequate decontamination of all physical areas exposed to pepper spray.
5. Identify and prohibit pepper spray use on children with chronic, serious respiratory problems or other serious health conditions that would make pepper spray exposure particularly dangerous.
6. Implement a system for review and oversight to ensure compliance with use of force and body-worn camera policies and procedures.

Behavior Management

1. Implement a systemwide positive behavior management program that:
   a) Offers meaningful incentives for positive behaviors;
   b) Provides a skills-based curriculum to teach the children skills needed to regulate their behaviors; and
   c) Includes appropriate consequences for negative behaviors.
2. Ensure consistent implementation of the positive behavior management program in all secure facilities throughout the day and across settings (unit, classroom, groups).
3. Implement a daily schedule in all facilities that includes an array of structured activities out of cells that are age-appropriate, available to all children, occur outside of school hours, and are led by staff that are adequately trained to lead the activities.

Isolation

1. Limit use of the RSU to brief periods of time for children who pose an imminent and serious threat to safety.
2. Implement a system for ensuring that children who are placed in the RSU are returned to the general population within twenty-four hours or as soon as they no longer pose a serious threat to safety.
3. Prohibit the use of isolation as punishment.
4. Implement a system for ensuring adequate mental health review of and input into RSU placement decisions.
5. Ensure children in the RSU receive adequate supports and services—including medical, mental health, and education—as well as adequate access to exercise, grievances, and hygiene facilities.
6. Adjust facility operational practices to reduce reliance on operational lockdown practices (shift change, unit cleaning, showers, etc.) and create a data tracking measure to monitor all forms of cell confinement.
7. Ensure adequate visual checks, at random intervals at least every fifteen minutes, of all children who are in any form of cell confinement.

Sexual Abuse

1. Ensure that housing and common areas are adequately supervised and monitored through direct supervision whenever and wherever children are present.
2. Review surveillance camera placement and implement changes necessary for identification of abuse.
3. Implement a system for review and oversight to ensure:
   a) Appropriate interactions between staff and children, including healthy
   b) boundaries and age-appropriate communications;
   c) Compliance with body-worn camera policy, and
   d) Adequate supervision of children.

Mental Health Care

1. Provide adequate mental health intake screening and assessments, including integration of trauma-related mental health difficulties in clinical formulations.
2. Provide adequate ongoing assessments of children's mental health needs at set time intervals and following behavior that indicates a current mental health difficulty or events likely to impact mental health (for example, where a child participates in an assault or is the subject of use of force).
3. Provide adequate mental health treatment to children, including timely counseling at appropriate intervals by practitioners who are licensed or license-eligible and actively clinically supervised by licensed practitioners with demonstrated competency in the treatment of the various populations held within TJJD's secure facilities.
4. Integrate mental health, psychiatric, substance use, and behavioral treatment programs and require multidisciplinary planning and information-sharing to allow for unified, individualized, coherent, consistent, and integrated plans and treatment across disciplines.
5. Create communication and information-sharing protocols between mental health, case management, and security to ensure that security responses and security- related discipline processes are informed by any underlying psychological causes of the child's behavior and their current mental health status and needs. Such a protocol should ensure that contraindicated security procedures are known and accounted for when staff engage in security measures and during the discipline decision making process.
6. Eliminate isolation and wide-ranging deprivations as uniform tactics in response to all threats of suicide and self-harm. Implement suicide screening protocols and responses that reflect individualized assessments of risk and the minimal necessary responses to address the determined risk.

Special Education and Related Services

1. Create an effective child find system that includes a reliable screening process to identify children who need initial evaluations and ensures

timely evaluations in all areas of need, including functional behavioral assessments.

2. Provide a full continuum of educational placement options appropriate to children's individualized needs.
3. Develop IEPs based on children's individualized needs that include:
   a) Accurate statements of current levels of performance;
   b) Appropriate goals that consider all areas of each child's individualized needs;
   c) Appropriate levels of services and supports to address all areas of need;
   d) Appropriate numbers of special education service minutes for each child's individualized needs; and
   e) A behavior intervention plan for any child whose behavior interferes with learning.
4. Provide adequate functional behavioral assessments for every child with a disability (or suspected of having a disability) who exhibits behavior that interferes with learning.
5. Provide adequate behavior intervention plans for every child with a disability (or suspected of having a disability) who exhibits behavior that interferes with learning.
6. Provide specially designed instruction and related services to children with disabilities based on their individualized needs.
7. Conduct triennial evaluations every three years.
8. Provide transition planning—including appropriate goals, courses of study, and a coordinated set of transition-related activities—to all children with disabilities ages 14 and up.
9. Track all classroom removals based on behavior, including children sent to any alternate setting, to determine when a manifestation determination review must be held.
10. Conduct a manifestation determination review whenever a child's behavior results in classroom removals totaling eleven days or more in the same academic year.
11. Conduct an IEP meeting for any child TJJD moves from their IEP's recommended educational placement (general education, inclusion, resource room, specialized class, or TJJD's self-contained specialized programs) to a different placement to determine whether the change is appropriate, given each child's individualized needs.
12. Ensure parents can meaningfully participate in the IEP decision making process.

13. Provide appropriate special education and related services to any children with disabilities who need to take online classes.

Disability Discrimination

1. Provide appropriate behavioral supports, including functional behavioral assessments and behavior intervention plans, to all children with disabilities in any setting where their successful completion of certain criteria is required to earn their release.
2. Ensure that information about a child's disability is reviewed and considered as part of:
   a) Any referral and placement decision involving the RSU or specialized programs; and
   b) Any review of a child's rehabilitative progress, including the Review & Release Panel for children with indeterminate sentences and program completion reviews for children with determinate sentences.
3. Implement a system for tracking disciplinary data that analyzes patterns of incident reports, referrals to the RSU, admissions to the RSU, and lengths of stay in the RSU involving children with disabilities. This system should also examine whether any disciplinary action occurs for behaviors related to children's disabilities.
4. Ensure that children with disabilities receive an equal opportunity to benefit from a full day of educational instruction in TJJD's self-contained units.
5. Implement a system for review and oversight to monitor TJJD's programs, services, and activities for disability discrimination.

Grievances

1. Implement a grievance system that ensures:
   a) Children have unimpeded access to grievance forms and the grievance hotline;
   b) Locked grievance boxes are accessible on all units and common areas of the facility;

c) The staff grievance coordinator makes daily rounds to collect grievances from the locked boxes and takes immediate action on emergency grievances (medical, mental health, and so forth); and
d) Defined, uniform grievance responses.

2. Eliminate the use of children as grievance coordinators and any other role in providing or collecting grievance forms.
3. Implement a system for review and oversight to ensure compliance with grievance policies and procedures.

Conclusion

DOJ has reasonable cause to believe that TJJD violates children's constitutional and federal statutory rights by subjecting them to excessive physical and chemical force, harmful isolation, and sexual abuse; failing to provide adequate mental health care; failing to provide appropriate special education and related services; and discriminating against children with disabilities. We look forward to working cooperatively with Texas to reach agreement on the remedies for these violations.

We must advise you that forty-nine days after issuance of this letter, the Attorney General may initiate a lawsuit under CRIPA to correct deficiencies identified in this letter if State officials have not satisfactorily addressed our concerns.[160]

This Report is a public document. It will be posted on the Civil Rights Division's website.

Appendix A: Specialized Treatment Programs

TJJD's secure facilities offer several types of programming:

- Violence Intervention Continuum. The Violence Intervention Continuum is designed to manage violent and aggressive behavior. It includes the Intensive Intervention Program, Redirect program, and Phoenix program. The Intensive Intervention Program is the lowest level of intervention available at Evins, Mart, and Gainesville. It provides a 30-day program to twelve children per housing unit.

---

[160] 42 U.S.C. § 1997b(a)(1).

Children in the Intensive Intervention Program are typically allowed to leave their unit for school and other essential services. Redirect is the next level of intervention and is available at Evins. It provides a 30-day program on self- contained units, meaning that children cannot leave their units. Phoenix is the most restrictive program and is available at Evins. It provides a 45-day program on self-contained units, ranging from six to ten children.

- Capital & Serious Violent Offender Treatment Program. This treatment program includes varied services to address risk factors specific to children with violent or aggressive offenses. There are three levels of intervention: Aggression Replacement Therapy, Power Source, and Capital Offender Group. Aggression Replacement Therapy is a 12-week program. Power Source is a
- 12- to 16-week program. Capital Offender Group is a 6- to 9-month program. Aggression Replacement Therapy and Power Source are offered at all five secure facilities, while Capital Offender Group is offered at Gainesville and Giddings only.
- Behavior Stabilization Unit. This self-contained unit is for up to four children with "immediate and significant mental health issues that engage in frequent aggressive event[s]." In 2022, the Behavior Stabilization Unit for girls was located at Ron Jackson, but by 2023, it had moved to Mart. The Behavior Stabilization Unit for boys is also located at Mart. It is designed to "[b]ehaviorally stabilize youth[,] with an emphasis on increasing safety towards self and others." TJJD conducts weekly treatment team meetings for children in the Behavior Stabilization Unit and provides "increased psychiatric oversight."
- Crisis Stabilization Unit. This self-contained unit is for up to eight children with "immediate and significant mental health issues that threaten the safety of themselves or others." The Crisis Stabilization Unit exists at Giddings only. It is designed to "[p]sychiatrically stabilize youth experiencing a behavioral health crisis" through "increased psychiatric oversight" and "onsite unit support from nurses." TJJD conducts weekly treatment team meetings for children in the Crisis Stabilization Unit to assess stabilization and reintegration plans to transition them to the Mental Health Treatment Program. According to TJJD policy, children must be transferred out of the

Crisis Stabilization Unit within ninety days after the admission hearing, unless an extension is granted.

- Mental Health Treatment Program. Children identified as having a high need for mental health services can be placed in the Mental Health Treatment Program. The boys' Mental Health Treatment Program is located at Giddings and the girls' Mental Health Treatment Program is located at Ron Jackson. The Mental Health Treatment Program provides normal programming with added mental health supports for up to eight children.
- Sexual Behavior Treatment Program. This unit-based program serves children whose offenses involve sexual behavior. It is offered at Gainesville only. The program is managed by a licensed sex offender treatment provider and offers individual, group, and family counseling.
- Alcohol & Other Drug. This treatment program provides services to children with a diagnosis of Substance Use Disorder and those identified as being at risk of developing the disorder. It is offered at all five secure facilities. The program includes individual and group counseling, life skills training, and Aggression Replacement Therapy.

Chapter 8

Mental Healthcare in the Texas Juvenile Justice System*

Texas Advisory Committee

U.S. Commission on Civil Rights

By law, the U.S. Commission on Civil Rights has established an advisory committee in each of the 50 states, the District of Columbia, and the five U.S. territories. The committees are composed of state citizens who serve without compensation. The committees advise the Commission on civil rights issues in their states that are within the Commission's jurisdiction. They are authorized to advise the Commission in writing of any knowledge or information they have of any alleged deprivation of voting rights and alleged discrimination based on race, color, religion, sex, age, disability, national origin, or in the administration of justice; advise the Commission on matters of their state's concern in the preparation of Commission reports to the President and the Congress; receive reports, suggestions, and recommendations from individuals, public officials, and representatives of public and private organizations to committee inquiries; forward advice and recommendations to the Commission, as requested; and observe any open hearing or conference conducted by the Commission in their states.

---

* This is an edited, reformatted and augmented version of Texas Advisory Committee to the U.S. Commission on Civil Rights Publication, dated February 2024.

In: Perspectives on Juvenile Justice: Legal, Social, and Policy Issues
Editor: David Y. Reyes
ISBN: 979-8-89530-669-7

Texas Advisory Committee to the U.S. Commission on Civil Rights September 2021 – September 2025

Merrill Matthews, Chairperson, Coppell
Joni E. Baker, Vice Chair, San Antonio
Jada L. Andrews-Sullivan, San Antonio
Josh M. Blackman, Houston
Charles Blain, Houston
Rogene G. Calvert, Houston
Cecilia R. Castillo, San Marcos
Ariel Dulitzky, Austin
Mark E. Harrington, Houston
Brandon Holt, Houston
Christopher Kulesza, Houston
Austin R. Nimocks, Austin
Ronald J. Smeberg, San Antonio
Barbara J. Walters, Plano
Jamilah Way, Houston

U.S. Commission on Civil Rights Staff

Brooke Peery,
Civil Rights Analyst & Designated Federal Officer

Angelica Trevino, Support Specialist
Madeleine Pattis, Civil Rights Analyst Intern

In Memoriam, Charles Z. Burchett (1949 – 2023)

The Committee would like to honor and remember the service of Charles Z. Burchett, who passed away on March 13, 2023, in the middle of this project. Charles has served as a dedicated member of the Texas Advisory Committee to the U.S. Commission on Civil Rights since 2002. In addition to the decades of service he gave to the Commission, he also served his community of Kirbyville as a pastor for 43 years. Specifically, the Committee would like to remember his years of advocacy in disaster management and the expertise he provided the Committee during their study of the Civil Rights Implications of Hurricane Harvey.

Introduction

In May 2022, the Texas Advisory Committee (Committee) to the U.S. Commission on Civil Rights (Commission) adopted a proposal to study the civil rights implications of mental health care in the Texas Juvenile Justice System. While other important topics may have surfaced throughout the Committee's inquiry, matters that are outside the scope of this specific civil rights mandate are left for another discussion.

As part of this inquiry the Committee heard testimony in person and via videoconferences held from August 2022 to April 2023.[1] The following report results from a review of testimony provided at these meetings, combined with written testimony submitted during the related timeframe.[2] It begins with a brief background of the issues the Committee considered and then identifies primary findings as they emerged from this testimony. Finally, it makes recommendations for addressing related civil rights concerns. This report and the recommendations included within it were adopted unanimously by the Committee on December 6, 2023.

Executive Summary

Allegations of civil rights violations and reports of abuse and mistreatment have long plagued the Texas Juvenile Justice Department (TJJD), which manages five state-operated secure facilities to serve those youth who have committed the most serious offenses and require specialized treatment services. However, it was clear from the testimony that the facilities create a challenging and often harmful environment for the youth.

Most youth in the Texas Juvenile Justice System have clear mental health needs. Not only are these needs not being adequately addressed, but being in state-run facilities may further traumatize the youth and exacerbate mental health needs.

---

[1] See Appendix A.

[2] TJJD submitted its written testimony after the record's scheduled closure. The Committee voted unanimously to accept the testimony in September 2023.

Facility understaffing and under-resourcing has long been a challenge, and was exacerbated by the pandemic. And while understaffing is improving, in part due to pay increases, it is still too low. We commend the Texas Legislature for taking steps to improve staffing and funding in the system, but it remains far short of what is needed to meet the needs.

We heard testimony that community-based services that prioritize a rehabilitative approach are proven to be the best way to address the needs of youth in the juvenile justice system. But TJJD continues to operate and invest in their five state-run facilities in rural areas that keep the youth far from their home communities. The Committee recommends that TJJD.

Finally, the Committee is concerned about the lack of clarity and communication about the rights of the youth in their care. Youth and their guardians need more clarity on what rights they have and the options they have for filing a grievance when they think those rights might have been violated.

This report provides the Commission with several recommendations for the Texas Legislature, the governor, and the Texas Juvenile Justice Department that the Committee believes would address many of these problems and vastly improve the outcomes for the youth assigned to the system.

Merrill Matthews
Chair of the Texas
Advisory Committee to the U.S. Commission on Civil Rights

Background

The Texas juvenile justice system has been afflicted with issues and challenges for decades. Many of the issues facing the system today are the same issues Texas has historically attempted to address. For example, in 1948, in response to reports of abuse, Richard Clenenden, Consultant on Training Schools for the U.S. Children's Bureau, advised the state to "close down most 'penal-type' facilities for juveniles located in isolated rural sites. Instead, he recommended smaller facilities located near urban centers, which would allow greater involvement in the rehabilitation process of juveniles' families and experts in relevant fields such as mental health, education, and psychiatry."[3]

---

[3] Dr. William Bush, Written Testimony submitted via email to the Texas Advisory Committee to the U.S. Commission on Civil Rights, p. 1 (hereafter cited as *Bush Written Testimony*).

In recent years, allegations of civil rights violations, state and federal investigations, and reports of abuse and mistreatment have plagued the Texas Juvenile Justice Department (TJJD). In October of 2021, the U.S. Department of Justice announced a statewide investigation into the conditions in the five secure juvenile correctional facilities run by TJJD. The investigation is examining whether Texas provides children confined in the facilities reasonable protection from physical, sexual, and emotional abuse by staff and other residents, excessive use of chemical restraints, and excessive use of isolation. The investigation is also examining whether Texas provides the youth with adequate mental health care.[4] At least 11 staff members of Texas facilities have been arrested for sexually abusing children in their care.[5] Some of the reported allegations include sharing pornographic material, having sexual relations with minors in custody, and sexual assault. Other examples of misconduct include reports of staff members allegedly paying children with drugs or cash to assault other children.[6]

The Sunset Advisory Commission of Texas provides regular assessment of all state agencies[7] and recently submitted a report on TJJD for the 2022-2023 legislative session.[8] The report found that staffing shortages are causing major instability and safety concerns within the Texas Juvenile Justice System, that key elements of TJJD's statute, rules, and procedures do not conform to common regulatory standards; and that the Office of the Independent Ombudsman needs clearer authority and formalized policies to better protect the rights of youth in the juvenile justice system.[9]

---

[4] Department of Justice Office of Public Affairs. "Justice Department Announces Investigation into Conditions at Five Juvenile Facilities in Texas." Wednesday, October 13, 2021 https://www.justice.gov/opa/pr/justice-department-announces-investigation-conditions-five-juvenile-facilities-texas.

[5] Sarah N. Lynch and Eric Beech. "U.S. Justice Department Opens Probe of Texas Juvenile Detention Facilities." Reuters. Thomson Reuters, October 13, 2021. https://www.reuters.com/world/us/us-justice-department-opens-probe-texas-juvenile-detention-facilities-2021-10-13/.

[6] Sarah N. Lynch and Eric Beech. "U.S. Justice Department Opens Probe of Texas Juvenile Detention Facilities." Reuters. Thomson Reuters, October 13, 2021. https://www.reuters.com/world/us/us-justice-department-opens-probe-texas-juvenile-detention-facilities-2021-10-13/; Brandi Grissom and Sue Ambrose. "Fights, sex, drugs: Texas juvenile lockup on the verge of crisis, reports show." Dallas Morning News, Nov. 16, 2017. https://www.dallasnews.com/news/investigations/2017/11/17/fights-sex-drugs-texas-juvenile-lockup-on-the-verge-of-crisis-reports-show/.

[7] TJJD website, Sunset Review (last accessed November 2023) https://www.tjjd.texas.gov/index.php/sunset-review#2-key-functions-performance.

[8] Sunset Advisory Commission Staff Report with Final Results, p. A1. Found here.

[9] Sunset Advisory Commission Staff Report with Final Results, pp. A11-A14. Found here.

Federal and State Law

The Due Process clause of the Fourteenth Amendment to the U.S. Constitution governs the standards for conditions of confinement of juvenile offenders.[10] Subjecting confined juveniles to undue restraint or excessive force violates the Due Process clause.[11] The Due Process clause also requires TJJD to keep juveniles reasonably safe from harm inflicted by third parties, including by other juveniles in the facility. They also must provide such minimally adequate training as reasonably may be required by these interests.[12]

The Department of Justice's investigation is conducted under the authority of the Civil Rights of Institutionalized Persons Act (CRIPA)[13] and the Violent Crime Control and Law Enforcement Act.[14] Both statutes give the Department of Justice the authority to investigate systemic violations of the rights of young people in juvenile correctional facilities. These laws can also be used to enforce other rights that youth have in the juvenile justice system, such as rights under the Americans with Disabilities Act and the Individuals with Disabilities Education Act.[15]

In the Texas juvenile justice system, a "juvenile" is legally defined as a person who was at least 10 years old but not yet 17 at the time he or she committed an act defined as "delinquent conduct" or "conduct in need of supervision."[16]

"Delinquent conduct" is generally conduct that, if committed by an adult, could result in imprisonment or confinement in jail. "Conduct in need of supervision" (CINS) is generally conduct that, if committed by an adult, could result in only a fine or would not even be considered a violation of the law. Examples include truancy or running away from home.[17]

A juvenile who engages in delinquent conduct or commits a CINS violation can be referred to juvenile court. The juvenile can be dealt with

---

[10] See Gary H. v. Hegstrom, 831 F.2d 1430, 1432 (9th Cir. 1987).

[11] See Youngberg v. Romeo, 457 U.S. 307, 73 L.Ed 2d 28, 102 S. Ct. 2452 (1982).

[12] *Id.;* see also J.H. ex rel. Higgin v. Johnson, 346 F.3d 788, 791 (7th Cir. 2003).

[13] 42 U.S.C. § 1997 et seq.

[14] H.R.3355 – 103rd Congress (1993-1994): Violent Crime Control and Law Enforcement Act of 1994, H.R.3355, 103rd Cong. (1994), https://www.congress.gov/bill/103rd-congress/house-bill/3355.

[15] Department of Justice Office of Civil Rights. Children's Rights in the Juvenile Justice System. https://www.justice.gov/crt/rights-juveniles.

[16] The Juvenile Justice System in Texas, Overview, Important Definitions. TJJD. http://www.tjjd.texas.gov/index.php/juvenile-system#important-definitions (accessed March 18, 2022).

[17] *Ibid.*

informally and returned home, but if the county decides to charge the juvenile with delinquent conduct, the juvenile is afforded the same legal rights as an adult charged with a crime. In certain circumstances, the county can request to have a youth certified as an adult. If such is granted, the person is considered an adult for criminal purposes and will no longer be in the juvenile justice system.

If the juvenile is adjudicated for delinquent conduct, there are several possible disposition options. The juvenile may be placed on probation; the juvenile may be sent to the Texas Juvenile Justice Department with an indeterminate sentence (only felony offenses); or the juvenile may be sent to TJJD with a determinate sentence (only certain offenses).[18]

In Texas, individual counties provide services to all youth referred to the juvenile courts and prosecute juvenile cases, either through their district or county attorney's office. County juvenile probation departments handle most of the sanctions and therapeutic interventions the courts may impose.

TJJD works in partnership with local juvenile boards and juvenile probation departments to support and enhance juvenile probation services throughout the state by providing funding, technical assistance, and training; establishing and enforcing standards; collecting, analyzing, and disseminating information; and facilitating communications between state and local entities. It also provides oversight of county-operated detention facilities.[19]

TJJD manages state-operated secure facilities and halfway houses to provide treatment services to those youth who have chronic delinquency problems and who have exhausted their options in the county. Additionally, youth who have committed the most serious offenses requiring specialized treatment services that counties are not equipped to provide are also likely to be committed to state-run facilities.[20]

There are also international standards for youth detention. The United Nations Rules for the Protection of Juveniles Deprived of their Liberty dictates the minimum standards for incarcerated youth.[21] The United States is the only

---

[18] The Juvenile Justice System in Texas, Overview, Referral to Juvenile Court and Possible Dispositions. http://www.tjjd.texas.gov/index.php/juvenile-system#referral-to-juvenile-court-possible-dispositions (accessed March 18, 2022).

[19] The Juvenile Justice System in Texas, Overview, State Agencies Involved in the Juvenile Justice System. http://www.tjjd.texas.gov/index.php/juvenile-system#state-agencies-involved-in-the-juvenile-justice-system.

[20] *Ibid.*

[21] Adopted by the General Assembly resolution 45/113 on December 14th, 1990 https://www.ohchr.org/en/instruments-mechanisms/instruments/united-nations-rules-protection-juveniles-deprived- their-liberty.

country that has *not* ratified this treaty and are therefore not subject to its standards.[22] The protections include a prohibition of solitary confinement and corporal punishment, a requirement that youth be kept separate from adults, the right to physical and mental health care, and a prohibition on the use of medicine as a form of restraint.[23]

The Juvenile Justice System in Texas

The Texas Juvenile Justice Department (TJJD) was created in 2012 when the Texas Youth Commission and the Texas Juvenile Probation Commission were merged. TJJD's responsibilities include operating five secured state facilities and supporting county probation departments by disbursing grants, providing technical support, and ensuring that all facilities are adhering to its guidance. TJJD is tasked with providing rehabilitative services including mental health treatment and quality educational instruction.

Since 2018, the number of youths in state-secured facilities has shrunk by more than a third.[24] There are currently five TJJD-secured facilities for youth: Evins Regional Juvenile Center, Gainesville State School, Giddings State School, McLennan County State Juvenile Correctional Facility, and the Ron Jackson State Juvenile Correctional Complex. During fiscal year 2023 the number of youth in state-secured facilities is around 590 total population.[25]

TJJD compiles detailed annual statistical reports regarding juvenile crime throughout the state. In a given year, more than 50,000 juveniles are arrested

---

22 National Juvenile Defender Center. International Human Rights: Law & Resources for Juvenile Defenders & Advocates. Fall 2012 https://njdc.info/wp-content/uploads/2013/11/International-Human-Rights_Law-and-Resources-for-Juvenile-Defenders-and-Advocates.pdf. United Nations, Treaty Series, vol. 1577, p. 3; depositary notifications C.N.147.1993.TREATIES-5 of 15 May 1993 [amendments to article 43 (2)]1; and C.N.322.1995.TREATIES-7 of 7 November 1995 [amendment to article 43 (2)]. https://treaties.un.org/Pages/ViewDetails.aspx?src=IND&mtdsg_no=IV-11&chapter=4.

23 National Juvenile Defender Center. International Human Rights: Law & Resources for Juvenile Defenders & Advocates. Fall 2012 https://njdc.info/wp-content/uploads/2013/11/Inter national-Human-Rights_Law-and- Resources-for-Juvenile-Defenders-and-Advocates.pdf.

24 Jolie McCullough. "Almost 600 Texas youths are trapped in a juvenile prison system on the brink of collapse." *The Texas Tribune*. August 2, 2022. Found here. TJJD, Written Testimony submitted via email to the Texas Advisory Committee to the U.S. Commission on Civil Rights, p. 2 (hereafter cited as TJJD Written Testimony).

25 TJJD Written Testimony, p. 2; Martin Martinez, testimony, *Briefing Before the Texas Advisory Committee to the U.S. Commission on Civil Rights,* Houston, TX, August 8, 2022. Transcript, pp. 21-22 (hereafter *Transcript I).*

in Texas or referred to the juvenile probation system.[26] Local county juvenile justice systems provide services for these youth, many of whom are diverted from further involvement with the juvenile justice system. The most serious offenders are committed to TJJD facilities. Reform measures enacted in 2007[27] greatly reduced commitments to state-run facilities by limiting them to youth with felony-level offenses only.[28]

Oversight & Accountability

Two independent groups are tasked with investigating alleged misconduct within TJJD: the Office of the Inspector General (OIG) and the Office of the Independent Ombudsman (OIO).

OIO for TJJD is a state agency established for the purpose of investigating, evaluating, and securing the rights of the children committed to TJJD.[29] OIO reports to the Governor and the Texas Legislature; it is not a part of TJJD and does not report to the Department's Executive Management or the TJJD Board.[30] To fulfill the duties of the office, staff regularly visit all TJJD secure facilities, halfway houses, parole offices, county post-adjudication facilities, and county contract care programs. In 2021, OIO was conducting regular site visits at 107 facilities and probation/parole offices that met the criteria expanded by Senate Bill 1630, 84th Legislative Session.[31] OIO periodically mails informational brochures regarding its services to the parents of youth newly committed to TJJD detention centers. To facilitate communications from youth in the facilities, as well as the public, OIO maintains a hotline that is answered 24 hours a day. The Deputy Ombudsman also distribute posters containing OIO's hotline number to the facilities that are routinely visited and educates youth on complaint procedures.[32]

---

[26] The Juvenile Justice System in Texas, Overview, The Numbers. http://www.tjjd.texas.gov/index.php/juvenile-system#the-numbers (accessed March 18, 2022).

[27] SB 103. Texas Legislature. 80th Session. https://capitol.texas.gov/tlodocs/80R/billtext/html/sb00103f.Htm.

[28] The Juvenile Justice System in Texas, Overview, The Numbers. http://www.tjjd.texas.gov/index.php/juvenile- system#the-numbers (accessed March 18, 2022).

[29] https://statutes.capitol.texas.gov/Docs/HR/htm/HR.261.htm.

[30] Independent Ombudsman, Overview, What is the Independent Ombudsman? https://www.tjjd.texas.gov/index.php/independent-ombudsman#what-is-the-independent-ombudsman (accessed March 18, 2022).

[31] Independent Ombudsman for the TJJD. Fourth Quarter Report FY 21. https://www.tjjd.texas.gov/index.php/doc-library/send/645-fiscal-year-2021/3070-fy21q4.

[32] *Ibid.*

OIO monitors and enforces 14 basic rights for post-adjudicated youth. Information on these rights is supposed to be provided to youth and their guardians upon entry to TJJD facilities and posted throughout the facilities. These are:

1) Right to equal treatment
2) Right to free speech and expression
3) Right to religious freedom
4) Right to personal possessions
5) Right to receive visitors
6) Right to access to mail and telephone
7) Right to earnings and monetary gifts
8) Right to protection from physical and psychological harm
9) Right to medical and dental care
10) Right to access attorneys
11) Right to be informed
12) Right to accuracy and fairness
13) Right to confidentiality of records
14) Right to file grievances and appeal decisions

OIG was created by the Texas Legislature and is charged with investigating TJJD regarding (1) crimes committed by department employees, including parole officers employed by or under contract with the department, and (2) crimes and delinquent conduct committed at a facility operated by the department, a residential facility operated by another entity under a contract with the department, or any facility in which a child committed to the custody of the department is housed or receives medical or mental health treatment.[33] The chief inspector is a commissioned peace officer and is authorized to appoint additional peace officers to fulfill the statutory duties of the office. The chief inspector is appointed by and reports directly to TJJD's Board. The inspectors general have all the power and duties afforded to peace officers under the Texas Code of Criminal Procedure.[34]

---

33 Agency Accountability, Overview. https://www.tjjd.texas.gov/index.php/accountability (accessed March 18, 2022).

34 Inspector General, Overview. https://www.tjjd.texas.gov/index.php/inspector-general#overview (accessed March 18, 2022).

Concerns About Safety and Civil Rights

Use of Force

In 2019, TJJD staff used force against incarcerated children almost 7,000 times.[35] TJJD defines "use of force" as "physical measures used to direct, compel, or restrain bodily movement of a noncompliant youth."[36] In the state facilities, the following methods are considered permissible under the use of force policy: mechanical restraints, manual restraints, chemical spray, physical escort, and planned team restraint.[37] Across all facilities, nearly half (47%) of all youth were subjected to the use of force.[38]

Juvenile facility staff may inappropriately use Oleoresin Capsicum (OC) (pepper) spray to respond to non-threatening conduct and behaviors that in fact are manifestations of mental illness or developmental disabilities, even when staff are trained to use OC spray as a last resort.[39] In fact, the Special Litigation Section of the U.S. Department of Justice's Civil Rights Division has found the inappropriate and excessive use of chemical agents on youth with disabilities, among other groups.[40]

Understaffing

The 2022-23 Sunset Commission review found that understaffing underscores "all other problems at TJJD, endangering youth and staff safety.[41] More

---

[35] Edgar Sandoval & Tim Arango. "Complaints Against Texas' Juvenile Prisons Include Violence and Sex Abuse" *The New York Times.* October 15, 2021. https://www.nytimes.com/2021/10/15/us/texas-juvenile-centers-investigation.html#:~:text=In%202019%2C%20prison%20staff%20used,who%20was%20confined%20that%20year.

[36] TJJD. General Administrative Policy Manual. 380.9723. Effective February 15, 2016. http://www.tjjd.texas.gov/index.php/component/jdownloads/send/498-ch380f-security-control/1744-380-%209723-use-of-force; 37 TAC Sec. §380.9723. https://texreg.sos.state.tx.us/public/readtac$ext.TacPage?sl=T&app=9&p_dir=F&p_rloc=166664&p_tloc=14619&p_ploc=1&pg=3&p_tac=&ti=37&pt=11&ch=380&rl=9727.

[37] TAC §380.9723.

[38] Brett M. Merfish and Beth Mitchell to Steven H. Rosenbaum, Chief, Special Litigation, Section of Civil Rights Division, U.S. Department of Justice. October 21, 2020. https://www. texasappleseed.org/sites/default/files/DOJ- FINAL-COMPLAINT-fin.pdf.

[39] Center for Children Law and Policy Factsheet, Chemical Agents in Juvenile Facilities. July 2019. https://cclp.org/wp-content/uploads/2019/07/Fact-Sheet-Chemical-Agents-Final-2019.pdf.

[40] *Ibid.*

[41] Sunset Advisory Commission Staff Report with Final Results, p. 20. Found here.

specifically, "chronic staffing shortages in state secure facilities affect nearly every aspect of committed youths' lives and perpetuate TJJD's problems with maintaining safety, providing treatment and services, and ensuring youths' due process rights.[42]

During the summer of 2022, at the height of the staffing crisis, TJJD secure facilities functioned at roughly 200% of their capacity; in September 2023, this dropped to 132% due to improved staffing among juvenile correction officers, not a decrease in youth admissions.[43]

Additionally, understaffing may lead to the overuse of lockdowns in secured facilities.[44] Due to low staffing levels, in order to meet requirements under the Prison Rape Elimination Act (PREA), lockdowns are sometimes utilized to meet the required ratio of 1 staff member for every eight youths.[45] The Sunset Advisory Commission found that bathroom breaks for youth in lockdown can take up to three or more hours due to these lockdowns.[46] The last full-day (22-23 hours) lockdown occurred in October 2022.[47]

Mental Health Care

The percentage of youth with moderate to severe mental health needs has grown significantly. Specifically, in 2014, at the point of intake, the TJJD identified 21% of youth as having moderate to severe mental health needs; in 2019, that percentage grew to 53%[48] and by 2022, it had risen to 84%.[49] In 2019, 138 youth were referred to security due to danger to self or suicide (which includes attempted suicide, injury to self, suicidal behavior, and suicidal ideation) a total of 271 times, a rate of almost two referrals per each youth. The rate of referrals was similar in 2018, with 186 youth referred a total of 417 times, a rate of two referrals per each youth.[50]

---

[42] Sunset Advisory Commission Staff Report with Final Results, p. 21-22. Found here.
[43] TJJD Written Testimony, p. 3.
[44] Sunset Advisory Commission Staff Report with Final Results, p. 23. Found here.
[45] *Ibid.*
[46] *Ibid.*
[47] TJJD Written Testimony, p. 3.
[48] Brett M. Merfish and Beth Mitchell to Steven H. Rosenbaum, Chief, Special Litigation, Section of Civil Rights Division, U.S. Department of Justice. October 21, 2020. https://media. disabilityrightstx.org/wp-content/uploads/2020/10/21154645/DOJ-FINAL-COMPLAINT. pdf.
[49] TJJD Written Testimony, p. 2.
[50] Brett M. Merfish and Beth Mitchell to Steven H. Rosenbaum, Chief, Special Litigation, Section of Civil Rights Division, U.S. Department of Justice. October 21, 2020.

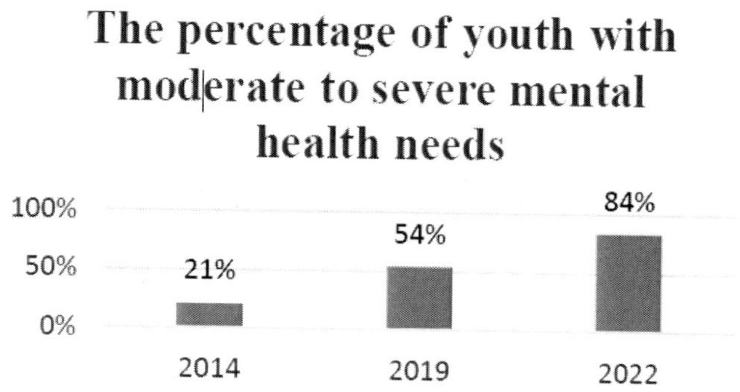

More recently, the Sunset Advisory Commission found that in fiscal year 2021, TJJD reported more than 6,500 suicide alerts in secured facilities, which represents an increase of about 40% since 2019.[51] Due to the extremely high level of risk in TJJD facilities, counselors spend roughly 30 hours a week solely on suicide risk assessments, resulting in far fewer hours to provide rehabilitative care.[52]

The increasing use of lockdowns due to lower staffing has had a negative mental health impact on youth in TJJD care in recent years.[53] TJJD itself cited full and partial lockdown as a cause of increases in suicide assessments in the fall of 2021.[54] The Sunset Commission heard accounts that youth regularly harm themselves while in lockdown in order to have adult intervention.[55]

Racial and Ethnic Disparities

All of these factors are made even more concerning by the racial and ethnic disparities found within Texas's juvenile justice system. In 2019, Black youth in Texas were 4.7 times more likely, and Latino youth were 1.6 times more likely, to be incarcerated than White youth.[56] Between 2015 and 2019, the

---

https://media. disabilityrightstx.org/wp-content/uploads/2020/10/21154645/DOJ-FINAL-COMPLAINT.pdf.

[51] Sunset Advisory Commission Staff Report with Final Results, p. 23. Found here.

[52] *Ibid.*

[53] *Ibid.*

[54] *Ibid.*

[55] *Ibid.*

[56] The Sentencing Project. "Black Disparities in Youth Incarceration: Racial Disparities Persist but Fall from All-Time High." July 2021. https://www.sentencingproject.org/wp-content/uploads/2017/09/Black-Disparities-in-Youth-Incarceration.pdf?eType =EmailBlastContent&eId=3678cc76-dab8-418b-b5cf-faa89e6baec9; The Sentencing

disparity between Black and White youth actually increased by 5%.[57]57 As of 2021, total new admissions to the TJJD system were 35% Black, 44% Hispanic, 20% White, and 1% other.[58]

Summary of Findings

Finding I: Most youth in the Texas Juvenile Justice System have clear mental health needs.

Finding II: Understaffing has been a major problem in the Texas Juvenile Justice System and has inhibited other efforts for reform. Staffing has been improving in the past year, but it is unclear if many of the longstanding issues with staffing will be resolved.

Finding III: There are not enough resources and staff to provide proper treatment for the mental health needs of the youth in the Texas Juvenile Justice Department's care.

Finding IV: Being in state-run facilities may further traumatize the youth and increase mental health needs.

Finding V: The state-run facilities provide an unsafe environment for both the youth and staff.

Finding VI: The Texas Juvenile Justice Department is transferring youth in their care to adult prisons rather than focusing on rehabilitative programming.

Finding VII: Youth benefit from individualized and asset-based mental health support, rather than the traditional punitive model currently in place in the Texas Juvenile Justice System.

Finding VIII: Youth facilities that are closer to home and incorporate community-based resources are more effective and better serve youth's mental health needs.

Finding IX: Texas communities do not have the resources required to support high-risk children who are ending up in Texas Juvenile Justice

---

Project. "Latinx Disparities in Youth Incarceration: Latinx Youth 28% More Likely Than Whites to be Held." July 2021.https://www.sentencingpro ject.org/wp-content/uploads/2017/10/Latinx-Disparities-in-Youth-Incarceration.pdf?eType=EmailBlastContent&eId=3678cc76-dab8-418b-b5cf-faa89e6baec9.

57 The Sentencing Project. "Black Disparities in Youth Incarceration: Racial Disparities Persist but Fall from All- Time High." July 2021. https://www.sentencingproject.org/wp-content/uploads/2017/09/Black-Disparities-in-Youth-Incarceration.pdf?eType=Email BlastContent&eId=3678cc76-dab8-418b-b5cf-faa89e6baec9.

58 Sunset Advisory Commission Staff Report with Final Results, p. 76. Found here.

Department care. Texas needs to invest more in upstream and preventive services to divert children who are currently being referred to the juvenile justice system.

Finding X: While the Texas Juvenile Justice Department has clearly defined rights for youth in their care, there remains confusion about what these rights are and/or if they are being adequately enforced.

Finding XI: Facilities' current grievance process and other accountability measures are insufficient and function poorly.

Finding XII: The Texas Legislature made some improvements to the Texas Juvenile Justice Department and its funding in the 2023 session, but there is much more reform and investment still needed.

Methodology

As a matter of historical precedent, and in order to achieve transparency, Committee studies involve a collection of public, testimonial evidence, and written comments from individuals directly impacted by the civil rights topic at hand; e.g., researchers and experts who have rigorously studied and reported on the topic, community organizations and advocates representing a broad range of backgrounds and perspectives related to the topic, and government officials tasked with related policy decisions and the administration of those policies.

Studies require Committee members to utilize their expertise in selecting panelists who are the most useful to the purposes of the study and will result in a broad and diverse understanding of the issue. This method requires Committee members to draw from their own experiences, knowledge, opinions, and views to understand the issue and possible policy solutions.

Committees are composed of volunteer professionals and advocates who are familiar with civil rights issues in their state or territory. Members represent a variety of political viewpoints, occupations, races, ages, and gender identities, as well as a variety of backgrounds, skills, and experiences. The intentional diversity of each Committee promotes vigorous debate and full exploration of the issues. It also serves to assist in offsetting biases that can result in the oversight of nuances in the testimony.

The Committee sees the perspective of the Texas Juvenile Justice Department as essential in understanding this issue and achieving a balanced project record. Many outreach attempts were made, and numerous invitations were extended, but unfortunately, TJJD declined to participate in this project until well after the deadline to submit testimony. However, because of the critical need for the agency's contribution, the Committee decided to reopen testimony to allow for TJJD's response to the Committee's preliminary report.

For the purposes of this study, Findings are defined as what the testimony and other data suggested, revealed, or indicated based upon the information collected by the Committee. Findings refer to a synthesis of observations confirmed by a majority vote of members, rather than conclusions drawn by any one member. Recommendations are specific actions or proposed policy interventions intended to address or alleviate the civil rights concerns raised in the related finding(s). Where findings indicate a lack of sufficient knowledge or available data to fully understand the civil rights issues at hand, recommendations may also target specific areas in need of further, more rigorous study. Recommendations are directed to the Commission; they request that the Commission itself take a specific action, or that the Commission forward recommendations to other federal or state agencies, policymakers, or stakeholders.

Findings

Finding I: Most youth in the Texas Juvenile Justice System have clear mental health needs.

Many of the youth who enter TJJD facilities are identified as having mental health needs.[59] In 2022, 84% of youth were identified at intake as having moderate to severe mental health needs, compared to only 21% in 2014.[60] Nationally, some studies suggest that two-thirds of youth in the juvenile justice system have diagnosable mental health disorders.[61] In

[59] Representative Gene Wu, testimony, *Briefing Before the Texas Advisory Committee to the U.S. Commission on Civil Rights,* remote panel via ZoomGov, December 7, 2022. Transcript, p. 7 (hereafter *Transcript III)*; Alycia Welch, testimony, *Briefing Before the Texas Advisory Committee to the U.S. Commission on Civil Rights,* Houston, TX, August 8, 2022. Transcript, pp. 15 (hereafter *Transcript I)*; Brittany Norman, testimony, *Briefing Before the Texas Advisory Committee to the U.S. Commission on Civil Rights,* Houston, TX, August 8, 2022. Transcript, p. 157 (hereafter *Transcript II)*.

[60] Martinez Testimony, *Transcript I*, p. 21; TJJD Written Testimony, p. 2.

[61] Liz Ryan, testimony, Briefing Before the Texas Advisory Committee to the U.S. Commission on Civil Rights, remote panel via ZoomGov, February 15, 2023. Transcript, p. 6 (hereafter Transcript IV).

December 2021 alone, TJJD reported they performed over 1,000 risk assessments for just 800 youth, with 500 of them at the Evins facility.[62]

Self-harm and suicide are on the rise, and in 2021, there were over 2,000 incidents of self-harm and 6,500 suicide alerts in Texas's state-secured youth facilities.[63] Over half of the youth in these facilities have been put on suicide watch.[64] For certain demographics, it's even higher; 63% of girls are on suicide watch, as well as 56% of youth under age 14.[65]

There is a correlation between mental health needs and experiences of trauma.[66] Up to 65% of youth in TJJD have had four or more adverse childhood experiences,[67] also called ACEs.[68] This figure is significantly higher than the general population.[69] Ninety youth in TJJD are identified as victims of sex trafficking.[70] Additionally, many of the behaviors that lead the youth to be in TJJD custody, particularly violence,[71] have mental health connections.[72]

Finding II: Understaffing has been a major problem in the Texas Juvenile Justice system and has inhibited other efforts for reform. Staffing has been

---

[62] Elizabeth Henneke, testimony, Briefing Before the Texas Advisory Committee to the U.S. Commission on Civil Rights, remote panel via ZoomGov, February 15, 2023. Transcript, p. 6 (hereafter Transcript IV).

[63] Ryan Testimony, Transcript IV, p. 4; Welch Testimony, Transcript I, p. 11; Henneke Testimony, Transcript IV, p. 7; Martinez Testimony, Transcript I, p. 24.

[64] Henneke Testimony, Transcript IV, p. 8; Welch Testimony, Transcript I, p. 11; Martinez Testimony, Transcript I, p. 22.

[65] Henneke Testimony, Transcript IV, p. 8; Martinez Testimony, Transcript I, p. 24.

[66] Jernard Brown, testimony, Briefing Before the Texas Advisory Committee to the U.S. Commission on Civil Rights, remote panel via ZoomGov, April 11, 2023. Transcript, p. 2 (hereafter Transcript V). Norman Testimony, Transcript II, p. 142; Welch Testimony, Transcript I, p. 9; Wu Testimony, Transcript III, p. 8; Henneke Testimony, Transcript IV, p. 8.

[67] Martinez Testimony, Transcript I, p. 21; Henneke Testimony, Transcript IV, p. 10; Ashley McFarland, Public Comment, Transcript V, pp.15-16.

[68] ACEs, or Adverse Childhood Experiences, are stressful or traumatic events that occur during a person's childhood and can have long-lasting negative effects on their physical and mental health. These experiences often include events such as abuse, neglect, household dysfunction, or other forms of adversity that can impact a child's well- being and development.

[69] Henneke Testimony, *Transcript IV*, p. 8; Martinez Testimony, *Transcript I*, p. 21.

[70] Henneke Testimony, *Transcript IV*, p. 8.

[71] Amnisty Freelen, testimony, *Briefing Before the Texas Advisory Committee to the U.S. Commission on Civil Rights,* Houston, TX, August 8, 2022. Transcript, p. 128 (hereafter *Transcript II);* Welch Testimony, *Transcript I*, p. 57; Henneke Testimony, *Transcript IV*, p. 10.

[72] Phyllis Becker, testimony, *Briefing Before the Texas Advisory Committee to the U.S. Commission on Civil Rights,* remote panel via ZoomGov, December 7, 2022. Transcript, pp. 4 (hereafter *Transcript III);* Freelen Testimony, *Transcript II*, p. 124; Brown Testimony, *Transcript V*, pp. 2-3; Welch Testimony, *Transcript I*, p. 59.

improving in the past year, but it is unclear if many of the longstanding issues with staffing will be resolved.

All five of TJJD's facilities have experienced chronic staff shortages.[73] For example, the Evins Regional Juvenile Center in Edinburg has been 200% over a proper youth-to-staff ratio, and the Giddings State School, which houses the Crisis Stabilization Unit, TJJD's mental health program, has been 150 percent% over a proper youth-to-staff ratio.[74] In June 2022, the agency had less than 50% of its full-time correction officer positions filled.[75]

Staffing levels have increased significantly in 2023, in part to additional investments by the Texas Legislature, including pay raises for all staff.[76] Two of TJJD's five secure facilities are now fully staffed, but three remain understaffed.[77]

In addition to the large number of vacancies, there is a very low staff retention rate. The turnover rate for correction officers was more than 70% in 2022.[78] In December 2021, the Texas Rangers were called in to help address the staffing shortages.[79] This issue of understaffing is not unique to Texas and is an issue nationwide.[80]

Low pay and the rural location of many of these facilities make it hard to recruit qualified individuals.[81] A 15% salary stipend for direct-care staff, including juvenile correction officers and case managers, was implemented in late 2022 to bring their pay to the same levels as adult correction officers.[82]

The understaffing at these facilities creates very difficult working conditions for the staff they do have.[83] They have been regularly asked to work 12-hour shifts for six or seven days a week to maintain minimum staffing requirements.[84] Other staff, such as teachers and case workers, have had to fill correction officer roles instead of providing their skilled services.[85]

---

[73] Martinez Testimony, *Transcript I*, p. 23; Welch Testimony, *Transcript I*, p. 12.
[74] Welch Testimony, *Transcript I*, p. 12.
[75] Welch Testimony, *Transcript I*, p. 12.
[76] TJJD Written Testimony, p. 2-3.
[77] Ibid.
[78] Martinez Testimony, *Transcript I*, p. 22; Welch Testimony, *Transcript I*, p. 12.
[79] Martinez Testimony, *Transcript I*, p. 65.
[80] Becker Testimony, *Transcript III*, p. 9.
[81] Norman Testimony, *Transcript II*, p. 135; Wu Testimony, *Transcript III*, p. 25.; Henneke Testimony, *Transcript IV*, p. 15.
[82] TJJD Written Testimony, p. 3.
[83] Layla Fry, testimony, *Briefing Before the Texas Advisory Committee to the U.S. Commission on Civil Rights,* Houston, TX, August 8, 2022. Transcript, p. 108 (hereafter *Transcript II)*; Henneke Testimony, Transcript IV, p. 15.
[84] Henneke Testimony, *Transcript IV*, p. 15.
[85] Henneke Testimony, *Transcript IV*, p. 13; Welch Testimony, *Transcript I*, p. 13.

These levels of understaffing mean that even when new policies are proposed and TJJD administration tries to address issues, the facilities are unable to fully benefit from these attempted reforms.[86]

Finding III: There are not enough resources and staff to provide proper treatment for the mental health needs of the youth in the Texas Juvenile Justice Department's care.

In addition to the overall understaffing of these facilities, there are even more unfilled positions for mental health care workers.[87] As of June 2022, TJJD had only 55% of its mental health positions filled across all facilities, and many of these professionals are unlicensed.[88] At the same time, Texas had a statewide shortage of mental health professionals reaching as high as 64%. In September 2023, TJJD has 52% of its mental health positions staffed.[89] TJJD testified they expect staffing their mental health positions to be an ongoing challenge as Texas struggles with a statewide mental health professional shortage.[90]

There is a months-long waitlist for mental health care across all facilities. At Giddings alone, there are 50 youth on the waitlist for the highest tier of mental health intervention.[91] TJJD has described this backlog of needs as a "pool they are emptying with a cup."[92] Not receiving treatment can result in youth staying in TJJD facilities for longer periods and inhibits rehabilitation efforts designed to minimize further justice system involvement.[93] Even when a youth is self-advocating for mental health care, they are frequently denied or left waiting for months.[94]

When youth are receiving mental health services, it is not always the appropriate treatment.[95] For example, evidence received by the Committee indicated a youth who needs a particular type of care (e.g., substance abuse treatment) might be offered a different type of mental health care (e.g., anger

---

[86] Welch Testimony, *Transcript I*, pp. 12; 43; 97; Norman Testimony, *Transcript II*, p. 133; Henneke Testimony, *Transcript IV*, p. 13.

[87] Welch Testimony, *Transcript I*, p. 13.

[88] Welch Testimony, *Transcript I*, p. 14; Norman Testimony, *Transcript II*, p. 13; Martinez Testimony, *Transcript I*, p. 25.

[89] Additional legislative appropriations allowed the department to improve its mental health professional-to-youth ratio from 1:16 to 1:12 in September 2023 which resulted a lower staffing rate despite an increase in new hires. TJJD Written Testimony p. 14.

[90] TJJD Written Testimony, p. 3.

[91] Welch Testimony, *Transcript I*, p. 14.

[92] Norman Testimony, *Transcript II*, p. 134; Henneke Testimony, *Transcript IV*, p. 6.

[93] Henneke Testimony, *Transcript IV*, p. 8; Norman Testimony, *Transcript II*, p. 133; Fry Testimony, *Transcript II*, p. 108.

[94] Norman Testimony, *Transcript II*, p. 140; Henneke Testimony, *Transcript IV*, pp. 9-10.

[95] Ryan Testimony, *Transcript IV*, p. 3; Henneke Testimony, *Transcript IV*, pp.7-8.

management treatment) because it's the only treatment that the facility has to offer at that time due to a lack of staff and funding.[96] TJJD testified that this piece of testimony might not be entirely true and that "many youth need multiple specialized treatments, and it is not uncommon for treatment programming to incorporate content learned in previous interventions."[97]

Lastly, there is inconsistent access to mental health prescriptions. Testimony received by the Committee suggested that there may be an overreliance by TJJD on medications for youth to compensate for the lack of other more appropriate treatments.[98]

Finding IV: Being in state-run facilities may further traumatize the youth and increase mental health needs.

TJJD was increasingly relying on isolating the youth in their cells to compensate for understaffing. The youth will sometimes spend 23 hours a day alone in their cell.[99] There are reports that youth did not have timely access to bathrooms during these lockdowns and resorted to relieving themselves in their cells.[100] In response to the isolation, youth are self-harming and exhibiting other disruptive behaviors just to leave their cell and receive treatment.[101]

Self-harm and other disruptive behaviors are frequently met with restraints and the use of force, including the use of OC spray (i.e., pepper spray) to stop youth from self-harming.[102] Youth who are experiencing a mental health crisis may escalate the situation by resisting, resulting in further trauma.[103] Youth need to feel safe before mental health needs can be effectively addressed.[104]

One population in TJJD custody that is particularly concerning is victims of human trafficking. As of February 2023, there were 90 youth in custody who were identified as survivors of sex trafficking, which was almost 25% of the total population.[105] Currently, the Texas criminal legal system incarcerates children whose crimes were a direct result of, or incident to, human trafficking,

---

[96] Henneke Testimony, *Transcript IV*, pp. 7; 23.

[97] The Committee was unable to provide any more analysis on these differing perspectives. TJJD Written Testimony, p. 14.

[98] Freelen Testimony, *Transcript II*, p. 126; Norman Testimony, *Transcript II*, p. 143.

[99] Martinez Testimony, *Transcript I*, p. 23; Welch Testimony, *Transcript I*, p. 10.

[100] Norman Testimony, *Transcript II*, p. 134; Welch Testimony, *Transcript I*, p. 11.

[101] Welch Testimony, *Transcript I*, p. 11; Norman Testimony, *Transcript II*, p. 139.

[102] Norman Testimony, *Transcript II*, p. 149. Martinez Testimony, *Transcript I*, p. 23.

[103] Ryan Testimony, *Transcript IV*, p. 3; Norman Testimony, *Transcript II*, p. 149.

[104] Becker Testimony, *Transcript III*, p. 4; Welch Testimony, *Transcript I*, p. 12.

[105] Henneke Testimony, Transcript IV, p. 8.

intimate partner violence, and other abuse.[106] These kids are much more likely to have mental health needs and less likely to be rehabilitated in a punitive system. For example, the Committee heard the testimony of a girl in a facility who had a history of sex trafficking and had also been a victim of sexual abuse in TJJD custody. She responded to an officer's use of force with panic and violence and consequently was charged with an additional crime and transferred to the adult justice system at the age of 16.[107]

Finding V: The state-run facilities provide an unsafe environment for both the youth and staff.

A high youth-to-staff ratio leads to unsafe conditions for both the youth and staff[108] and is a "recipe for disaster."[109] Safety concerns include increased violence, unsanitary living conditions, and lack of basic health care and medical attention. With inadequate staff-to-youth ratios, the staff only have time to triage the youths' needs.[110] It was reported that in July 2022, TJJD halted the intake of youth into its facilities because it would not have been able to guarantee their safety.[111] TJJD has made improvements in the last year, and it decreased the number of committed youth awaiting transfer to state custody from about 160 in July 2022 to about 70 in September 2023; during that timeframe, over 400 youth were moved off of the waitlist.[112]

The Sunset Advisory Commission found that understaffing led to increased safety risks for both youth in TJJD care and staff, due to abuse of youth by staff and threats of physical violence.[113]

Between 2019 and 2021, there were 10,000 violations identified as assaults on youth and staff in secure facilities; 20% of these assaults resulted in bodily harm.[114] In the same period, assaults on staff increased by 23%.[115]

---

[106] Henneke Testimony, *Transcript IV*, p. 9.

[107] Henneke Testimony, *Transcript IV*, p. 9.

[108] Welch Testimony, *Transcript I*, p. 41; Martinez Testimony, *Transcript I*, p. 55; Becker Testimony, *Transcript III*, p. 10.

[109] Ashley McFarland, public comment, *Briefing Before the Texas Advisory Committee to the U.S. Commission on Civil Rights,* remote panel via ZoomGov, April 11, 2023. Transcript, pp. 15-16 (hereafter *Transcript V*).

[110] Henneke Testimony, *Transcript IV*, p. 22; Welch Testimony, *Transcript I*, p. 9; Martinez Testimony, *Transcript I*, p. 41.

[111] TJJD Director Shandra Carter quoted in: Jolie McCullough. "Almost 600 Texas youths are trapped in a juvenile prison system on the brink of collapse." *The Texas Tribune.* August 2, 2022. Found here.

[112] TJJD Written Testimony, p. 3.

[113] Sunset Advisory Commission Staff Report with Final Results, p. 22. Found here.

[114] Ibid.

[115] Ibid, 25.

The instability in staffing levels decreases peer monitoring, which can increase opportunities for predatory staff to engage in abuse or exploitation.[116] There has been an increase in dangerous incidents involving the use of force and sexual violence.[117] From 2020 to 2022, there was an increase in sexual misconduct investigations by the Office of Inspector General at four of the five secure facilities.[118] One study reported that between January and August 2020, the five facilities reported using restraints on youth a total of 2,947 times.[119]

The Committee heard accounts from youth and former youth in facilities that during their time with TJJD, they felt unsafe, were further traumatized, and were "destroyed."[120]

Finding VI: The Texas Juvenile Justice Department is transferring youth in their care to adult prisons rather than focusing on rehabilitative programming.

TJJD is referring some youth who turn 16 and older to adult prison systems, where the children do not have age-appropriate care or supervision.[121] This goes against the evidence backed model of child-focused mental health care which prioritizes treating children as children and keeping them out of adult systems and prisons.[122] Rather than having a culture of rehabilitation, TJJD is preparing youth for transfer to adult prison.[123] Without age appropriate supervision and care, TJJD youth in adult systems are extremely vulnerable to abuse and increased self-harm.

Finding VII: Youth benefit from individualized and asset-based mental health support, rather than the traditional punitive model currently in place in the Texas Juvenile Justice System.[124]

Children with mental health challenges benefit from a model that is grounded in supporting the youth and families, focusing on strengths, assets, and needs.[125] Mental health services for children operate better when services can be individualized and youth are in smaller settings.[126] One beneficial

---

116 Ibid.

117 Welch Testimony, *Transcript I*, pp. 11,56; Henneke Testimony, *Transcript IV*, p. 9.

118 Henneke Testimony, *Transcript IV*, p. 9.

119 Russell Testimony, Transcript I, p. 37.

120 Brown Testimony, Transcript V, p. 2; Henneke Testimony, Transcript IV, p. 9; Norman Testimony, Transcript II, p. 137; Welch Testimony, Transcript I, p. 11; Freelen Testimony, Transcript II, p. 125.

121 Freelen Testimony, Transcript II, p. 123; Henneke Testimony, Transcript IV, p. 11.

122 Ryan Testimony, *Transcript IV*, p. 4.

123 Freelen Testimony, *Transcript II*, p. 127.

124 Becker Testimony, *Transcript III*, p. 17.

125 Becker Testimony, *Transcript III*, p. 5.

126 Norman Testimony, *Transcript II*, p. 189.

model the Committee heard testimony about is Multisystemic Therapy (MST), a counseling model which involves the entire family and works to solve behavioral concerns within the family dynamic.[127] However, even if youth are receiving proper therapy, in an unsafe environment, treatment is often compromised.[128]

The Committee heard testimony that TJJD may over-rely on the use of medications for treatment of youth in their care; 69% of youth in TJJD care have been prescribed some form of psychotropic medicine.[129] While use of psychotropic medicine can be part of a care plan for a child with mental health challenges, the use of medicine in TJJD is often inconsistent and may change frequently.[130]

Finding VIII: Youth facilities that are closer to home and incorporate community-based resources are more effective and better serve youth's mental health needs.

Studies show that community-based programs positively impact youth behavior and reduce re- offending. These programs generally emphasize therapeutic or educational approaches and build accountability.[131] Communities can maintain smaller facilities, which can be more effective in addressing mental health needs.[132] Additionally, research has shown that large incarceration facilities are not effective for youth and increase the likelihood of recidivism.[133] States that are transitioning to regional-based programs are seeing better outcomes for youth and lower costs in the long term.[134]

Currently, most youth are in facilities that are far from their home, isolating them from their family and communities.[135] Children in crisis need stability, and maintaining a connection to homes and communities is important.[136] Being far from home also makes it hard to ensure youth will have community-based resources to help them after they are released from custody.[137]

---

[127] Wu Testimony, *Transcript III*, p. 18.
[128] Becker Testimony, *Transcript III*, p. 4.
[129] Martin Martinez, T1, p. 21; Norman Testimony, *Transcript II*, p. 143.
[130] Freelen Testimony, *Transcript II*, p. 126.
[131] Ryan Testimony, *Transcript IV*, p. 4.
[132] Norman Testimony, *Transcript II*, p. 189; Martinez Testimony, *Transcript I*, p. 30.
[133] Ryan Testimony, *Transcript IV*, p. 4; Martinez Testimony, *Transcript I*, p. 22; Welch Testimony, *Transcript I*, p. 17.
[134] Welch Testimony, *Transcript I*, p. 17; Becker Testimony, *Transcript III*, p. 12; Ryan Testimony, *Transcript IV*, p. 3; Norman Testimony, *Transcript II*, p. 137.
[135] Martinez Testimony, *Transcript I*, p. 20.
[136] Ryan Testimony, *Transcript IV*, p. 3.
[137] Becker Testimony, *Transcript III*, p. 12.

TJJD has already made great efforts to keep more youth close to home and has reduced the number of youth in state custody drastically over the last 10 years.[138] But the state continues to invest a significant portion of the TJJD budget in both the existing and new state facilities.[139] Given the decades of struggles these facilities have faced, it is unclear why TJJD continues to send the most at-risk youth to the facilities with the greatest safety and care concerns.

Harris County is an example of a county that has already made improvements in how it addresses the mental health needs of the youth in its juvenile justice system.[140] It has implemented a Multisystemic Therapy (MST) approach to reduce criminal activity, which includes coordinated services to address behavior, mental health needs, academics, and other needs of the whole family.[141] Harris County judges are aware of mental health needs while hearing a youths' case.[142] They have also utilized diversion programs to address mental health needs before the youth is officially involved in the justice system.[143] Harris County has decreased the number of youth sent to secure confinement by half in the past four years.[144]

Finding IX: Texas communities do not have the resources required to support high-risk children who are ending up in Texas Juvenile Justice Department care. Texas needs to invest more in upstream and preventive services to divert children who are currently being referred to the juvenile justice system.[145]

Community-based mental health services could serve children being referred to TJJD before they interact with law enforcement.[146] Outcomes for youth in community-based programs are far better than those who are incarcerated, especially in programs that incorporate the family in treatment and therapy.[147] Community-based services also recognize how important

---

138 TJJD Written Testimony, p. 2.

139 TJJD Written Testimony, p. 8.

140 Leah Wolfthal, testimony, *Briefing Before the Texas Advisory Committee to the U.S. Commission on Civil Rights,* Houston, TX, August 8, 2022. Transcript, p. 152 (hereafter *Transcript II);* Wu Testimony, *Transcript III*, p. 7; Fry Testimony, *Transcript II*, p. 162; Ryan Testimony, *Transcript IV*, p. 4.

141 Fry Testimony, *Transcript II*, p. 111; Martinez Testimony, *Transcript I*, p. 27; Ryan Testimony, *Transcript IV*, p. 4.

142 Martinez Testimony, Transcript I, p. 27; Welch Testimony, Transcript I, p. 59.

143 Wolfthal Testimony, *Transcript II*, p. 117; Martinez Testimony, *Transcript I*, p. 27.

144 Ryan Testimony, *Transcript IV*, p. 4; Martinez Testimony, *Transcript I*, p. 40; Wu Testimony, *Transcript III*, p. 7.

145 Norman Testimony, *Transcript II*, p. 182.

146 Ryan Testimony, *Transcript IV*, p. 3.

147 Ryan Testimony, *Transcript IV*, pp. 12, 18. Becker Testimony, *Transcript III*, p. 3.

basic necessities such as food, clothing, shelter, stability, and safety are to a child's development and wellbeing.[148] By working with these children at an earlier point of need, organizations can reduce the number of kids in the prison system by making sure behaviors leading to incarceration do not escalate.[149] Currently there is no one system connecting Texas schools, mental health services, juvenile justice, etc.[150]

The current system across Texas is not equipped to prevent and respond to mental health crises occurring in communities.[151] More youth in crisis are presenting at emergency rooms or are being arrested.[152] In many cases, parents call police when their child is having a mental health crisis as there are no other community resources, but this can result in the youths' arrest and incarceration.[153]

Finding X: While the Texas Juvenile Justice Department has clearly defined rights for youth in their care, there remains confusion about what these rights are and/or if they are being adequately enforced.

TJJD policy states that youth and their guardians receive information about their rights when admitted to TJJD facilities and have access to these rights in their student handbook and on posters hung around the facility.[154] But the Committee heard testimony from former youth, parents, and lawyers that this is not always fully implemented.[155] Additionally, it is hard to find the 14 basic rights youth have in TJJD online. The Committee only received this information directly from TJJD and were not able to find it independently on the agency website or in other TJJD materials.[156]

Even when youth are given access to information on their rights, it may not be presented in a way that is understandable or empowering to youth.[157] For example, in TJJD's "Youth Complaint & Grievance Guide," there is no mention of the right to adequate mental health care or an explanation of what a violation of that right might look like. The rights in both the poster displayed in facilities and the brochure are not written in age-appropriate language, using

---

[148] Becker Testimony, *Transcript III*, p. 4; Wolfthal Testimony, *Transcript II*, p. 120.
[149] Wu Testimony, *Transcript III*, p. 7.
[150] Becker Testimony, *Transcript III*, p. 19.
[151] Fry Testimony, *Transcript II*, p. 111.
[152] Fry Testimony, *Transcript II*, p. 123; Norman Testimony, *Transcript II*, p. 132.
[153] Freelen Testimony, *Transcript II*, p. 159.
[154] TJJD Written Testimony, p. 12.
[155] Norman Testimony, *Transcript II*, p. 179; Brown Testimony, *Transcript V*, p. 11.
[156] While this does not mean it does not exist online or on their website, it does suggest that it is not easily accessible.
[157] Norman Testimony, *Transcript II*, p. 139.

words such as "confer," "correspond," "discrimination," and "extent."[158] Additionally the translated Spanish version of the flyer may cause confusion. For example, "youth rights specialist" in English is translated to "especialistas en derecho juvenil" and may be hard to understand for native Spanish speakers.

There are some noticeable rights that the youth have that are missing from the list of basic rights, for example a right to education or the right to protection from retaliation.[159] Additionally, the flyer distributed to youth should not discourage reporting in any way. The final section on the "Youth Complaint & Grievance Guide" may unduly cause youth to second-guess if they should make a complaint or not.[160]

The Committee is particularly concerned about the "right to protection from physical and psychological harm." There has been significant evidence that youth have been subject to both unsafe conditions and at risk of further psychological trauma under TJJD's protection.[161] For example, the Committee heard testimony about a child with pus streaming from their arm from having inserted items under the skin. This was present on over two visits spanning two weeks apart with no apparent medical treatment.[162] Youth should be given clearer information about what violations of their physical and psychological rights look like in the juvenile detention context.

Lastly, while TJJD has been facing the difficult challenge of staffing shortages and a lack of resources that are largely out of their control, they should reevaluate their procedures for when staffing is low. TJJD's testimony indicated that understaffing was the source of many of the Committee's human and civil rights concerns. The practice of isolation; ceasing educational, spiritual, and recreational activities; and increasing the use of force should not be acceptable outcomes of understaffing.

Finding XI: Facilities' current grievance process and other accountability measures are insufficient and function poorly.

TJJD has an Office of the Independent Ombudsman that conducts routine inspections of all five state-secured youth facilities. The office is also required to conduct routine inspections of county-level facilities.[163]

---

158 TJJD Written Testimony, Appendices.
159 TJJD Written Testimony, p.17.
160 Ibid.
161 Welch Testimony, *Transcript I*, p. 10,12; Becker Testimony, *Transcript III*, p. 4.
162 Henneke Testimony, *Transcript IV*, p. 7.
163 TJJD Written Testimony, p. 6.

There is currently little to no anonymity for youth in the grievance-filing process.[164] The youth can access the ombudsman via phone, but only in the facility's common spaces with no privacy.[165] Additionally, access to common spaces may be limited at times due to understaffing.[166]

TJJD testified that it has clear procedures and safeguards to make sure all grievances are responded to in a fair and transparent manner.[167] But testimony received by the Committee questioned the neutrality of many of these grievance investigations.[168] They are concerned that complaints are investigated by staff who work in the same facility or by staff who have existing relationships with those they are investigating.[169] One parent testified that they feared retribution for their child if they filed a complaint about their child's treatment.[170]

Few complaints address mental health care. TJJD's data from 2019 indicates that one percent of grievances were for specialized treatment programs and less than one percent of the grievances were for mental health.[171] However, the youth may not understand that this is something they can complain about, and the onus is currently on the youth to make the complaint.[172]

Even when complaints are made and investigated, there may not be enough resources or staff to address the concerns.[173] This is especially true for mental health care and when the grievance concerns missing or inadequate care.[174]

Finding XII: The Texas Legislature made some improvements to the Texas Juvenile Justice Department and its funding in the 2023 session, but there is much more reform and investment still needed.

In the past few years, TJJD has had budgeted funds diverted from it several times.[175] Additional funding for the agency may continue to address the

---

164 Norman Testimony, *Transcript II*, p. 136; Martinez Testimony, *Transcript I*, p. 45.
165 Martinez Testimony, *Transcript I*, p. 45; Norman Testimony, *Transcript II*, p. 135.
166 Welch Testimony, *Transcript I*, p. 46.
167 TJJD Written Testimony, pp. 5-6.
168 Brown Testimony, *Transcript V*, p. 6; Norman Testimony, *Transcript II*, p. 179.
169 Henneke Testimony, *Transcript IV*, p. 19.
170 Freelen Testimony, *Transcript II*, p. 178.
171 Norman Testimony, *Transcript II*, p. 138; Martinez Testimony, *Transcript I*, p. 46.
172 Norman Testimony, *Transcript II*, p. 138.
173 Welch Testimony, *Transcript I*, p. 45; Henneke Testimony, *Transcript IV*, p. 23; Norman Testimony, *Transcript II*, p. 139.
174 Welch Testimony, *Transcript I*, p. 45.
175 Welch Testimony, *Transcript I*, p. 41.

department's most pressing issue, understaffing.[176] Improved programming and treatment for youth cannot be successful without adequate investment.[177]

In the 2023 session, the legislature approved $31.9 million in targeted salary increases for direct- and non-direct-care staff, nursing staff, and OIG positions, on top of the other salary increases given last year. Historically, although there have been pay increases to address employee retention issues in TJJD, these proved to be short-term fixes rather than long-term improvements to staffing levels.[178] Increased pay may not address other concerns, such as the rural location of many of these facilities, the availability of qualified individuals, or unfavorable working conditions.[179]

Increases in the TJJD budget also included $30.7 million in increased placement funding and probation grants to expand local diversion opportunities and community-based programming, as well as $60 million in increased appropriations for county juvenile probation departments to better fund their work with youth shallow in the system to prevent commitment to state custody.[180] However it should be noted, that many of the increases to the budget in FY2022 were subsequently reduced in FY2023.[181]

Recommendations

Among their duties, advisory committees of the Commission are authorized to advise the Agency (1) concerning matters related to discrimination or a denial of equal protection of the laws under the Constitution and the effect of the laws and policies of the Federal Government with respect to equal protection of the laws, and (2) upon matters of mutual concern in the preparation of reports of the Commission to the President and the Congress.182 In keeping with these responsibilities, and given the testimony heard on this topic, the Committee submits the following recommendations to the Commission:

The U.S. Commission on Civil Rights should issue the following recommendations to the U.S. Department of Justice:

---

[176] Welch Testimony, *Transcript I*, p. 61; Sunset Advisory Commission. Written Testimony, submitted via email on April 14, 2023.
[177] Norman Testimony, *Transcript II*, p. 137; Welch Testimony, *Transcript I*, p. 42.
[178] Martinez Testimony, *Transcript I*, p. 60; Norman Testimony, *Transcript II*, p. 136.
[179] Becker Testimony, *Transcript III*, p. 20; Ryan Testimony, *Transcript IV*, p. 12.
[180] TJJD Written Testimony, pp. 8-9.
[181] Ibid.

1) Provide more transparency and report the progress on your ongoing investigation into the Texas Juvenile Justice Department.

The U.S. Commission on Civil Rights should issue the following recommendations to the Governor of Texas and the Texas Legislature:

1) Invest in the staff of all TJJD facilities, including:
   a) Improve the salaries of staff to a competitive rate and in recognition of the essential and challenging roles these staff fill.
   b) Require additional training for correction officers and ensure the training is developmentally appropriate for youth and considers their unique mental health needs.
   c) Increase the number of specialty staff, including teachers, medical personnel, and mental health care workers. Ensure these specialists are being used for their expertise and are not required to fill in for corrections officers.
   d) Require more mental health care workers to be properly licensed in order to ensure a high caliber of care.
2) Invest in the local and county-level juvenile systems and incentivize these community- based programs to treat youth closer to home, including:
   a) Expanding multidisciplinary programs to address all the needs of youth, such as Multisystemic Therapy (MST).
   b) Incorporate families in all mental health care programming.
   c) Develop a regionalized system that can offer better support and funding to the many rural counties in Texas.
   d) Consider participation in the Department of Justice's Community-Based Alternatives to Youth Incarceration Initiative,183 which supports states and localities as they close large, under-capacity youth prisons.
3) Prioritize rehabilitation over punishment in all future investments and program changes to TJJD.
4) Mandate that TJJD provide multiple avenues for youth and their families to submit grievances and appoint investigators external to the facility to investigate all complaints.
5) Raise the age youth are considered a juvenile and increase the age that a youth can be transferred into the adult corrections system.

The U.S. Commission on Civil Rights should issue the following recommendations to the Texas Juvenile Justice Department:

1) Prioritize the human and civil rights of all the youth in its care.
2) Increase efforts to educate the youth in its custody and their parents and/or guardians on their rights and their avenues for grievance. The grievance process should be more available to youth, be private, and be adjudicated by neutral parties.
3) Invest in additional mental health care resources that can begin to address the needs of youth in its custody in the short term, including:
   a) Consider additional remote resources such as 24/7 mental health hotlines that could support both the youth and staff in crisis and offer additional capacity for understaffed facilities.
   b) Develop relationships with national resources such as the National Alliance on Mental Health and Substance Abuse and the Mental Health Services Administration.
   c) Utilize telehealth in its full capacity to provide mental health care to youth. This includes one-on-one therapeutic services, not large group therapy sessions.
4) Reduce the use of isolation. When isolation is deemed necessary, ensure it is used sparingly and for the least amount of time possible. Increase mental health support during and after periods of isolation.
5) Require all staff to be trained in trauma-informed care and ensure that all policies recognize the potential trauma experienced by the youth and their mental health needs.
6) Provide additional crisis prevention training to staff to improve their de-escalation skills to prevent violent situations.
7) Accept all avenues of additional funding, including accepting all federal funds available and pursuing additional grants.
8) Consider the use of peer support services from individuals who have previous experience in the juvenile justice system but who have been rehabilitated and trained in crisis and behavioral management.
9) For youth who age out of or are released from state-secured facilities, conduct family assessments to ensure that the youth are returning to a safe environment and that family members are receiving support services as needed.
10) Raise the age youth are considered a juvenile and increase the age that a youth can be transferred into the adult corrections system. Reduce the practice of transferring youth to the adult system.

11) Review and revise the language of your rights brochures and other materials to include more age-appropriate language, proper translations, and a more comprehensive explanation of rights.

Appendix

A. List of Panelists
B. Panel Agendas, Minutes, Presentation Slides, & Transcripts
C. Written Testimony

Appendix A – List of Panelists

Panel 1 – August 8, 2022, Houston, TX

Alycia Welch,
The University of Texas at Austin Martin Martinez, Texas Appleseed
Dr. Kristan Russell, Prairie View A&M University

Panel 2 – August 8, 2022, Houston, TX

Layla Fry, Meadows
Mental Health Institute
Leah Wolfthal, Center for Urban Transformation Amnisty Freelen, Parent Advocate
Brittany Norman,
Disability Rights Texas

Panel 3 – December 7, 2022, Virtual

State Representative Gene Wu, Texas House of Representatives Phyllis Becker, Missouri Division of Youth Services

Panel 4 – February 15, 2023, Virtual

Liz Ryan, Office of Juvenile Justice and Delinquency Prevention, U.S. Department of Justice Elizabeth Henneke, Lone Star Justice Alliance

Panel 5 – April 11, 2023, Virtual

Jernard Brown, Collective Action 4 Youth

Appendix B - Panel Agendas, Minutes, Presentation Slides, and Transcripts

Documents found at:
https://securisync.intermedia.net/us2/s/folder?public_share=409J0xbKeIQ2vuMJBvQond0011ef 58&id=L1RYL0p1dmVuaWxlIEp1c3RpY2U%3D

Appendix C – Written Testimony

All written testimony can be found at:
https://securisync.intermedia.net/us2/s/folder?public_share=409J0xbKeIQ2vuMJBvQond0011ef 58&id=L1RYL0p1dmVuaWxlIEp1c3RpY2U%3D

Testimony submitted by:
Alycia Castillo
Amanda Burnitt Rachel
Gandy Natalia Oakes
Sarah L. Martin
Dr. William Bush
Texas Juvenile Justice Department

Index

E

F

G

H

I

J

L

M

N

P

R

S

T

U

V

Y